Medieval Literature: An Introduction to Type-Scenes

This is the first book-length exploration of the type-scenes of western medieval literature from the ninth to the fifteenth centuries, spanning both the Latinate and Germanic traditions. Type-scenes are the recurring, stock scenes comprising the basic structure and cognitive guidance for narrative. These formulaic scenes enabled medieval poets to express originality while honoring tradition. Central to medieval poetic invention, type-scenes form the vital "internal organs" of narrative, each serving a specialized function while working in concert with other organs to create and sustain the story. This accessible and engaging guide to medieval type-scenes consists of three parts: Part I is a compendium of the type-scenes commonly found in medieval narrative, including analyses of examples from individual poems. Part II explores combinations of type-scenes within single works of literature for purposes of chronology, characterization, or virtuosity. Part III examines how a single type-scene manifests across multiple poems, adapting to a variety of settings and periods, while maintaining its original intent. This volume kindles in scholars, teachers, and students alike a new and refreshing awareness of the foundational narrative strategies of medieval literature.

Dominique Battles holds a Ph.D. in English from the University of Virginia and an M.A. in Medieval Studies from University of York (UK). Her previous publications include *The Medieval Tradition of Thebes* (2004) and *Cultural Difference and Material Culture in Middle English Romance: Normans and Saxons* (2013) as well as numerous articles on medieval literature. She has been a professor of English and Medieval Studies at Hanover College since 2001.

Medieval Literature
An Introduction to Type-Scenes

Dominique Battles

NEW YORK AND LONDON

Designed cover image: The Dream of Sir Lancelot at the Chapel of the Holy Grail, 1896 (oil on canvas), Burne-Jones, Edward Coley (1833–98)/Southampton City Art Gallery, Hampshire, UK/ Southampton City Art Gallery/Bridgeman Images

First published 2025
by Routledge
605 Third Avenue, New York, NY 10158

and by Routledge
4 Park Square, Milton Park, Abingdon, Oxon, OX14 4RN

Routledge is an imprint of the Taylor & Francis Group, an informa business

© 2025 Dominique Battles

The right of Dominique Battles to be identified as author of this work has been asserted in accordance with sections 77 and 78 of the Copyright, Designs and Patents Act 1988.

All rights reserved. No part of this book may be reprinted or reproduced or utilised in any form or by any electronic, mechanical, or other means, now known or hereafter invented, including photocopying and recording, or in any information storage or retrieval system, without permission in writing from the publishers.

Trademark notice: Product or corporate names may be trademarks or registered trademarks, and are used only for identification and explanation without intent to infringe.

ISBN: 9781032439587 (hbk)
ISBN: 9781032439570 (pbk)
ISBN: 9781003369592 (ebk)

DOI: 10.4324/9781003369592

Typeset in Sabon LT Pro
by Apex CoVantage, LLC

For my students

Contents

Notes on Permissions ix
Acknowledgments x
Introduction xi

PART I
A Compendium of Type-Scenes of Medieval Literature   1

Arming of the Hero 3
Beasts of Battle 7
Blason 9
Catalog of Warriors 19
Conciliar Debate 22
Contending Throng 25
Council of the Gods 27
Crowd of Onlookers 31
Dawn Song 35
Descent into the Underworld (katabasis) 39
Disguise and Infiltration 44
Ekphrasis 49
Epic Descent 53
Exile 57
Flyting 60
Hero on the Beach 66
Inventio 68
Joy in the Hall 71
Lady with the Mead Cup 72
Loathly Lady Encounter 74
Locus Amoenus 80
Magic Ring 86

Open Heavens 89
Outlaw Gathering 90
Paraclausithyron 93
Rash Promise 96
Scop's Repertoire 100
Sleeping After the Feast 102
Teichoscopia (Teichoscopy) 104
Traveler Recognizes His Goal 107
Wise Woman 109

PART II
Type-Scene Sequences within Single Works — 113

I Sequencing for Chronology: Boccaccio's Use of the Epic Type-Scene in the *Teseida* — 115

II Sequencing Type-Scenes for Characterization: Anglo-Saxon as Other in the Middle English *Athelston* — 126

III Sequencing for Virtuosity: The "Sleeping After the Feast" Type-Scene in *Beowulf* — 136

PART III
One Type-Scene in Three Different Works — 147

Medieval Cultural Profiling: The Wise Woman Type-Scene in Middle English Romance — 149

Bibliography — 199
Index — 212

Notes on Permissions

Part II, section I, "Sequencing for Chronology: Boccaccio's Use of Epic Type-Scenes in the *Teseida*," originally appeared in modified form in *The Medieval Tradition of Thebes* (Routledge, 2004). Used by permission of the publisher.

Part II, section II, "Sequencing for Characterization: Anglo-Saxon as Other in the Middle English *Athelston*," originally appeared in modified form in "The Middle English *Athelston* and 1381: Part I: The Politics of Anglo-Saxon Identity," *Studies in Philology* 117 (2020): 1–39. Copyright © 2020 University of North Carolina Press. Used by permission of the publisher, www.uncpress.unc.edu.

Part II, section III, "Sequencing for Virtuosity: The 'Sleeping After the Feast' Type-Scene in *Beowulf*," is adapted from unpublished and published work on this scene by Paul Battles—notably, "'Sleeping After the Feast' Scenes in *Beowulf*, *Andreas*, and the Old English Poetic Tradition," *Modern Philology* 112(3) (2015): 435–57. Used by permission of the author.

Acknowledgments

My first and sincerest thanks goes to my students at Hanover College. This book was their idea. My understanding of medieval type-scenes developed over the years in the classroom, in conversation with students. Their perennial interest in type-scenes and persistent urgings that I collect these ideas in a book has resulted in this volume. For their insights on type-scenes, I am especially grateful to Kimberly Koch-Fonzo, Erin Chandler, Jenaba Wabby, Emma Copeland, Rob Allega, Patrick Spears, Abigail Fulton-Caress, Melissa May Lepley, Stephanie Rathbun, Tyler Blaker, Anna Cooley, Brett Lowen, Kylie Miller, Angelena Pierce, Shelby Edington, Kelly Poston, Geneva Dischinger-Smedes, Katarina Rexing, Kassidy VanGundy Katherine Booker, Catherine Brassell-Mills, Anya Polito, Kegan Mixdorf, Benjamin Kugler, Chelsie Bruther, Kayla Pyle, Lance Bruer, Allyson Howard, Meredith Shepherd, Emily Sanders-Whiteley, Hayden Rinker, and Victoria Zwilling. I think of this book as very much our collaborative endeavor.

Thanking my husband, Paul Battles, has become a type-scene in my own life. This time, in addition to expressing my deepest gratitude—yet again—for his abiding support as a partner and colleague over the years, I would like to thank him for his contributions to the Old English material in this book. I must also thank our son, Perry Battles, for his enthusiasm and good humor about this and all my projects.

The editors at Routledge, Michelle Salyga and Bryony Reece, have been models of cheerful, timely, and encouraging professionalism. I would also like to thank our archivist at the Hanover College Duggan Library, Jennifer Duplaga, for her assistance in securing permission for the cover image of this volume.

Introduction

We talk a lot nowadays of embodied cognition, the vital and previously overlooked role our physical bodies play in how we think, reason, and feel. Recent work in the field of intelligence has moved beyond the brain and into the body, revealing how our bodies have their own intelligence, and our guts harbor a second brain.[1] Contrary to an earlier tendency to separate the functions of the brain and body, and to inflate the brain's status over that of the body, we have come to appreciate how much we depend on healthy liver function or improved circulation or the microbial community in our guts for optimal cognitive performance, a humbling yet necessary paradigm shift not just for the future of the "knowledge economy" but also for our better selves. In the field of literary studies, we might think of the network of type-scenes—the recurring scenes that form the infrastructure of a given narrative—as making up the "body" of the story, and the individual type-scenes themselves, as the "vital organs" of the narrative. Just as each of the organs of the body serves a specialized function in the system as a whole, so, too, each of the type-scenes in a story serves a specialized function in how the story unfolds, and just like our vital organs, type-scenes are essential to the life of the story.

Like the wider culture, the field of literary studies has grown top-heavy, privileging the "brain," or the theoretical dimension of stories over their bodily parts, so that, just as we take for granted our pituitary gland or spleen or left lung on any given day, though none of us could survive without them, we have come to overlook the value, or indeed, the very presence of the humble organs of stories—their type-scenes. Their familiar, recurring nature often makes them invisible to students and scholars alike, hiding their quiet complexity and variability within their specialized task, and obscuring the subtle messages concerning each individual story they contain. Just as "the substrate of the mind is not the brain alone, but the entire body," the life of a story begins with the infrastructure of its type-scenes and works outward from there.[2] As students and scholars, we therefore form a more grounded understanding of a text when we study its actual groundwork. This book is intended to revitalize our understanding and appreciation of type-scenes in medieval literature, a tradition-bound body of literature that relies heavily on these recurring structures, drawn from earlier literary practice, to construct and convey meaning. As sites where tradition and innovation intersect at the deepest level of story, type-scenes have their own hidden intelligence, and I have found repeatedly that, through the inner workings of its type-scenes, a story gives up its secrets.

What Is a Type-Scene?

In simplest terms, a type-scene is a recurring scene that conveys meaning through a predictable configuration of characters, setting, and action—elements that are, themselves, predictable. The scene may or may not contain dialogue, as the familiar choreography alone can sufficiently signal to the audience what is happening and why. Type-scenes recur because they do necessary work in advancing the narrative, both structurally, in upholding the plot, and conceptually, in shaping understanding of the story. In the classroom, I illustrate how type-scenes work by telling my students to watch carefully what I do and then to tell me who and where I am, what is happening, and why. I position my feet wide, place my palms on my hips, squint, strut forward three paces, and slowly turn to the left and pretend to spit. I have said nothing. Immediately, the students blurt, "It's the wild west!" They know that my hands rest on holsters, each containing a six-shooter, I am about to engage in a shoot-out with the bad guy, and the year is 1850. The whole thing takes about three seconds. Encoded into the scene are broader concomitant frontier values of rugged individualism, rough justice, and self-reliance.[3] The shoot-out scene evokes the genre of the Western and forecasts other scenes we would expect of this story type. It also conjures a mindset of austerity and grit and an emotional script at once expansive and cautious. Types-scenes are the weight-bearing beams that hold up the story, and their placement, individually and collectively, tells us what kind of building we are in—or "genre," in narrative terms—and therefore, what kind of experience we can expect.

Type-scenes occupy the mid-tier in story architecture. At the macro-level, we have the basic plot line of a story-type (e.g., a romance), which divides itself into smaller units, or "episodes," or narrative units of action bound temporally and spatially, which are similarly formulaic and imitative.[4] In his study of episodic structure in medieval romance, Peter Haidu defines the "episode" as "a syntactical unit of narrative structure," across multiple texts, that indicates a "shared consciousness of textual structure," coalescing into a genre.[5] An episode can span up to weeks, or even months, and will typically include various scenes of dialogue, combat, celebration, and other action, and these scenes can take place in multiple locations. For example, in Chrétien's *Yvain*, the magic spring episode early in the story includes Yvain's journey to the spring, his fight with Esclados the Red, his entry into the castle barbican, Lunete's offer of the magic ring, Yvain's first sight of Laudine, his evasion of detection as Lunete negotiates with Laudine to accept Yvain as a new husband and protector of the spring, and finally, his marriage to Laudine. The episode spans many days, involves several modes of interaction, and takes place in multiple locations in and around the castle. Later episodes include the hero's "madness episode," the "lion episode," and his quest to reform himself through a series of challenges where he serves the interests of women.

Within a larger episode, a type-scene forms a smaller moment in time and space. It is one of many scenes that make up the episode. (In the episode of *Yvain* mentioned earlier, one type-scene is the blason of Laudine.) At the same time, a type-scene distinguishes itself from other scenes in the episode in that it has been seen before, many times. Its components, configuration, and choreography are all familiar to the reader—features that come prescribed from its earlier occurrences in other texts within the genre. For this reason, it strikes a higher pitch of formality in that its conventionality lends it a ceremonial and reflective quality. In early oral epic, conventional type-scenes can occur densely, with formal scenes of journeys, arrivals, feasting, and challenge that follow close upon one another through stylized repetition.[6] In the newer genre of medieval romance, whose scenes are as yet emergent, type-scenes may be more thinly distributed across an episode. Nonetheless, for the reader, the familiarity of the type-scene brings a contemplative awareness to the larger episode, as it distills and attributes meaning to what has been happening. In *Yvain*, the blason of Laudine defines the meaning of the entire magic spring episode by re-orienting the hero to the woman who will remake his identity.

Within or around type-scenes, we find smaller units of narrative. For example, there is the "plot device" of the magic within the type-scene of that name. There is the "motif" (i.e., recurring theme) of the undercover king in the Disguise and Infiltration type-scene.[7] Likewise, the Old English "trope" (i.e., verbal formula) of the Traveler Recognizes his Goal gets applied to the wise men arriving in Bethlehem.[8] The "theme" (i.e., a recurring topic or central idea/moral) of the impermanence of life can suffuse and reverberate throughout the narrative, including its type-scenes. While specific definitions of these narrative elements vary somewhat among scholars, none of these things by themselves constitute a unified scene incorporating setting, characters, and action.

Another helpful way to configure the type-scene and its place within a story is as a *narrative ritual*, a scene not unlike a wedding, baptism, or graduation whose meaning derives from the formalized repetition of movement, words, costume, and often, music. While we can have a degree of variation on the constituent elements of a ritual, we all know a wedding dress when we see one, and it only adorns a bride at a wedding. Like rituals, type-scenes recur and are recognizable when they do. Like rituals, type-scenes honor and affect *change* in a character through repetition, just as a woman becomes a bride and a child becomes a graduate. Indeed, many of them, such as the Arming of the Hero or Flyting scenes, serve as rites of passage for the hero as he assumes greater responsibility. Specifically, like ritual, type-scenes operate not only through repetition but through stylized elements of setting and choreographed action. In this sense, according to Manuel Aguirre, in his study of the type-scenes of nineteenth-century Gothic literature, these scenes render what is otherwise invisible, inner change—change of heart or role or direction—visible to the reader, and the character emerges transformed from the scene.[9] Also, Aguirre notes how type-scenes, like ritual, honor the individual and his unique agency in the narrative, ironically, while diminishing it by simultaneously subjugating his agency to a larger "narrative order which prevails over characters' intentions."[10] Like a ritual, a type-scene records both the timely and the timeless, the momentary and the universal, so that the present moment participates in cosmic time. So, too, just as ritual marks a pause and integration within the main action of life, a type-scene, while including its own action, marks a pause and integration of meaning within the main action of the episode in which it falls. Therefore, the formulaic nature of type-scenes, far from reducing significance and beauty, magnify those things through both variation *and* repetition. Aguirre's analysis of type-scenes suggests how we might think of the *variations* on the scene as inscribing the particular, timely meanings of the story itself and the *infrastructural repetition* as "the prism which makes meanings possible," as with a wedding or a baptism.[11] Predictability and spontaneity work in unison, affecting change within prescribed norms, change for both the characters within the story, and within the genre itself.

With an eye to maximum utility, as well as scholarly integrity, I conceptualize the "type-scene" as a recurring scene involving repetition of the following features (usually in combination): verbal formulae; characterization; character configuration; choreography; setting; and purpose. I have found this constellation of features does justice to concurrent notions of "theme," "trope," "motif," or "plot device," as they so often occur together, and generally incarnate as scenes.

Type-Scene Analysis Then and Now

The concept of the type-scene is an old idea first applied to the oldest literature. It originated in Homeric studies with the foundational 1933 work of Walter Arend, *Die typischen scenen bei Homer*.[12] Around the same time, A.B. Lord, following Milman Parry's work on Homer, developed the similar organizing narrative concept of the "theme" as "a subject unit, a group of ideas, regularly employed by a singer, not merely in any given poem, but in the poetry as a whole."[13] Seeking to understand Homer's compositional practices, Lord studied living, South Slavic oral poets, who still recited long, epic poems from memory, employing "themes" as units of composition. He then applied the methods of oral composition observed among these living poets to poetic composition of the ancient and medieval past.[14] Lord emphasized the utility of such narrative set-pieces as both memory aids for oral composition (both ancient Homeric and contemporary Serbo-Croat) and as tools for preserving and transmitting cultural tradition through story. This early foundational work paved the way for more specialized analyses of individual type-scenes in Homer, such as the arming motif, guest reception, catalogs of warriors, messenger scenes, battle revenge, and return and recognition scenes, to name a few.[15] Type-scene analysis in Homeric studies gained most recent thoroughgoing treatment in the work of Mark Edwards, who incorporates not only identification and classification but also the specialized and subtler workings of type-scenes, individually and in concert, while extending their applicability into wider theoretical discourse.[16]

While type-scenes form the familiar building blocks of early narrative, they have fallen into obscurity within the wider field of literary studies. Early scholars express a working understanding of these narrative structures. They acknowledge type-scenes as the functional infrastructure behind the drywall of a story; however, they used type-scene analysis primarily as a tool for classification, focusing on the conventionality of the scene, compared with established models.[17] They also used type-scenes to trace the genealogy of subject matter, as with Jean Bodel's famous classifications of the "Matter of France" (*chanson de geste*), the "Matter of Rome" (romances of antiquity), and the "Matter of Britain" (the tradition of King Arthur).[18] Such studies enabled scholars to track the intertextual relationships within a given genre and to situate a work within the larger medieval literary corpus.

This early emphasis on literary conventionality deterred many later scholars from type-scene analysis, who saw it primarily as a tool for pigeonholing literary works, thereby obscuring their originality. Type-scene analysis for purposes of classification became tantamount to scholarly taxidermy, turning a living poem into a museum piece. Consequently, modern scholars more interested in poetic originality tend to overlook or dismiss type-scenes as merely "formulaic," a term of contempt in literary criticism.[19] They are not entirely wrong. As recurring scenes that generate meaning through repetition, type-scenes are, by definition, "formulaic," ostensibly the antithesis of "original." To be "formulaic" is to be common, derivative, and therefore, beneath consideration. One of the most common dismissals of a type-scene, in whole or in part, is to relegate it to "folkloric," a vast, undifferentiated realm of nondescript material. As recurring blocks of narrative, type-scenes are often consigned to the realm of poetic "standard issue," hardly worthy of serious academic inquiry. Moreover, with the cultural shift away from the traditional and toward a modernist aesthetic, we have lost both our appetite and our eyes for tradition-bound narrative as cliché. Hence the absence of any book-length study of type-scenes, *per se*, for nearly a hundred years.[20] As a result, most contemporary scholars and students have little awareness of the diagnostic and interpretive power of type-scenes to reveal distinctive treasures of narrative design and sympathy—as tools of originality.

Type-scenes have gained new interpretive vitality in the field of cognitive poetics, where they denote the very nature of thought and language. Using the joint lens of psychology and linguistics, cognitive poetics demonstrates how we instinctively organize experience in story form, and that these stories, themselves, organize into "schemas," or "bundles of information" that render the world (including the world of a story) recognizable, and therefore, navigable.[21] Schemas apply to every level of story, from literary genre to fictional episodes to specific imagined characters within the episode. Schemas appeal to readers precisely for their familiarity. They provide cognitive security through their repetition of the familiar (the known), while also using that familiar space to introduce the new (the unknown), not unlike introducing a stranger to a child within the safety of the family circle.[22] The new becomes a source of open curiosity rather than of closed anxiety.

Type-scenes participate in this structuring and expansion of human experience. As a schema—a repeated unit of narrative—a type-scene certainly preserves and reenforces existing knowledge, but it can also become a vehicle of innovation, either through accretion (the addition of new facts to the schema that enlarge its scope or explanatory range) or through tuning (the modification of facts or relations within the schema) or, less often, through restructuring (the creation of new schemas based on old models).[23] I would add to these innovative techniques within a type-scene the idea of placement, as poets often craft a "textbook example" of a type-scene only to deliberately misplace it within the narrative, thereby changing its traditional function. In all these poetic modifications, familiarity forms the base note upon which the entire chord is built, and the gate of entry for the new.

Why Do Type-Scenes Matter for the Study of Early Literature?

Type-scenes matter to students and scholars of early literature because they mattered to early poets themselves. Medieval poets crafted their stories around traditional type-scenes, utilizing these familiar literary formulae to establish genre, propel plot, and foster readerly sentiment. We know that ancient and medieval poets practiced formulaic methods of composition, first, from the poetic record itself. Early poets created (self)portraits of the oral poet at work, portraits that, themselves, became type-scenes. In the *Odyssey* VIII, Homer attests to Odysseus' reputation as a master tactician by depicting Demodocos, a blind minstrel (an oral poet like Homer himself) in the palace of King Alcinous, who sings three songs, interspersed with festivities, of the Trojan war.[24] Odysseus, a king in disguise, hears his recent exploits now set to music. The scene dramatizes the dynamic process of a poet incorporating new material of recent events, related in scenic snapshots, into the traditional medium of oral poetry used for transmitting cultural experience. This transposition of feats on the battlefield into song in the feasting hall transforms Odysseus himself from refugee to restored king; hence, these scenes often dovetail with disguise, recognition, and emerging identity.[25]

Similar scenes depicting the making and performance of poetry occur in Germanic tradition throughout Old English and Middle High German poetry. In a type-scene known as the "*scop*'s repertoire," we witness an oral poet (*scop*) transmitting ancient songs through traditional oral recitation while also innovating within the form by incorporating—and interpreting—recent events affecting the hero.[26] Like Odysseus, Beowulf finds himself the subject of story and song shortly after his victory over Grendel, as the *scop* in the feasting hall commemorates his triumph in verse, elevating Beowulf as a hero.[27] In the OE *Andreas*, the poet explicitly pronounces his practice of composing in narrative units, as the poet promises to relate the saint's final triumphs through "a portion of words of verse in short episodes" (*lytlum sticcum leoðworda dæl*).[28] Thus, early poets acknowledge their reliance on formulaic structures, including type-scenes, by depicting it fictionally and admitting it personally.

Later poets formalized and prescribed composition through formulaic means, including type-scenes, in written manuals intended for fellow poets commonly known as the *ars poeticae*, dating mostly from the twelfth century. Geoffrey of Vinsauf's *Poetria Nova*, surviving in some fifty manuscripts, instructs aspiring poets on how to "describe, in amplified form, a woman's beauty" (the type-scene of the blason) or how to describe a feast or a tearful farewell of lovers.[29] Similarly, Matthew of Vendôme's *Ars versificatoria (The Art of the Versemaker)* provides guidelines and illustrations for writers on how to describe a woman's beauty or the seasons of the year or a place—descriptions that either become type-scenes themselves (e.g., the blason) or that form vital ingredients within type-scenes (e.g., the Spring Opening).[30] So influential were these treatises for medieval writers that even a highly original poet like Chaucer would frame his own poetic methodology using metaphorical imagery of the builder's craft drawn from Geoffrey of Vinsauf, clearly deriving inspiration for the new from poetic practices of old.[31]

Useful Ways to Think About Type-Scenes

Type-Scenes Are About Thresholds

As a rule, fictional type-scenes originate in frontier conditions in actual life. As new spaces of exploration and inhabitance open up, new literary forms emerge. For example, the Western arose with American westward expansion, and Science Fiction with scientific advancements. New frontiers generally create conditions where lots of unrelated strangers, often with diverse histories, converge from disparate areas into newly sprouted settlements. Consequently, there is a general spontaneity and lawlessness of conduct, given the absence of a shared past in the population. All sorts of new things emerge. American westward expansion brought prominence to certain foods (beef jerky, hardtack, hominy), new art forms (patchwork quilting), and new narrative genres (the Western, and the captivity narrative).[32]

Within the Western, we have new type-scenes that capture—and render navigable—the conditions of uncertainty, lawlessness, and austerity of the new terrain. For instance, we get the "saloon scene," where a cowboy arrives in a strange town, walks into the town saloon full of suspicious eyes, and encounters a hostile challenger that he must contend with before doing business there.[33] The setting includes the tinny sounds of an upright piano, circles of rough men at gambling tables, smoking and drinking, and seductive women. The weapons are six-shooters. Frontier conditions are always temporary, as settlement of the new territory, along with the attendant social networks of familiarity and shared governance, generally follows. The "baseline" type-scene has the closest proximity, culturally, chronologically, and geographically, to the frontier. The closer the type-scene occurs to its point of origin, the more it can withstand repetition, relatively unchanged, with no loss of its charm for audiences. With regard to medieval romance, for instance, the basic narrative formula—its plot and episodes—persisted through three generations of texts, running from Chrétien de Troyes to the introduction of interlacing design.[34] Territorial frontiers, such as the American west, tend to be short-lived, as itinerant communities give way to established settlement, enhancing their mystique for writers and audiences, and solidifying the type-scenes associated with them. Thus, frontier conditions become growth spurts in narrative, giving rise to new genres that require new type-scenes to construct them.

Frontiers that give rise to new literary forms, and thus new type-scenes, can be conceptual, technological, or cultural as well as territorial, as with the advent of medieval chivalric romance. The genre of romance that blossomed in twelfth-century France tracks the changes in economic and social life that enabled women to become powerful patrons and consumers of the arts, including literature, featuring numerous female characters who drive the plot and form the hero.[35] It also reflects the rise of court culture and the new ranks of landless noblemen who must prove themselves through means other than landed wealth, through interior and invisible refinements of "character" (e.g., courtesy, liberality, humility, generosity, piety), cultivated in the privacy of one's own heart.[36] The genre of romance introduces new type-scenes that come to typify the genre. For example, we have the blason (formal description) of the heroine, reflecting the centrality of women in the hero's maturation. While the blason of female beauty is part and parcel of a new poetic inclination for description, especially for the exotic, nonetheless, the pronouncement of the leading lady through a formal blason is distinctive with medieval romance.[37] By contrast, earlier figures, like Dido of the *Aeneid*, or Calypso and Penelope of the *Odyssey*, receive no formal blason, given their ancillary though formative role for the hero. More commonly, existing scenes such as flyting, a formal exchange of insults between a hero and a challenger originating in epic, take on a new choreography that becomes standardized for the genre; rather than returning an insult for an insult, the medieval Christian hero "turns the other cheek" and disarms his challenger by de-escalating the conflict for now, reflecting the Christian ethics underlying the chivalric code.

If type-scenes emerge at frontiers of civilization, they also mark thresholds within stories. Each significant inflexion point of a story will be announced with a formal type-scene. For example, the blason of the beautiful woman will come when the hero first sets eyes on her and reorients himself around winning her love. Likewise, the formal arming of the hero scene occurs just prior to a pivotal battle that will make or break the hero's reputation. So, too, the *locus amoenus* ushers the protagonist into a new way of thinking and feeling within story-types about personal transformation. A scene like the Wise Woman will afford a close-up portrait of the "problem" the hero must contend with in the story. Thus, through their familiar configuration of setting, characters, and action, type-scenes honor the defining moments of the hero's (and the story's) development.

Type-Scenes Are About Emotion

Type-scenes essentially mechanize emotional affect within narrative. They record what characters are feeling, and in doing so, signal appropriate feelings of sympathy or its opposite in the reader. A grieving character gains our sympathy, while a vituperative character loses it. More than that, type-scenes tend to specialize in an emotional state. Again, the physiological metaphor of vital internal organs proves apt. Traditional Chinese Medicine associates various human emotions with specific organs of the body. For example, anger is processed through the liver; grief, through the lungs; fear, through the kidneys; and joy, through the heart and small intestine.[38] Similarly, in stories, the blason triggers the orienting response; when applied to a woman, it accesses the hero's feelings of love, and when applied to a monster, it triggers fear. Flyting concerns the reflex response of anger as either retaliation or retreat. The Arming of the Hero scene tempers fear, as the hero centers himself mentally and physically for the challenge ahead. The Beasts of Battle scene amplifies the desire for carnage. The *paraclausithyron* scene renders poignant the grief of the rejected lover. As we watch the characters navigate emotional states, our sympathies as readers become harnessed to theirs. Thus, type-scenes take the emotional "vital signs" of the characters at any given point in the story.

In consolidating and dictating emotional experience through repetition, type-scenes tap into the deepest strata of culture. Forty years ago, Franco Moretti showed how convention is the very fabric of literature, woven with the threads of cultural values. He writes, "Rhetorical forms, and their larger combinations which organize long narratives, are . . . of a piece with the deep, buried, invisible presuppositions of every world view."[39] Type-scenes are one of these "larger combinations" forming the subfloor of a narrative. Far from being ornamental or merely aesthetic, rhetorical structures like type-scenes do real work in "enlisting support for a *particular* system of values."[40] To that end, these scenic units depict action in order to direct our sympathies, either toward a character who upholds those values or away from a character who threatens them. More recently, film scholar Greg M. Smith anchors the emotional life of a story to what he calls "micro-scripts." He asserts how "the most significant genre scripts with relation to emotion are not the broad expectations for the overall shape of the film, but genre micro-scripts, intertextual expectations for sequences and scenes."[41] These "micro-scripts" translate into type-scenes that writers use to foster emotion and direct our sympathies. Which is not to reduce the work of type-scenes to didacticism (though they can do that). Rather, in gathering and directing sympathy, a scene, depending on its handling, can just as well challenge as uphold "the law" embedded in its structure. For example, by some measure, the *inventio* scene of the ME *St. Erkenwald* garners faith and devotion by way of challenging the ecclesiastic "orthodoxy" represented by the bishop of the poem. Thus, within the confines of convention, dutifully observed, a type-scene can have a mind of its own.

Type-Scenes Are About Innovation Within—Not Despite—Tradition

Type-scenes are formulaic in the same way that all human thumbs share the same basic anatomy, and yet, each human thumbprint is unique. We can consider type-scenes as hubs in the story that consolidate clues to its meaning and mystery. Sherlock Holmes can read the clues on an ordinary men's hat to piece together the peculiar, idiosyncratic life of its owner. Likewise, video gamers know to search a new room for clues and resources. So, too, we can close-read the subtle clues embedded in type-scenes to glean the singular aspirations of a given tale. Small details of a blason can indicate the woman to be gained or the woman to be lost. An Arming of the Hero can emphasize the hero's offensive potential or his defensive position. A Catalog of Warriors can mark absence as well as attendance. The Flyting scene can express the hero's ferocity or his humility, depending on the genre. In other words, the same scene can have diverse meanings and produce unprecedented effect.

To illustrate how type-scenes innovate within tradition, we have a scene from the Western set in outer space, infusing novelty into the scene. The new setting and modifications of character alter the underlying meaning of the scene. Such is the case in the cantina scene in *Star Wars: A New Hope* (1978), set in Mos Eisley on the (suitably dusty) planet of Tatooine. The basic elements assume new forms: most of the rough customers in the cantina are aliens; the cowboys are Jedi who carry light sabers in place of six-guns. A jazz band of aliens substitutes for the tinny, upright piano. These novel substitutions of setting renew the type-scene and generate delight quite on their own. However, director George Lucas innovates with the saloon scene at a deeper level of characterization. The Western tends to feature a savvy, rugged hero with a supportive but less capable sidekick.[42] Lucas reverses this dynamic by making the hero, Luke, a young, inexperienced, provincial, and orphaned boy—the opposite of rugged—and his companion a seasoned Jedi, Obi Wan Kenobi, acting as a father figure to Luke. To achieve their aims, Obi Wan and Luke must team up with, rather than oppose, one of the rough customers in the cantina, the roguish Han Solo, who himself mentors Luke throughout the story.[43] Through Luke's eyes, the scene is, therefore, less about survival in a rough world than about discovery of a wider world. The scene is emotionally receptive rather than defensive, open rather than closed, well-suited to the larger theme of a "new hope," which Luke represents for the Jedi Order and for the galaxy.

In its formulaic construction, medieval literature resembles contemporary "genre fiction" in that it is convention-bound and rule driven.[44] The rules pertain to both form and content, and type-scenes distill these rules by structuring and embodying otherwise invisible beliefs and sentiments in predictable ways. At the same time, however, poets varied these type-scenes ingeniously to redirect and reframe familiar story patterns and to explore new vantages. In essence, "originality" in medieval literature emerges primarily through unusual handling of the usual—that is, fresh renditions of familiar type-scenes, enabling us to see what was new about any given work at the time, despite its seemingly conventional form. Awareness of these literary type-scenes enables us to look through the eyes of the medieval poet, and therefore, provides a vital, foundational stage of literary analysis that can then dovetail into any number of interpretive directions, even among beginners.

How to Use This Book

In working with type-scenes, it is helpful to distinguish between "observation" and "interpretation." The observation stage simply involves seeing what is there and taking field notes. This raw observational data can then serve literary interpretation of any persuasion, and at any level, from first steps to Olympian. As students grow familiar with these type-scenes, they can use them as stars to navigate by when exploring new texts and traditions. Advanced scholars can use type-scene analysis to validate and deepen emerging interpretations at a fundamental level. To that end, I have organized the present volume to model the various levels of type-scene analysis.

Part I, the compendium of type-scenes most commonly encountered in medieval literature, models the observational stage and works with individual scenes. For each scene, I provide a working definition of the type-scene and number its main components to sensitize the reader's eye to the "molecular structure" of the scene. Following the definition, I provide brief close readings of different instances of the type-scene from disparate corners of the canon, numbering the scenic components to track each poet's specific handling of the elements. Simultaneously, I connect the micro-level detail to macro-level themes of the work or of its larger poetic tradition. These readings, thus, venture into the interpretive stage and demonstrate how a work's larger concerns manifest in the inner workings of the scene. These readings are not intended to be definitive in any way, and my understanding of these scenes continues to evolve. Rather, the readings are designed to make visible the structure and constituent components of the scene, with an eye to the ingenuity of each successive iteration. Editions and translations of primary texts cited in Part I can be found in the bibliography.

Just to clarify, the compendium is not an encyclopedia. The list of scenes featured is by no means exhaustive. Rather, it features those type-scenes students are most likely to encounter in the literature of western medieval Europe and in texts commonly taught in college classrooms. I have also adhered to texts and traditions I know—namely, the literature of English, French, and Italian tradition—and have avoided literature less familiar to me, such as the medieval Celtic, Norse, and Spanish traditions. My hope is that scholars in those adjacent fields will be inspired to develop similar guides to the type-scenes governing those literatures.

Part II applies a wider lens to type-scenes, stepping away from the individual scenes to view how poets coordinate multiple type-scenes across a single work to produce unique effects. Type-scenes often fall into predictable arrangements that ensure logical stories, like the standard ingredients of a cookie. However, a skilled poet can innovate by making unusual combinations of type-scenes. He might take a familiar grouping of scenes and change their usual order, as Boccaccio's does with epic type-scenes in the *Teseida*. The poet might take several type-scenes, from mutually distinct genres that almost never occur together, and place them in the same narrative as a sustained diatribe of the protagonist, as the poet of the Middle English *Athelston* does. Or, the poet might reiterate a single-scene over and over, achieving effects from dread to humorous delight using the same scenic components, as the *Beowulf*-poet does with a scene of fatal feasting. Each poet uses predictable scenes in unpredictable configurations, highlighting the creative potential of the medium and of the poet himself.

Part III takes a wider perspective, still, on type-scenes. Here, I identify the Wise Woman scene *as* a formal type-scene for the first time, and show its prevalence across several Middle English romances that share an ideological program of political and cultural expansionism. While scenes of female counsel occur throughout medieval literature, the particular and recurring configuration of setting, character, and action in the Wise Woman scene not only distinguishes it from other scenes of female counsel but also helps to define the stories in which it occurs as a distinct story-type involving matters of foreign policy. Each story containing this type-scene depicts a different political or cultural frontier. By introducing this domestic type-scene, which originates in crusading literature, the medieval poet announces the problem personality representing a problematic culture in need of reform. The single intimate scene invokes the "big picture" of the narrative and of the nation.

xxiv *Introduction*

The beauty and mystery of type-scenes rests in their paradoxical nature. Their ritualistic purpose brings opposites into complementarity, opposites of past and future, stasis and change, tradition and innovation, stillness and action, old and new identities, the effable and the ineffable, and the microcosm and the macrocosm. While stories are full of working scenes of dialogue, travel, combat, and diplomacy that move the plot, type-scenes do the higher work of bringing awareness to what the other scenes are doing. It is through its type-scenes that a story achieves consciousness.

Notes

1. See Guy Claxton, *Intelligence in the Flesh* (New Haven, CT and London: Yale University Press, 2015). Michael Gershon, *The Second Brain* (New York: Harper Perennial, 1999); Emeran Mayer, *The Mind-Gut Connection* (New York: Harper Wave, 2018).
2. Claxton, *Intelligence in the Flesh*, 4.
3. On the "Code of the West" in the Western, see John Truby, *The Anatomy of Genre: How Story Forms Explain the Way the World Works* (New York: Picador, 2022), 419–20.
4. Peter Haidu, "The Episode as Semiotic Module in Twelfth-Century Romance," *Poetics Today* 4 (1983): 655–81, 660–63.
5. "The Episode as Semiotic Module in Twelfth-Century Romance," 680.
6. See Brian Toohey, *Reading Epic* (London and New York: Routledge, 1992), 13–16. Also, Matthew Clark, "Formulas, Metre and Type-Scenes," in Robert Fowler, ed., *The Cambridge Companion to Homer* (Cambridge: Cambridge University Press, 2004), 117–38, 134–37; Mark W. Edwards, "Homer and Oral Tradition: The Type-Scene," *Oral Tradition* 7(2) (1992): 284–330.
7. Ernst Robert Curtius discusses several themes and motifs germane to medieval literature under "topics." See *European Literature and the Latin Middle Ages*, trans. Willard R. Trask, Bollingen Series 36 (Princeton, NJ: Princeton University Press, 1990), 79–105.
8. See Philip J. Deloria and Alexander I. Olson, *American Studies: A User's Guide* (Berkeley: University of California Press, 2017), 188–90.
9. See Manuel, "'The Voice of Thunder': The Formulaic Nature of the Gothic Type-Scene," *Gothic Studies* 25 (2023): 93–111, 107.
10. Ibid.
11. Ibid., 98.
12. Walter Arend, *Die typischen scenen bei Homer* (Berlin: Weidmann, 1933).
13. See A.B. Lord, "Homer and Huso II: Narrative Inconsistencies in Greek and Southslavic Heroic Song," *Transactions of the American Philological Association* 69 (1938): 439–45, 440.
14. Lord published his joint work with Milman Parry as *The Singer of Tales* (Cambridge, MA: Harvard University Press, 1960).
15. J. Armstrong, "The Arming Motif in the *Iliad*," *American Journal of Philology* 79 (1969): 337–54; M. Bailey, "Homeric Guest-Reception and Ritual Handwashing," *American Philological Association Abstracts* (1987): 126; C.W. Shelmerdine, "The Pattern of Guest Welcome in the *Odyssey*," *Classical Journal* 65(3) (1969): 124; C.R. Beye, "Homeric Battle Narrative and Catalogues," *Harvard Studies in Classical Philology* 68 (1964): 345–73; H.D. Kolias, "The

Return Home: A Study of Recognition in the *Odyssey*," *Dissertation Abstracts* 44(8) (1984): 2464A; N. Richardson, "Recognition Scenes in the *Odyssey*," in F. Cairns, ed., *Papers of the Liverpool Latin Seminar* 4 (1983): 219–35.
16 See Edwards, "Homer and Oral Tradition: The Type-Scene," 284–330; also "Type-scenes and Homeric Hospitality," *Transactions of the American Philological Association* 105 (1975): 51–72; also "Convention and Individuality in *Iliad* 1," *Harvard Studies in Classical Philology* 84 (1980): 1–28; also "The Structure of Homeric Catalogues," *Transactions of the American Philological Association* 110 (1980): 81–105; "The Conventions of a Homeric Funeral," in J.H. Betts, J. T. Hooker, and J.R. Green, eds., *Studies in Honor of T.B.L. Webster* (Bristol: Bristol Classical Press, 1986), 84–92; also *Homer: Poet of the Iliad* (Baltimore, MD: Johns Hopkins University Press, 1987); "*Topos* and Transformation in Homer," in J.M. Bremer, I.J.F. de Jong, and J. Kalff, eds., *Homer Beyond Oral Poetry* (Amsterdam: Grüner, 1987), 47–60.
17 For example, the studies detailing the courtly landscape settings of the May festival and the *minnegrotte* episodes in Gottfried von Strassburg's *Tristan and Isolde* as instances of the type-scene involving the *locus amoenus*. See Frederic C. Tubach, "The *Locus Amoenus* in the *Tristan* of Gottfried von Straszburg," *Neophilologus* 43 (1959): 37–42; Michael S. Batts, "The Idealised Landscape of Gottfried's *Tristan*," *Neophilologus* 46 (1962): 226–33. Both scholars apply the paradigm of the *locus amoenus* as identified by Ernst Robert Curtius, *European Literature and the Latin Middle Ages*, 195–200.
18 See Emmanuèle Baumgartner, "Romance," in William Kibler and Grover A. Zinn, eds., *Medieval France: An Encyclopedia* (New York: Garland Publishing, Inc., 1995), 811–13, 811.
19 Haidu notes a similar prejudice against the narrative unit of the episode. See "The Episode as Semiotic Module in Twelfth-Century Romance," 655.
20 I refer to Walter Arend's 1933 *Die typischen scenen bei Homer*. Essential related studies include Stith Thompson's pioneering *Motif-Index of Folk Literature* (Bloomington: University of Indiana Press, 1955–58); Charles Muscatine, *Chaucer and the French Tradition* (Berkeley: University of California Press, 1957), for Chaucer's use of courtly poetic convention; Ernst Robert Curtius, *European Literature and the Latin Middle Ages*.
21 See Peter Stockwell, *Cognitive Poetics: An Introduction*, 2nd ed. (London and New York: Routledge, 2020), 106–9.
22 Ibid., 106.
23 Ibid., 106–7.
24 Homer, *The Odyssey*, trans. Robert Fagles (London: Penguin Books, 1996), Book VIII.
25 See Brian Toohey, *Reading Epic* (London and New York: Routledge, 1992), 50–52. For the matter of identity in this and related scenes, see Bernard Fenik, *Studies in the Odyssey* (Wiesbaden: Steiner, 1974), 5–130.
26 See Paul Battles and Charles D. Wright, "*Eall-feala Ealde saege*: Poetic Performance and 'The *Scop*'s Repertoire' in Old English Verse," *Oral Tradition* 32 (2018): 3–26.
27 *Beowulf*, ll. 867b-876. Battles and Wright, "*Eall-feala Ealde saege*: Poetic Performance and 'The *Scop*'s Repertoire' in Old English Verse," 6–7.
28 Ibid., 9–10.
29 Excerpted in O.B. Hardison, Alex Preminger, Kevin Kerrane, and Leon Golden, eds., *Medieval Literary Criticism* (New York: Frederick Unger Publishing, Inc., 1974), 123–44, 123, 133–34.

30 Matthew of Vendôme, *Ars Versificatoria (The Art of the Versemaker)*, trans. Roger P. Parr (Milwaukee: Marquette University, 1981), 36–38, 55, 55–57.
31 See *Troilus and Criseyde*, I.1065–71, in Larry D. Benson, ed., The Riverside Chaucer, 3rd ed., (Boston: Houghton Mifflin, 1987). Chaucer echoes the opening lines of Geoffrey's "General Remarks on Poetry" of the *Poetria Nova*. See Hardison, et al., *Medieval Literary Criticism*, 128. Also, Martin Carmargo, "Chaucer and the Oxford Renaissance of Anglo-Latin Rhetoric," *Studies in the Age of Chaucer* 34 (2012): 173–207.
32 On the form and variations of the Western novel, see James K. Folsom, *The American Western Novel* (New Haven, CT: College and University Press, 1966).
33 For a recent discussion of the structural and philosophical components of the American Western, see Truby, *The Anatomy of Genre*, 403–61; also, Jane Tompkins, *West of Everything: The Inner Life of the Western* (New York: Oxford University Press, 1992), 23–130. On the stock scenes of the western, see Deloria and Olson, *American Studies: A User's Guide*, 196.
34 Haidu, "The Episode as Semiotic Module in Twelfth-Century Romance," 655.
35 Roberta L. Krueger, "Questions of Gender in Old French Courtly Romance," in Roberta L. Krueger, ed., *The Cambridge Companion to Medieval Romance* (Cambridge: Cambridge University Press, 2000), 132–49; W.R.J. Barron, *English Medieval Romance* (London and New York: Longman 1987), 25–27.
36 Barron, *English Medieval Romance*, 28–29; Kenneth Varty, "Medieval Romance," in Alex Preminger and T.V.F. Brogan, eds., *The New Princeton Encyclopedia of Poetry and Poetics* (Princeton, NJ: Princeton University Press, 1993), 751–54; W.P. Ker, *Epic and Romance: Essays on Medieval Literature* (New York: Dover Publications, 1957), 321–70.
37 Ker, *Epic and Romance*, 328–33; Jan Ziolkowski, "Avatars of Ugliness in Medieval Literature," *The Modern Language Review* 79 (1984): 1–20.
38 This is known as the "Five Element/Five Phase Theory." See Harriet Beinfield and Efrem Korngold, *Between Heaven and Earth: A Guide to Chinese Medicine* (New York: Ballantine Books, 1991), 96–97.
39 *Signs Taken for Wonders: On the Sociology of Literary Forms* (London: Verso, 1983), 6.
40 Ibid., 3.
41 See *Film Structure and the Emotion System* (Cambridge: Cambridge University Press, 2007), 48.
42 On the styling of the cowboy hero in nineteenth-century popular fiction of the American frontier, see Mody C. Boatright, "The Beginnings of Cowboy Fiction," *Southwest Review* 51 (1966): 11–28; Truby, *The Anatomy of Genre*, 416–18; Folsom, *The American Western Novel*, 99–140.
43 On the influence of the western on *Star Wars: A New Hope*, see Deloria and Olson, *American Studies: A User's Guide*, 198–200.
44 See Haidu, "The Episode as Semiotic Module in Twelfth-Century Romance," 680 and 659.

Part I

A Compendium of Type-Scenes of Medieval Literature

Arming of the Hero

The equipping of the hero with weapons and armor in preparation for battle, of both Classical and Germanic origin. A quiet, meditative, and ritualistic scene without dialogue marking the hero's transition from accepting to enacting his mission as the hero prepares himself physically and mentally for the martial challenge ahead. The scene consists of 1) the hero; 2) an atmosphere of silence, even in company; 3) sometimes, an attendant who arms the hero; 4) a catalog of the armor and weapons placed on the hero. We later see the hero use these items in the thick of battle. The nature of the weapons and armor, who bestows them, and who owns them signify aspects of the hero's identity and the nature of his mission.

The OE *Beowulf* contains memorable scenes of the Arming of the Hero prefacing each of his fights with the monsters of the poem: Grendel, Grendel's mother, and the Dragon. The first such scene (ll. 671–76) is actually a *dis*arming scene, as Beowulf (1), in the presence of his men, silently (2) removes his helmet and his corslet, along with his splendid sword (4), and hands them to a servant (3) for safekeeping in preparation to fight Grendel, illustrating two aspects of his nobility: the strength of his bare hands (proven repeatedly) and his insistence on a fair fight (as Grendel fights without weapons). Beowulf's disarming doubles as a preparation for sleep as well as battle, as it prefaces the Sleeping After the Feast* type-scene containing Grendel's attack on Heorot; hence, the reversal of the Arming scene. During the fight, we see Beowulf overcome Grendel with the "weapon" of his bare hands, closing the formula. A second Arming of the Hero scene occurs at the edge of the mere (ll. 1441b-1491) as Beowulf prepares to dive in to encounter Grendel's mother. The hero (1) silently (2) dons his famous mail shirt, crafted by Wayland (the blacksmith god of Old Norse tradition), his helmet hung with chain mail, and the sword, Hrunting, lent him by Unferth (3)(4). Beowulf's gear distills key aspects of Anglo-Saxon cultural identity. Each of these items is described as skillfully hand-crafted and attributed with sentient feelings of duty and loyalty, knowing how to guard, protect, and serve, reflecting not only the defensive nature of this and all the other fights in the poem but also the animism characteristic of Anglo-Saxon belief. The mail shirt crafted by Wayland indicates not only the epic warrior's singular status but also the Anglo-Saxon roots in Norse religion. The helmet incorporates the boar imagery common to Anglo-Saxon warrior culture, and the sword lent by Unferth reflects the centrality of gift-giving and reciprocity in early English society. True to the formula, the gear features in the fight, but interestingly, the sword fails, while a giant sword discovered in the lair supplements the hero's equipment, outperforming Hrunting, and again, proving the hero's superhuman strength through his ability to wield it. A similarly unique item appears in the final Arming scene (l. 2336ff.) as Beowulf (1) prepares to avenge the dragon's attacks on his people. He instructs the smith (3) to make a shield entirely of iron to withstand the fire-breathing serpent, again proving his physical strength. The poet varies the scene by having Beowulf speak (2) of the gear he takes into the barrow: a tempered sword (Naegling), his corslet, and the iron shield (4). He indicates only bringing a sword because he cannot use his bare hands against the fire-armed foe, though the sword snaps in the powerful grip of his hand, again proving his superior strength.

Chretien de Troyes includes a brief Arming of the Hero scene early in *Erec and Enide* (l. 707 ff.), which illustrates the new priorities of chivalric romance, where combat serves female interests and the hero's individual emotional development thereby. Erec pursues the knight Yder to the town of Cardigan, where he meets Enide, his future wife and the primary agent of his growth. Up to this point, Erec has been unarmed and unprepared for heroic exploit, and the Arming scene illustrates his first step into masculine maturity, as defined by the genre. In facing the sparrow-hawk challenge against Yder, Erec borrows choice armor from Enide's father, an older, seasoned veteran, taking on the vavasor's mature masculine identity. The Arming scene at Enide's home contains the standard elements of the hero (1) being armed silently (2) with items of armor and weapons forming a catalog (greaves laced with deer-hide thongs; a hauberk of chain mail laced onto the ventail; a helmet; a sword laced at his side; a horse; a shield and a lance) (4). At the same time, Chrétien varies the scene by having Enide, herself, assume the role of the servant (3) arming the hero from head to foot, indicating not only the amorous goal of Erec's upcoming challenge but the unusually active role Enide will play in his quest through dangerous encounters, where she continues to handle horses and weapons. Erec's victory against Yder is marked by his *dis*arming of the other man by forcibly tearing off his helmet, untying his ventail, removing the armor from his face and head, though refusing the offer of his sword. Though Erec presumably returns the borrowed armor to the vavasor, the disarming scene pertains to Yder, not to Erec, suggesting the hero's emerging identity and the enemy's loss of his. A longer, more detailed and ritualistic, Arming of the Hero scene occurs once Erec and Enide are married and living at court (ll. 2620–60). Erec arms himself this time in his own armor, for a quest to dispel rumors about him as a lovestruck lay-about. Without explanation, Erec (1) orders a servant (3) to bring his gear, steps onto an image of a leopard on a carpet and dons his costly armor piece by piece (4) before a silent (2) and bewildered crowd of knights. While a servant assists with the final stages of arming, Enide assumes an even more prominent role in "arming" herself, on Erec's orders, in her finest gown to accompany him on his quest, luring hostile challengers to Erec so he can prove himself worthy of this royal armor and of his future role as king.

Gottfried von Strassburg includes a ceremonial Arming of the Hero scene in *Tristan and Isolde* (ll. 4860ff.) prior to Tristan's return to Parmenie to avenge his father's death. Gottfried employs an unusual amalgam of literary traditions, genre, and imagery to fashion Tristan as a new kind of hero. The dialogue-free scene (2) differs from other Arming scenes in being more rhetorical than practical, concerned more with Tristan's literary, rather than his personal or political, identity. In Tristan's (1) investiture at Mark's court, Gottfried invokes (in the conditional) the classical figures of Apollo, the Camenae, Vulcan (the maker of Aeneas' armor), and Cassandra as would-be participants in Tristan's arming, yet indicates his shield bears the image a boar, the iconic image of the Germanic warrior, thus blending classical and Germanic heroic literary traditions. Gottfried then pairs the boar imagery of ancient Germanic epic with the image of a Fiery Dart of love on the hero's helmet (4), thus incorporating the newer literary tradition of French chivalric romance. Tristan's arming scene presages his unique identity as a romance figure, the famed lover of Isolde, who, nevertheless, consistently fights along the pattern of the epic warrior on behalf of men and usually in matters of state, rather than "for the girl," distinguishing him from his French counterparts and thereby elevating Love to the highest status within the medieval literary hierarchy.

Sir Gawain and the Green Knight contains a well-known Arming of the Hero scene that both fulfills and varies the formula from chivalric romance. Predictably, the scene occurs early in the narrative (Fitt II, ll. 566–669) as Gawain prepares to leave Camelot in search of the Green Chapel to face the Green Knight. True to the scene, Gawain (1) is armed in silence (2). The poet varies the familiar scene, however, in several ways. First, the arming is done partly by Gawain himself and partly by unnamed others, indicating the communal rather than strictly personal nature of his mission as he defends the honor of King Arthur and the court. Second, the poet greatly extends the catalogue of armor (4), describing each item for its design, quality, and craftsmanship, and by staging the arming on a red carpet, making the scene especially meditative and ceremonious, and validating the inherent honor of the court unfairly insulted by the challenger. Third, the poet describes the "arming" of Gawain's horse, Gringolet, detailing its embroidered, silken accoutrements (4) made by many women over seven years. Fourth, the Arming scene ends with an Ekphrasis* of Gawain's shield, which, rather than exhibiting a personal family crest, displays (on the outside) a pentangle whose points distill universal, collective aspects of Christian piety (the five wounds of Christ; the five pure joys of Mary) and the chivalric virtues. As a defensive item, the shield also reveals the defensive nature of his mission, underscored by no mention of a sword here. Likewise, the shield's interior displays an image not of the hero's personal beloved woman but of the Virgin Mary, indicating a more holy and universal love—a variant (and possible critique) on the female orientation of the French hero. Unlike his French counterpart, the English Gawain arms not for future gain but for ultimate loss, for what he believes will be his death through his encounter with a half-giant against whom he cannot wage any resistance; hence, the solemnity of the scene.

Geoffrey Chaucer satirizes the Arming of the Hero type-scene in *Sir Thopas* (ll. 845–89) as the hero prepares himself to fight the giant, Olifaunt. Its absurdities include its excessive length (31 lines) and its precise yet mis-matched materials, including a gold shield with a carbuncle, an ivory sword sheath (but no sword), a brass helmet, cypress spear, and dappled gray horse (4), all drawn from popular romances of the time. Rather than having a formal, quiet tone, the Arming takes place in the raucous atmosphere of a feast (2), with the hero (1) swearing on ale and bread about his upcoming fight, while accompanied by minstrels and bards rather than by a servant (3).

Further Reading

Derek Brewer, "The Arming of the Warrior in European Literature and Chaucer," in Edward Vasta, Zacharias P. Thundy, and Theodore M. Hesburgh, eds., *Chaucerian Problems and Perspectives: Essays Presented to Paul S. Beichner, C.S.C.* (Notre Dame: University of Notre Dame Press, 1979), 221–43.

Stephanie J. Hollis, "The Pentangle Knight: 'Sir Gawain and the Green Knight'," *The Chaucer Review* 15 (1981): 267–81.

Helmut Nickel, "Arthurian Armings for War and Love," *Arthuriana* 5 (1995): 3–21.

Beasts of Battle

Prominent in Old English poetry, a narrative ornament used to embellish a battle-scene, involving mention of a wolf, eagle, and/or raven, singly or in combination, as beasts attendant at a scene of carnage. Mention of the beasts may occur as a harbinger of ensuing carnage, an after-effect of carnage completed, accompaniments of current battle, or in the subjunctive as a predictable and recurring pattern of bloody events. As a narrative element attending a battle-scene, the Beasts of Battle formula consists of 1) mention of a carrion-eating beast(s) 2) who is eager for, or rejoicing in, a corpse 3) and usually howling, screaming, singing, or talking 4) in a setting of carnage. While most instances of the scene contain all four elements, the single mention of a raven swooping and screaming/singing can synecdochally imply the remaining elements of the scene. The scene forebodes bloody and decisive events, and the beasts' eagerness/rejoicing, though neutral in the conflict, intensifies the emotional effect of the scene either by emboldening the participants in the conflict or by instilling fear and dread of a doomed outcome. At least nine poems and twelve scenes contain mention of the Beasts of Battle in Old English, including the *Battle of Brunanburg*, *Beowulf*, *Elene*, *Genesis A*, the *Wanderer*, *Finnsburg*, *Judith*, the *Battle of Maldon*, and *Exodus*. In Middle English, it features in Chaucer's "Legend of Philomela," in the *Legend of Good Women*.

The Beasts of Battle occurs three times in the OE *Elene* (27b-30; 52; 110b-14a). In the first instance, Emperor Constantine (not yet Christian) rides out to battle the Huns, and a forest wolf (1) "sang its war-song" (*fyrd-leoð agol*) (3) and made no secret of "its hope for a corpse" (*wael-rune ne mað*) (2), while an eagle (1) "raised its song in pursuit of the foe" (*sang ahof/laðum on laste*) (3) on the battlefield (4), as fighting is about to commence. As the troops advance further (4), a raven (1) circles over the assemblage, screaming (3). When fighting erupts (4), a raven (1) "rejoiced in the work" (*weorces gefeah*) (2), while an eagle (1) watched the marching troops (4) and a wolf "raised its song" (*sang ahof*) (3). The scene promises bloody triumph.

In *Beowulf* (ll. 3024b-27), the Beasts of Battle scene takes the subjunctive, as a likely consequence of enemy tribes hearing of Beowulf's death. The poet artfully pictures a raven (1), poised over men fated to die (4), talking a lot (3) with an eagle (1) about its meal, while it and a wolf (1) plundered the slain. In this sense, the scene presages doom rather than triumph. The ominous Beasts of Battle can also cast similar doom on interior spaces (i.e., halls), as in this compressed reference to the scene in *The Fight at Finnsburg* (l. 34–5a), where "[the screaming eagle moved about,] the raven circled, black and dark glistening" ([*Hwearf hlacra earn,*] *hraefn wandrode/sweart* and *salu-brun*), where the brief image of screaming (3) beasts (1) swooping among the rafters sets the tone for the scene.

Geoffrey Chaucer employs the poetic device of the Beasts of Battle in the "Legend of Philomela" in the *LOGW*, as part of his larger portraiture of the cruel, unjust, and primitive King Tereus of Thrace, who rapes his wife's sister, Philomela, and then cuts out her tongue and imprisons her to prevent her from ever revealing the crime. Chaucer adapts the story and this scene from the sixth book of the *Metamorphoses* of Ovid, who casts a shadow over the wedding of Tereus and Procne (Philomela's sister) by describing an owl—a sign of misfortune—perched/sitting (*sedit*) silently on the (external) roof (*culmine*) over the marriage chamber. Chaucer modifies the image so that, rather than huddling stationary, the owl (1)—a prophet of despair (l. 2254, "That prophete is of wo and of myschaunce")—flies in circles (indoors) among the beams all night (l. 2253, "The oule al nyght aboute the balkes wond") during the fateful wedding feast (4), with the continuous song (3) of the party (l. 2255, "This revel, ful of song...") providing the element of singing commonly associated with the scene, evoking the early English imagery of the Beasts of Battle portending decisive and bloody suffering in this portrait of a barbaric king.

Further Reading

Thomas Honegger, "Form and Function: The Beasts of Battle Revisited," *English Studies* 79 (1999): 289–98.

Stephen C.E. Hopkins, "Snared by the Beasts of Battle: Fear as Hermeneutic Guide in the Old English *Exodus*," *Philological Quarterly* 97 (2018): 1–25.

Francis P. Magoun, Jr., "The Theme of the Beasts of Battle in Anglo-Saxon Poetry," *Neuphilologische Mitteilungen* 56 (1955): 81–90.

Blason

A head-to-toe description of a character. Of French origin. While often associated with Renaissance, Petrarchan literary tradition, in which the blason denotes a descriptive poem in praise or blame of an object or person, the blason, in fact, has its roots in medieval narrative, where it functions as a type-scene, typically occurring early in a narrative, to introduce the character pivotal to the plot and central to the hero's task. The scene consists of 1) a person/creature who catalyzes the plot; 2) a catalog of the person/creature's physical features; and 3) a viewer, the person most impacted by the subject described. The scene marks a pause in the main action, and the "action" of the scene is viewing the pivotal person/creature. As a blason occurs most often within the genre of romance, the type-scene typically applies to the beautiful woman whose hold on the hero's heart generates the plot, and therefore, we experience the blason through the eyes of the male lover. Other common subjects of blasons include monsters, whose dangerous threat creates the central conflict of the narrative. Blasons of beauty and monstrosity merge in the figure of the Loathly Lady*, a beautiful young woman trapped in the form of a repulsive hag, vividly described. As a snapshot of the catalyst of the story, the nature of the blason, its items, order of elements, and placement within the narrative, often distills the main priorities of the text.

The literary formula of the blason becomes codified in a group of texts known as the *artes poeticae* (arts of poetry), including two twelfth-century poetic treatises, Geoffrey of Vinsauf's *Poetria Nova*, and Matthew of Vendôme's *Ars versificatoria (The Art of the Versemaker)*, both handbooks for aspiring poets. Under *amplificatio* (Amplification), Geoffrey includes the subsection of *descriptio* (Description), where he prescribes how "to describe, in amplified form, a woman's beauty" (133). Starting at the top and working downward, Geoffrey recommends "let the color of gold give a glow to her hair, and lilies bloom high on her brow. . . . Let her nose be straight . . ." and "let her eyes . . . be radiant with emerald light, or with brightness of stars" (133). Working through the details of her face, including mouth, lips, teeth, and chin, the poet moves downward to neck, shoulders, arms, fingers, and hands. Her breast should capture "the image of snow" with "its twin virginal gems," while her waist should be small enough to encircle with two hands (134). Skipping over the parts for which "the mind's speech is more apt than the tongue's," Geoffrey moves to her legs, concluding with her "tiny foot," emphasizing balance and symmetry at each stage. While Geoffrey allows for additional description of clothing and jewelry, "her beauty will be of more worth than richness of vesture" (134).

Matthew of Vendôme's *Ars versificatoria*, whose entire first book is devoted to modes of description, applies this same model of portraiture to Helen of Troy (I.56–57), dwelling especially on the radiant details of her face. Matthew then follows this description of female beauty with an example of an ugly woman, Beroe, "a mangy cur, a pallid social outcast," working downward from her "bald head" and "menacing brow" to her "mangy shins" and "gouty feet" (I.58), again emphasizing the physical features of this monstrous female. In describing men, however, Matthew minimizes the physical in order to showcase the intellectual and psychological, working less head to toe than inside out. Of Ulysses, for example, we learn of "the glory of his intellect," "his mighty tongue" and "sound judgment," which are wedded to his "integrity," and he is praised for how he perceives, comprehends, and speaks, so that "the inner man is the faithful master of the outer man" (I.52). In this sense, Matthew prescribes not simply a mode of description for women, monsters, and men but also a way of envisioning their agency and impact in narrative. Thus, the *Poetria Nova* and the *Ars versificatoria*, intended for students and practitioners of the poetic arts, delineate what soon becomes a stock scene in both lyric and narrative poetry from that point on. Nevertheless, despite the *Poetria Nova*'s orderly and stylized method for scribing a beautiful woman, creative variation of the various elements of the literary blason became a signature move among medieval poets right at the outset.

Chrétien de Troyes includes two blasons in *Yvain, the Knight with the Lion* (c. 1180), one of a monstrous peasant, "ugly and hideous in the extreme" (298), and the other of Laudine, the love interest of the hero (313). Both occur early in the narrative, at the beginning of the hero's quest to avenge the dishonor of his cousin, Calogrenant, at the hands of Esclados the Red, the knight of the spring. On route to the spring, Yvain (3) encounters a "peasant who resembled a Moor" (1), described in the head-to-toe poetic formula, including his unkempt hair, excessively wide forehead, hairy ears "as huge as an elephant's," eyes of an owl, nose of a cat, jaws of a wolf, and teeth of a boar (289)(2). The rest of his body comes into view as he stands up on a stump, wielding a club. Rather than fighting this creature, as readers might expect, Yvain asks for directions to the nearest adventure, effectively transitioning the narrative away from feats of brute strength as a measure of heroic merit, toward internal, emotional, and spiritual challenges—the heart of chivalric romance. Chrétien announces this new challenge with a second blason, this one of Laudine (1), the noblewoman whose husband Yvain has just killed. The new heroic priorities of the romance hero in matters of the heart, rooted equally in classical Ovidian tradition and medieval Christianity, become modeled in the blason of Laudine, as we look through the hero's eyes. Upon first spying her through a window, Yvain (3) senses the pain of his fresh wounds, pale in comparison to the newly inflicted emotional wounds of Love, "which are more enduring than those from lance or sword" (311), echoing Ovid's dictum "*militat omnis amans, et habet sua castra Cupido*" ("Every lover is a soldier, and Cupid keeps his own camps," *Amores*, 1.9). Further, Chrétien grounds this seemingly secular experience of Love in Christian teachings, as Yvain resolves to "love my enemy forever" (312), the widow of the man he just killed. Thus, Chrétien aligns the blason with enlightened thinking. External appearances give way to internal truths through a series of comparisons, as Yvain sees beyond Laudine's tear-stained, disheveled face into her innate beauty, which draws upon him powerfully. Thus, he grieves her "beautiful hair, which surpasses pure gold as it glistens," despite her "tearing and pulling it out"; though "they are filled with unceasing tears, there never were more beautiful eyes"; though she is "doing injury to her face. I've never seen a more perfectly shaped face"; "why does she wring her beautiful hands and strike and scratch at her breast?"; concluding "she is so beautiful even in anguish" (313)(2). In his ability to perceive and be moved by the feminine and reorient himself accordingly, Yvain models the romance heroic ideal. Thus, Chrétien uses the literary blason, both individually and in combination, to distill the core tenets of chivalric romance, the genre he pioneered.

Roughly contemporary with Chrétien, Marie de France employs the blason in equally innovative ways with regard to both the transforming character (the subject of the blason) and the one being transformed (the object of the blason). In the *Lai de Lanval*, for example, she omits a formal blason of the Fairy Princess (1) upon the hero's (3) first, intimate encounter with her, suggesting that he is already worthy of the lady's love rather than in need of inner transformation. Instead, Marie moves the blason of the Fairy Princess to the end of the narrative, in a public setting, as she disrupts the legal proceedings wrongfully incriminating Lanval for crimes against the queen, accusations that hold not only the hero but the entire court hostage to corruption. On the brink of the verdict, the Fairy Princess (1) approaches on horseback, and we view her through the collective perspective of Arthur's entire court (3), whose faulty perceptions of Lanval are dispelled by the living truth of the fairy's beauty, which exonerates the hero. The court, more than the hero, undergoes inner transformation. The fairy's disruptive influence on the court accounts for the disordered arrangement of the elements of the blason: rather than descending from head to toe, the blason starts at her torso, with the "white tunic and shift, laced left and right so as to reveal her sides," moves down to her hips, up to her neck and face, detailing her bright eyes, mouth, nose, and eyebrows, and ending with her "curly and rather blond" hair (80)(2). The unusual order of elements captures the disorienting sexual appeal she has for King Arthur and his courtiers, overshadowing Guinevere, while the recurring images of whiteness and brightness indicate the righteousness of her cause. In essence, Marie challenges the narrowly personal honor espoused by chivalric romance by using the blason to rectify public corruption.

In his *Tristan and Isolde* (c.1210), Gottfried von Strassburg uses the blasons of both Tristan and Isolde to craft the "hero" role distinctive to the *liebestod* tradition. Unlike the hero and heroine of a chivalric romance, who spend most of the narrative navigating closer proximity to one another up to marriage, the couple of the *liebestod* tradition solidify their bond early in the narrative, and spends the remainder of the story defending that bond against insurmountable odds that ultimately cause the double-death of the couple. The more collaborative nature of the *liebestod* couple joins the "hero" and "heroine" into a single "hero" as they face adversity together. Gottfried expresses this new hero-type in the blasons of Tristan and Isolde, reversing markers of gender in each. For example, upon Tristan's (1) arrival at the court of King Mark (3), we get a formal blason of him that could easily characterize a young woman: "His form . . . was shaped as Love would have it. His mouth was as red as a rose, his colour radiant, his eyes clear; his hair fell is brown locks, crimped at the ends; his arms and hands were shapely and dazzling white; his figure was tall to the right degree," and only in his feet and legs "in which his beauty most appeared," does Gottfried remind us that this blason details "such praise as a man may give a man" (85) (2). This girly description of Tristan, moreover, contradicts his later profile as the indominable warrior who defeats Morold. The feminized description of Tristan contrasts with the blason of Isolde, which exudes power and authority along with feminine appeal. As Isolde (1) enters into the public view (3) accompanied by her mother, Gottfried emphasizes not her physical form but the costly attire covering her form: "She wore a robe and mantle of purple samite cut in the French fashion and accordingly, where the sides slope down to their curves, the robe was fringed and gathered into her body with a girdle of woven silk. . . . Her robe fitted her intimately, is clung close to her body . . . clinging between her knees as much as each of you pleases. Her mantle was set off by a lining of white ermine with the spots arranged diaper-fashion" (185) (2). Gottfried highlights royal colors and materials (purple and ermine) and craftsmanship; the robe is "cut to perfect measure," "the sable and the ermine curved all along its seam," with her hand accentuating the pearls near the clasp, not vice versa (185)(2). The blason pronounces the royal wealth and power Isolde commands in the public eye (3). Thus, her eyes peer out like those of a "falcon" of Love, whose "rapacious feathered glances . . . [go] in search of prey," robbing "many a man of his very self!"

(185) (2)(3). The blason ends not at the feet but at the crown, describing the literal "circlet of gold" atop her head, upstaging her hair which merely "resembl[ed] gold" (186)(2). If the earlier blason of Tristan feminizes the hero, the blason of Isolde masculinizes her as a formidable royal. They become equalized and unified as a single "hero" in a misperceiving world; hence, the public lens of each blason (3).

The literary blason prevailed into the Middle English romances of the thirteenth and fourteenth centuries, where it, nonetheless, reflects different values. In *Sir Orfeo* (c.1325), the blason of Orfeo's beloved wife (ll. 102–116), Heurodis, follows convention in falling early in the narrative, upon her first appearance, and cataloging her beauty from the head down through the perspective of the hero, Orfeo. Nevertheless, as in *Yvain*, the blason occurs amidst trauma, after the queen (1) is threatened by the Fairy King. And, as in *Yvain*, the blason contrasts her emotional distress with her physical beauty. Orfeo (3) notes her body, which "was so white y-core,/ Wiþ þine nailes is al to-tore"; "þi rode, þat was so red,/Is al wan . . ."; "þine fingres smale/Beþ al blodi"; "þi louesom eyȝen to/Lokeþ so man doþ on his foe!" (ll. 105–12; "was so fair before, is all torn with your nails; your face, that was so red, is all pale; your small fingers are all bloody; your lovely eyes look as a man does on his foe") (2). As in *Yvain*, the blason of Heurodis records altered beauty, prefiguring imminent changes for the hero. As in *Yvain*, the heroine's distraught appearance contrasts with the hero's mental image of her captivating beauty. However, whereas, in *Yvain*, the contrast creates a "both-and" effect of distress *and* beauty, in *Sir Orfeo*, the contrast creates a "before and after" effect, as Orfeo recalls aspects of Heurodis' beauty, now lost. Loss—of wife, of kingdom, of community, of status—permeates the entire poem, a theme introduced in the blason. Orfeo's personal loss doubles as collective loss for the kingdom; hence, the semi-public nature of the blason, spoken aloud by King Orfeo before his closest men (3). Thus, rather than ushering in a new love for the hero, as in *Yvain*, the blason in *Sir Orfeo* spells the loss of an established love that soon cascades into many losses—military, political, and social as well as personal.

Sir Gawain and the Green Knight employs two blasons: one, of the green intruder into Arthur's hall at Camelot; and the other, of Lady Bertilak and Morgan le Fey at Bertilak's castle Hautdesert. The *Gawain*-poet innovates on the blason by grafting incompatible elements together, creating incoherence rather than clarity. The first blason of the poem describes the Green Knight (1), whose size, color, appearance, and behavior all indicate a monster. Indeed, the poet refers to the Green Knight as "aghlich" (l. 136, "terrifying") and "Half-etayn" (l. 140, "half-giant"), a word derived from the Old English *eoten*, the same word used to describe Grendel in

Beowulf (l. 761a). Moving from top down, the poet focuses on the Green Knight's torso, tracing his "mesure hyghe" (l. 137, "great height"), "swyre to the swange" (l. 138, "neck to the waist"), "his lyndes and his lymes" (l. 139, "his loins, and his limbs"), and moving back up to his "bak" and "brest" (l. 143, "back" and "breast"), stressing the size and strength of each, and we later see that, like Grendel, who has eyes like fire (*ligge gelicost*, l. 727), the Green Knight has "rede yȝen" (l. 304, "red eyes")—all vocabulary derived overwhelmingly from the Anglo-Saxon. Grafted onto this giant are elements of the late-medieval English, mounted aristocrat. Again focusing first on the torso, the poet retraces the same form but with contradictory imagery, so that the "sware" (l. 138, "strongly built") waist now appears "worthily smale" (l. 144, "properly slim"), and the same body parts that struck terror now sport elegant clothing, including a fitted tunic, a fur-trimmed cloak, tights, and gold spurs on bases of embroidered silk (ll. 151–64), conjuring a "clene" (146, 163, "elegant") man, vocabulary derived overwhelmingly from the Anglo-Norman (2). The grafting technique of the blason continues (ll. 168–98), as the portrait of the green man merges seamlessly with that of his green horse, each with groomed hair and costly adornments, simultaneously contributing to the animalistic impression he strikes in the hall, while completing his characterization as a mounted nobleman. The dual portrait of the Green Knight, uncivilized and civilized, correlates to the items he carries in each hand: a giant axe, (redolent of the giant sword in Grendel's lair) and a holly branch of peace, both part of his beheading "gomen" (l. 283, "game"). Like the Fairy Princess in Marie's *Lanval*, the Green Knight exerts a collective disorienting impact on Arthur's court (3) (including Gawain), who all bear his demeaning insults, but unlike the Fairy Princess, who resolves a conflict by clarifying truth, the Green Knight generates the conflict through mixed messages of the blason. Like Grendel, the Green Knight forms the *telos* of the hero's journey, equally shrouded in expectations of death.

The second blason of the poem occurs through the eyes of Gawain (3), who ventures into not a monster's lair but a castle. There, Gawain sees Lady Bertilak (1), whose description combines inimical elements in this double-blason of her and her older escort, Morgan. The blason moves from the top down but also back and forth between two women, contrasting the one's appeal and the other's repulsiveness: ". . . if the yonge was yep, yolwe was that other;/Riche red on that on rayled aywhere,/Rugh, ronkled chekes that other on rolled" (ll. 951-2, "if the young one was youthful, yellow was the other;/ hues rich and red adorned the former,/ rough, wrinkled cheeks hung in folds on the latter"). The shining throat and breast of Lady Bertilak contrast with the black chin and brows and bare lips (ll. 958–62) of the old crone (who receives more coverage than the Lady), with her protruding nose, stumpy body, and big buttocks (2). The blason catalogs feminine ugliness more than beauty. If the public perspective of the blason of the Green Knight captures the primacy of community and collective endangerment, the intimate perspective of Lady Bertilak and Morgan through the eyes of the hero presages the personal threat they pose to him.

In the Middle English *Erl of Tolouse*, the blason serves as much to signal nascent, amorous inclination as to safeguard it against criticism, given its adulterous circumstances. The poem revolves around the territorial dispute between the German Emperor, Sir Dyoclysyan, and Bernard of Tolouse, a costly and pointless conflict with no end in sight. Dame Beaulybon (1), the beautiful wife of the emperor, emerges as an intercessor between the two feuding men. Disguised as a hermit, Bernard (3) sneaks into the chapel where she worships and views her from a distance, generating the blason (ll. 334–57). Everything about the blason—its setting, arrangement, direction, and larger context—announce the heroine as a chaste political peacemaker more than a love object. It takes place in a chapel, with Bernard disguised as a hermit, and the ring she gives him constitutes "alms" rather than a love token. The scenic elements obviate suspicions of potential adultery. The blason's elements follow convention, but its direction conjures the shape of a cross: starting at her head, then her face, eyes, mouth, nose, and forehead, downwards to her "syde longe, hur myddyll small" (l. 352, long side and small middle), and then upwards towards her shoulders, arms, hands, and fingers, and likening her to "an aungell of hevyn" (l. 350, "an angel of heaven") (2). Experienced through the eyes of the hero, disarmed by her beauty and dressed in a hermit's garb, within an ecclesiastical space, the blason charts a new direction for the hero away from the conflict and toward peaceful reconciliation with the emperor by means of his wife. Hence, the final "kysse" (l. 1182) happens between the two men long before Beaulybon and Bernard ever marry.

The Middle English *Havelok the Dane* (c.1295–1310), relating the struggles of the dispossessed heirs of England and Denmark, contains a brief blason unusual for its subject, perspective, placement, and orientation. Throughout the poem, Havelok and the glow in his mouth when he sleeps attract voyeurism, and the blason follows this pattern. Rather than an introductory blason of the heroine, Goldeboru, through the eyes of an enamored hero, the blason depicts Havelok (1) through the eyes of another man, Ubbe (3), preoccupied with matters of national security rather than love, who sees in Havelok a valuable leader and warrior. Like the romance heroine, Havelok is the agent of transformation, and the blason provides a thumbnail of Havelok's emerging purpose in the narrative. He has abandoned his disguise as a fisherman and reclaimed his royal identity as a prelude to reclaiming the kingdoms of Denmark and England from usurpers. Ubbe, commander of Denmark's patrol, spies "Hu he was wel of bones maked/Brod in þe sholdres, ful wel schaped,/Picke in þe brest, of bodi long; He semede wel to ben wel strong" (ll. 1646–49) and thinks to himself how better suited such a man would be bearing "Helm on heued, sheld and spere" (l. 1653), superimposing military purpose onto the hero's frame and anticipating Havelok's imminent role (2). Whereas most blasons dwell on the woman's face, this one dwells on the man's shoulders and chest, focusing on Havelok's strength and its new application—not as a laborer, as if "he were a best" (l. 944), but as a fearsome warrior. The perspective of the blason through the eyes of Ubbe, a security official of Denmark and friend to Havelok's wronged father, King Birkabeyn, reframes Havelok as heir to Denmark, no longer an orphan. Finally, Ubbe's mental blason of Havelok fulfills Grim's earlier prophetic vow to protect him until "'þat þu conne ful wel bere/Helm on heued, sheld and spere'" (ll. 623–4), connecting Havelok to his royal destiny, a status he will now use on behalf of both Denmark and England. That the blason belongs to Havelok rather than Goldeboro (who receives no formal blason), reverses the usual hero-heroine/love object orientation of romance and forefronts Goldeboro as the protagonist of the poem and Havelok as the means by which she will achieve her end, in this instance, more political than amorous.

Blasons appear throughout the works of Geoffrey Chaucer, spanning every genre, from the portrait of the inappropriately beautiful Prioress in the General Prologue to the *Canterbury Tales* to the modest description of Emelye (mostly from behind) in the *Knight's Tale* (ll.1049–55) to the amorously unlucky classical heroines in the *Legend of Good Women* and the caricatured portraits of Diomede, Criseyde, and Troilus at the *end* of the *Troilus* (V.799–833), figures already well known to us. In each instance, Chaucer experiments with perspective, placement, and content, sometimes using this tool of praise in order to blame or using it to ambiguate rather than clarify. Two of Chaucer's blasons, however, warrant special attention for their signature ingenuity: that of Blanche, Duchess of Lancaster, in the *Book of the Duchess*, and that of Alisoun in the *Miller's Tale*. Chaucer's *Book of the Duchess* is deeply indebted to French poetic tradition, and the blason of Blanche forms one its crowning gestures thereof. Intended to commemorate the deceased Blanche (1), it stands to reason that her blason forms the bulk of the poem and the center of its drama. Chaucer dutifully follows the poetic model in its broadest conceit of moving from head to toe, but several features of the blason make it unprecedented in poetic tradition, French or English. First, whereas the blason of the heroine typically occurs early in the narrative, praising a live woman who will shape the future of the hero's experience, the blason of Blanche describes a dead woman who shaped the past experience of the Man in Black (3), becoming a retrospective rather than a prediction. He speaks the blason to the narrator, making his private experience a shared one (3). Second, while most blasons consist of roughly a dozen lines, the blason of Blanche runs for one hundred forty-three lines (ll. 817–960), often circling back to specific features, like her eyes, giving us a sustained look at her rather than a brief snapshot. Third, whereas the blason typically represents a verbal still-life of the woman's physical features (eyes, lips, cheeks, and so on), the blason of Blanche captures both the beauty of her physical features and her benevolent use of those features through movement and gesture, revealing her inner beauty of character. Thus, forty-five lines (ll. 840–85) describe how with her lovely eyes she "wolde/Have mercy," extending "pure lokyng" (ll. 866–7 and 870). Chaucer devotes nineteen lines not to her mouth but to her "softe speche" (l. 919, "soft speech"), elegant, kind, and truthful. The blason returns from its poetic cadenza by closing with a predictable catalog of her neck, throat, shoulders, long torso, arms, hands, nails, round breasts, and hips (ll. 939–57), but only after beginning the blason with the Black Knight's recollection of seeing her dance, sing, laugh, and play (ll. 848–50), infusing movement, voice and personality into an otherwise static poetic portrait (2). (Chaucer, perhaps, borrows from Matthew of Vendôme's prescription for describing men, highlighting action and character over physique.) Effectively, Chaucer uses his poetic artistry to bring the dead Blanche back to life, honoring the tradition of eulogy by breaking tradition.

Chaucer continues to break with the convention of the blason in the *Miller's Tale*, both in terms of the figure described and the one doing the describing. Most often, the blason forms a tool of praise reserved for women deemed most praiseworthy; namely, first-estate women, whose various physical features recall delicious, fragrant, smooth, and radiant things (e.g. apples, cherries, roses, polished marble, stars, and golden sunshine), a feast for the senses. In the *Miller's Tale*, Chaucer applies the blason to Alisoun (1), a country "wenche" (l. 3254), replacing comparisons of sensual refinement with ones of sensual instinct. Rather than starting customarily with her head, Chaucer starts at the hips, with the "barmcloth" (l. 3236, "apron") covering her "lendes" (l. 3237, "loins"), full and shapely, given the generous cut of the apron. He moves to her dress, embroidered in front "and eek behynde" (l. 3239), affording an unconventional glimpse backside (2). The blason of Alisoun announces the "business end" of this common adulteress in the tale. The blason then rises to her collar, black silk "withinne and eek withoute" (l. 3240), her bonnet and headband, before settling on her "likerous ye" (l. 3244, "lecherous eye"), suggesting how Alisoun will use her "body gent and smal" (l. 3234), doing looking (2).

Rather than characterizing a mature, rare, and ennobling beauty, the blason of Alisoun catalogs her youthful, common, and animalistic appeal through a list of young barnyard animals, including a weasel (l. 3234), a barn swallow (l. 3258), a kid and a calf (l. 3260), and a colt (l. 3263). Even the conventional imagery of flowers and fruit smacks of the farm, including the "hoord of apples leyd in hey or heeth" (l. 3262), the "new pere-jonette tree" (l. 3248, "newly blossomed pear tree"), and the wildflowers of primrose and cuckooflower (l. 3268), the last image presaging the story's theme of adultery. Above all, Chaucer's blason of Alisoun tells us less about her than about the one looking at her, the Miller (3), a shrewd villager with an eye for money and sex. Rather than seeing priceless natural beauty, the Miller notices Alisoun's pricey garments (apron, dress, collar, bonnet, headband, purse), including socially restricted accoutrements such as silk (ll. 3240, 3243, 3251), embroidery (l. 3238), and a brooch (l. 3265). Her complexion is likened to a newly minted gold coin from the Tower of London (l. 3256–6) (2). The Miller perceives not ornamental beauty but the functional sex-appeal of a woman "For any lord to leggen in his bedde,/ Or yet for any good yeman to wedde" (ll. 3269–70). His subsequent, more conventional, blason of Absolon (ll. 3312–25) further satirizes the blason by feminizing the lovestruck clerk. And yet, the Miller's unexpected command of the descriptive blason elevates him as a serious storyteller.

Further Reading

Alice M. Colby, *The Portrait in Twelfth-Century French Literature: An Example of the Stylistic Originality of Chrétien de Troyes* (Geneva: Vittorio Klostermann, 1965).

Walter Clyde Curry, *The Middle English Ideal of Personal Beauty; As Found in the Metrical Romances, Chronicles, and Legends of the XIII, XIV, and XV Centuries* (Baltimore, MD: J.H. Furst Company, 1916).

James Wimsatt, *Chaucer and the French Love Poets: the Literary Background of the* Book of the Duchess (Chapel Hill: University of North Carolina Press, 1968).

Jan Ziolkowski, "Avatars of Ugliness in Medieval Literature," *Modern Language Review* 79 (1984): 1–20.

Catalog of Warriors

A roster of fighting men distinctive to epic tradition, intended to unify and rally opposing armies prior to a pivotal battle. Of classical origin, with Germanic and Celtic counterparts. The catalog typically features men from disparate regions gathered for a common cause, showcasing the collective martial talent of each army. The scene fosters an inclusive and universalizing effect, elevating the significance of the conflict. Classical examples include the Greek and Trojan forces in Homer's *Illiad* II, the Argive forces under the seven commanders attacking Thebes in the *Thebaid* IV, and the Italian forces of *Aeneid* VII, which closes with a woman warrior, Camilla. The type-scene consists of 1) a setting on or anticipating a battlefield where 2) two armed contingents gather forces in preparation for battle, whose key participants are announced through a 3) list of warriors, including name, place of origin, and often, father's name and past exploits. In classical tradition, the Catalog of Warriors type-scene glorifies the war and warriors alike, albeit sometimes tragically. Some medieval renditions of the catalog similarly extol the martial event, as in the *Roman d'Enéas* (ll. 3897–4084), where the catalog of warriors assembling for Turnus closes with the catalog of feminine beauty in the blason of the warrior Camilla, who leads a contingent of knights. Other poets question the cause through a partial or questionable catalog.

Giovanni Boccaccio includes a catalog of warriors in Book Six of his *Teseida* (1339–41), which spans the roughly twenty-year period between the Theban and Trojan wars. Two Theban kinsmen, Palamone and Arcita, survivors of the Theban war and now prisoners of war of Theseus of Athens, prepare to settle their dispute over their mutual love for Emilia through an armed contest organized by Theseus. Boccaccio varies the epic catalog in ways that compromise rather than edify the conflict at hand: the setting of the conflict is not a battlefield but a "theater" (7.108–111) (1) formerly used for gladiatorial contests, downsizing the event to a martial "game" (7.4), with each side limited to one hundred fighters. The two armed contingents (2) arrive in Athens in a spirit of gaiety rather than rivalry, joining in festivities and martial practice in the weeks leading up to the event (6.6–11). Palamone and Arcita themselves renew their friendship during this time, casting artifice over the conflict and highlighting the inglorious Theban pattern of civil strife where no one wins. The catalog of warriors (3) itself marks absences as well as presences, featuring obscure figures from Thebes as the sole remnants of the Theban war, even noting absentees—Narcissus and Leader—mythological figures being among the few survivors. Boccaccio also uses the catalog to transition between the Theban and Trojan wars, as warriors from Thebes encounter future heroes of Troy (Peleus, Agamemnon, Menelaus, Castor, and Pollux). As fellow

Greeks, the two contingents (2) represent not so much two sides of one conflict as one meeting of two wars. The scanty Theban arrivals record casualties through blank omission, foreshadowing similar losses at Troy. This changing of the guard between Thebes and Troy parallels and diminishes both the present conflict over Emilia (*si poca di cosa*, "such a small thing"), and by extension, the future conflict at Troy—yet another war over a woman. Thus, the recreational nature of the catalog of warriors in the *Teseida* suggests pointlessness rather than high purpose.

Chaucer intensifies the disenchantment surrounding the battle over Emelye in the *Knight's Tale*, his adaptation of the *Teseida*, where the catalog of warriors becomes disquieting. Unlike Boccaccio, Chaucer uses the story of Palaemon and Arcite to perpetuate rather than alleviate Theban dysfunction, removing the many intimations of reconciliation between the two Thebans that pepper their rivalry in the *Teseida*. The Catalog of Warriors scene exposes Theseus' well-intentioned, though naïve, attempts to contain the incorrigible Theban character. As in the *Teseida*, the contest between Palaemon and Arcite takes place in an arena (1), one specially commissioned by Theseus for the event, suggesting a gesture of statecraft, built in record time (l. 1896) at considerable expense (ll.1881–1913). Chaucer also incorporates the disturbing temples of Mars, Venus, and Diana, with their foreboding imagery, directly into the arena complex (ll. 1914–2092), a proximity unspecified in the *Teseida*. As in Bocaccio, the opposing contingents (2) serve competing kinsmen, whose rivalry in Chaucer goes unabated until the end, in keeping with the Theban tradition of internecine strife. The catalog (3) itself concentrates Theban disfunction. Rather than alternating portraits of dignified pomp and ferocity, as Boccaccio does, Chaucer features only the leaders, whose dubious appearance undercuts Theseus' diplomatic hopes for the event. The knight-narrator promises a pageant of European knightly elegance (ll. 2105–16) only to present two exotic, non-knightly, opposing leaders for each side who defy chivalric respectability: leading Palamon's contingent is Lycurgus, King of Thrace, grim with the reddish-yellow eyes of a griffon, black hair of a raven, and an old bear pelt with yellow claws in place of armor (ll. 2129–54); leading Arcite's men is Emetrius, King of India, whose rich clothing from the East barely compensates for his strange physical features of curly golden hair, yellow eyes, and ruddy, freckled complexion (ll. 2155–78) (3). Chaucer excises from the ranks the famous names associated with Troy found in Boccaccio, removing any familiar grandeur that might soften the undercurrent Theban gloom at the tournament. Routine protocol replaces pageantry as attendance of nameless participants is taken for both sides on the morning of the event (ll. 2594–6) (3). Thus, Chaucer's catalog of warriors in the *KT* reveals Theseus' well-intentioned, but futile, political attempts to regulate and reform the ungovernable Theban character.

Malory introduces a variant of the catalog of warriors in his fifteenth-century *Le Morte Darthur*, portraying Arthur's knights of the Round Table. In the "healing of Sir Urry" episode of the Winchester MS, Malory summons one hundred and ten of his knights (forty were away) to approach the wounded Sir Urry, whose wounds will reveal the relative holiness of each knight, depending on whether they bleed or close, becoming an authenticating miracle for the moral character of each man. The catalog differentiates the knights not as inflictors of wounds but as healers (2). The story comes late in the narrative, and Malory uses the catalog as a closing retrospective, rather than an opening, anticipatory scene, to mark their cumulative achievement. Each knight is introduced by name, and sometimes by place of origin (e.g. "King Carydos of Scotlande") or by destiny (e.g. "Sir Alysaundir le Orphelyn, that was slayne by the treson of kynge Marke"), joining them in common service of Arthur (3). However, the story pivots toward decline from here, as the Round Table transitions from their days of harmony and unity into disharmony and open civil war, leading to the dissolution of the Round Table. Therefore, the catalog prefaces a battle ahead (1) that will destroy rather than inaugurate an empire. Thus, Malory's Catalog of Warriors profiles what will be lost rather than gained at this twilight of an age.

Further Reading

David Anderson, *Before the Knight's Tale* (Philadelphia: University of Pennsylvania Press, 1988).

Stephen C.B. Atkinson, "Malory's 'Healing of Sir Urry': Lancelot, the Earthly Fellowship, and the World of the Grail," *Studies in Philology* 78 (1981): 341–52.

Dominique Battles, "Boccaccio's *Teseida* and the Destruction of Troy," *Medievalia et Humanistica, New Series* 28 (2001): 73–99.

Conciliar Debate

A gathering of political and military advisors to devise a strategy, found in both classical and Germanic traditions. For medieval audiences, scenes of conciliar debate predominate in the chronicle tradition, particularly of the First Crusade and the challenges of siege warfare. The type-scene consists of 1) a wartime setting, often a siege, at an impasse, prompting a 2) leader to convene a council; 3) two advisors propose 4) conflicting strategies (e.g., fighting vs. diplomacy; advance vs. withdrawal), 5) one of which is adopted, unifying the perspectives. The scene consolidates and potentiates the will of the army by showing their ability to reconcile their differences as they enter a new phase of the conflict.

Scenes of conciliar debate occur throughout the plot of the OF *Roman de Thèbes*, scenes modeled on chronicle accounts of the First Crusade. Whereas Statius includes four scenes of conciliar debate in his first-century *Thebaid*, the OF poet renders seventeen such scenes in the *Thèbes*, portraying the forces of Pollinicés and Ethïoclés as crusaders vs. infidels, respectively. During the siege of Montflor (Mora-Lebrun, ed., ll. 3181–3220), whose citizens refuse to surrender outright (1), the army of Pollinicés encamped around the city convenes to strategize (2). Pollinicés (3) argues the futility of ever taking the city and proposes withdrawal. Thideüs (3), a fellow commander, emphasizes the strategic necessity of the city as the entrance to the kingdom of Thebes and argues for escalation of attack, berating Pollinicés as a coward (*coart*) and blockhead (*bricon*) in the process (4). Adrastus, King of Argos, commends Thideüs's nobility and seconds his suggestion, which they adopt (5). The type-scene of conciliar debate at Montflor, amidst a lesser siege *en route* to the final siege of Thebes, echoes similar scenes in the chronicle accounts of lesser sieges leading up to the major sieges of Antioch and Jerusalem. It also serves the same function: to remotivate the forces of Pollinicés before their final battle at Thebes. The scene also highlights an innovation in this first vernacular rendition of the Theban War: to create a "right" and "wrong" side out of the indistinguishably misguided sides of the classical Polynices and Etiocles and to profile Thideüs (Tydeus) over the incestuously conceived Pollinicés as the hero of the story. The debate resolves both the military strategy on the battlefield and the moral strategies of the poem.

Chaucer satirically adapts the type-scene of conciliar debate to serve matters of love, thereby aligning love and war, private and public. Forms of debate occur throughout the *Merchant's Tale* (ll. 1469–1576), one of which conforms to the type-scene of conciliar debate, where January (2) ponders the pros and cons of marriage late in life. The impasse of the heart replaces that of the battlefield (1). He consults two "brethren," Placebo and Justinus (3), representations of the flatterer and the truth-teller. Both men give self-interested advice, and their opposition concerns the process rather than the content of advising (4). Placebo, the consummate courtier (ll. 1492–1505) intent on job security, refuses to debate a nobleman, on principle (l. 1496). The advisor refuses advice, for his own sake, exposing his uselessness. Justinus, a mouthpiece of the recently married Merchant-narrator, challenges Placebo's cowardly intellectualism. Speaking from experience, he advises caution in marrying and dispels ideals of the perfect wife, citing his own marital misery (ll. 1544–5). Marriage, he says, is "cost and care" (l. 1547). January resolves the conflict by ignoring the warning and following his desires, with Placebo's rhetorical agreement, unifying them in folly (5). Chaucer's scene of conciliar debate highlights the climatic impediments to honest debate—namely, subjectivity—and therefore, the rarity of sound advice. The type-scene typical of narratives of war and empire coordinates with the ominous references to Theban history during the wedding of January and May (e.g., Amphion, Theodamas, and Bacchus—patron god of Thebes, ll. 1716-22), never a harbinger of joy. True to the type-scene about strategy, January and May each strategize within the marriage, with him ever advancing and her ever evading.

In *Troilus and Criseyde*, Chaucer again applies the scene of Conciliar Debate to love, fusing the public and the private. Set during the siege of Troy (1), the poem suitably contains a scene of conciliar debate (IV.141–96). King Priam calls a parliament (2) to consider the Greek request for a prisoner exchange, Antenor for Criseyde, the daughter of Calchas, a Trojan seer and defector. Chaucer innovates on the type-scene by stressing what is *not* known to the assembly and what is *not* said, thereby ending in disunity rather than unity. The parliament readily assents to the exchange but remains unaware of the future treason of both Antenor and Criseyde, one political (war) and the other personal (love), both against Troy on some level. In restoring Antenor in exchange for Criseyde, they double the betrayal—of Antenor's betrayal of Troy and Criseyde's betrayal of Troilus. Gaps in knowledge accompany gaps in the debate. While the scene includes the requisite opposing arguments for and against the exchange, with Hector defending Criseyde's right to remain in Troy and the council challenging him (176–95) (4), the main strategy crafted during the council is *un*spoken and *un*debated, as Troilus mentally plans to circumvent the exchange (ll. 148–75), infusing interiority into this normally public scene. The scene concludes with disunity rather than unity; while the parliament votes for the exchange, Troilus' counterplans prevent resolution and fragment the Trojan effort (5). Meanwhile, King Priam must pursue a plan contrary to both his sons' wishes, suggesting political division at the top. Unlike the forces of Pollinicés in the *Thèbes*, who advance to some degree of victory, the Trojans move closer to annihilation. Chaucer uses this type-scene of strategy to highlight the unseen forces to the best-laid plans.

Further Reading

Dominique Battles, *The Medieval Tradition of Thebes: History and Narrative in the* OF Roman de Thèbes, *Boccaccio, Chaucer, and Lydgate* (New York: Routledge, 2004).

Tison Pugh, "Gender, Vulgarity, and the Phantom Debates of Chaucer's Merchant's Tale," *Studies in Philology* 114 (2017): 473–96.

Contending Throng

A crowd, typically of soldiers or servants that competes to serve, defend, or attack the central character of the narrative, often their lord. Predominant in Old English poetry and echoed in Middle English poetry. The scene consists of 1) individual members of the crowd, joined in common purpose, who nonetheless 2) compete (vie, contend) with one another to be the first to serve, defend, or attack 3) the most prominent and/or beloved person of the narrative. Generally, the members of the crowd remain anonymous individually, equal in their desire to out-perform the rest, as the scene concerns crowd dynamics that convey the importance of the person commanding its attention, whether that be a warrior-king or a holy person. The crowd embodies the ideal of the *comitatus*, or retainer-band who honors and serves the lord, who protects and serves them in return. In Old English, the scene utilizes a stable vocabulary across iterations: *þringan* + (*georne*) + *hwilc hie/hwa* + (superl.) + infinitive + *magan/motan*. The scene occurs in the OE *Descent into Hell*, *Christ I*, *Andreas*, and *Battle of Maldon* as well as in the ME *Seinte Katherine* and *Cursor Mundi*.

In Old English tradition, the contending throng scene applies equally to peace and war and the amalgamation of heavenly war. In the *Battle of Maldon*, where Byrhtnoth and his men assemble to fight off Viking invaders at the Battle at Maldon in 991, his men (1) contend (*swa stemnetton*, l. 122) to be the first to avenge (2) the death of Byrhtnoth's (3) nephew. Interestingly, the individuals comprising this band of warriors are not all anonymous, as Eadweard rises to strike revenge on behalf of his lord, one among many named warriors of the poem. In the OE *Christ I* (ll. 391b-399), the crowd consists of nameless seraphim (1) guarding and serving Christ (3) who vie to see who can fly closest to the Lord (2). In *Descent into Hell* and *Andreas*, native images of warfare come to serve heavenly purposes, as Christ (3) takes on the role of a warrior-king bestowing gifts of sword, byrnie, helmet and war-gear (ll. 72a-73a) and protection (l. 75) on John the Baptist in *Descent*, while St. Matthew (3) in *Andreas* becomes a "holy hero . . . famed in battle" (ll. 143–46) facing down a throng of (nameless) heathen warriors (1) who vie with one another to attack him (2). In *Beowulf* (ll. 2864-74b), the throng of warriors (1) contending to serve their lord (2) forms an absent presence in the dragon episode, where Wiglaf chastises the band of cowards who abandoned (rather than contending for) their lord, Beowulf (3), as they approached the dragon's barrow-lair, contrasting Beowulf's generosity toward them with their own abdication of duty, his "fellow warriors" (*fyrdgesteallum*) unworthy of praise.

The fourteenth-century, Middle English *Cursor Mundi* contains an entry (ll. 21127-28, 21130-36) concerning the Apostle James, the son of

Alphaeus, and "our lauerd sistur sun" ("our Lord's sister-son"), whereby men call him "vr lauerd broþer" ("our Lord's brother") and the first bishop of Jerusalem. In conveying James' great holiness, the poet describes how "Þat folk ilkan wald oþer stemm,/Qua rin moght titest on his hemm" ("that people would vie [each] with the other to see who might first touch his garment's hem"), the word "stemm" echoing the word "stemnetton" of Old English renditions of this scene. In this case, the crowd dynamic of the Contending Throng type-scene dovetails with that of the Crowd of Onlookers* of hagiographic tradition, with the collective (and competitive) action of "contending" substituting for the collective (and non-competitive) emotional pathos of the Crowd of Onlookers, with both scenes portraying a group of anonymous people joined in common purpose and directing attention and praise to the holy person.

Further Reading

Paul Battles, "'Contending Throng' Scenes and the *Comitatus* Ideal in Old English Poetry, with special attention to *The Battle of Maldon* 122a," *Studia Neophilologica* 83 (2011): 41–53.

Council of the Gods

Common to classical epic, a meeting of the gods, including the chief god, Jupiter (Jove, Zeus), usually in wartime, to negotiate the progress of events below on earth, with each god championing a particular character. Also referred to as "Parliament of the Gods," "Divine Assembly," and "Divine Council." The scene occurs early in the narrative, contextualizing the main action, providing the reader with the "big picture" of events, including the ending—a privileged vantage not afforded to the characters themselves. The Council of the Gods type-scene consists of 1) a gathering of the gods in heaven, 2) early in the narrative, 3) to debate events happening on earth, 4) with certain gods advocating for specific human characters 5) while disclosing the larger divine plan governing events; 6) various gods compromise for mutual gain, and 7) achieve their desired outcome. The scene mechanizes the epic concept of Fate, as planned events unfold inexorably, and often tragically, despite human countermeasures, so that history shapes people more than vice versa. Human characters, notably the hero, fulfill divine will. Medieval western audiences would have encountered the Council of the Gods in the openings of Virgil's *Aeneid* and Statius' *Thebaid*, in which leisured, divine orderliness contrasts with desperate earthly chaos. In Virgil, ends justify means; long-term advances in human civilization, as professed by the gods, compensate for short-term human tragedy. In Statius, divine oversight replaces foresight, and noble ends remain elusive. The divine council scenes in Virgil and Statius became the prototypes for medieval poets.

The Council of the Gods scene as a tool of divine foresight occurs in the first book of Virgil's *Aeneid* (I. 304–410), as a revisionist, optimistic libretto for the future of the Trojan race following their fall at Troy. Just after the Invocation (2), we see Jupiter standing "on heaven's height," joined by Venus (1), who questions his plans for the Trojans fleeing the burning city below (3), particularly for her son, "my Aeneas" (4). Jupiter reassures her by disclosing "'secret fated things to come'" (l. 354) that will glorify Aeneas, who will establish "'empire without end'" (l. 375) (5), suggesting a compromise for their mutual gain (6). The successful completion of Aeneas' destiny (7) forms the remainder of the narrative. Divine confidence above contrasts with miserable human uncertainty below, with noble ends justifying harsh means. Virgil's gods remain loyal to the Trojans, using Aeneas as their earthly agent, and Jupiter and Venus alike play the part of loving parents to the hero, forgiving his transgressions and keeping him on the track of his destiny in founding Rome, conveying order within chaos.

Statius' *Thebaid* (ll.197–302) contains a comparable Council of the Gods scene in its opening sequence. As in Virgil, we see the chief god,

Jove, convening with other gods in heaven (1), early in the narrative (2), to discuss earthly circumstances below (3). Juno challenges Jove's intention to punish the Thebans, yet again, for the most recent incidents of deviant conduct going back generations (4 and 5). Rather than compromising with Juno for all parties' best interest, Jove reluctantly insists on further punishment for Thebes (6), which consumes the remainder of the narrative (7). While retaining its essential structure, Statius varies the Council of the Gods scene at its heart. Statius divides the majestic heavenly realm from the depraved human realm more sharply than in Virgil. The pointless suffering of the civil war between the sons of Oedipus (Etiocles and Polynices) replaces the purposeful suffering of the Trojan defeat in Virgil, redirecting the Council of the Gods scene. Unlike in Virgil, where noble ends carried out by a noble hero compensate for painful means, in Statius, means and ends are equally painful and futile. In place of Virgil's "empire without end," Statius inserts "madness unlimited" (l. 37). Instead of dutiful Aeneas, Statius presents "the tyrant pair" of Etiocles and Polynices (l. 37), the sons of Oedipus, who will die treasonously by mutually inflicted wounds. Instead of Rome emerging from the ashes of Troy, we get "cities undermined by death for death" (l. 40–1). Jove's serene confidence in a glorious future in Virgil transmutes into Jove's patient resignation, chronically helpless in taming the incorrigible Theban race. Ironically, as Jove stands higher above the earth in the *Thebaid*, he exercises less positive influence over its affairs. The Council of the Gods scene, therefore, limits itself to damage control in human affairs, and gods and humans alike share in the same disempowerment.

Jove's power in the Council of the Gods type-scene becomes further eroded in the twelfth-century OF *Roman de Thèbes* (Constans, ed. appendix II, ll. 9577ff.). Here, the divine-human divide all but collapses. Rooted in the ethos of the First Crusade, the *Thèbes* incriminates the pagan gods alongside the house of Thebes as part of the problem rather than the solution to the disfunction of the Theban race. The Council scene itself grows dysfunctional, undercutting each of its core elements. Rather than an orderly meeting of a few high-ranking gods sitting on high, we have a confusing assembly of all of the gods voicing their grievances as Jove listens—a scene that blurs seamlessly with the equally chaotic earthly scene in Thebes (1). Rather than occurring early in the narrative to organize the whole, the Council scene occurs late in the narrative, in the thick of the civil war (2), and alongside Capaneus' famously irreverent speech discrediting the gods, as yet another sign of moral decay in the poem. Rather than focusing on the war, the gods air their personal dramas (9483–6; 9517–20) (3) and advocate only for themselves (4), their speeches upholding no political or moral agenda (5 and 6). Finally, Jove entreats his council (ll.9585–88) for advice in words that echo Ethïoclés' entreaty to his council (ll. 7801–5), creating an unflattering likeness between the chief pagan god and the equally clueless main enemy chieftain of the poem. The events that follow, therefore, cannot be attributed to divine intent or oversight (7).

Giovanni Boccaccio includes a Council of the Gods in *Il Teseida* (9.2–9), the first epic in the Italian language, which covers the intervening period between the Theban and Trojan wars, combining characters and plot elements from both conflicts. The Council of the Gods scene in the *Teseida* thematizes disorder. Pluto, god of the Underworld, rather than Jove, heads the council, which takes place in "the dark realms of blazing Dis," rather than in heaven (1), where Venus ventures to advocate for Palamone in his conflict with Arcita (3, 4). The scene occurs late in the tale (2), disrupting rather than organizing events that have already occurred (Arcita's apparent triumph over Palamone) (5). Pluto exerts little control over the scene, as Venus and Mars have already negotiated terms (6) prior to the meeting below, and Venus acts unilaterally to unleash Furies into the arena who cause Arcita's ignoble death by accident (7). Subjective, short-term godly agendas obscure any long-range goals, and divine intervention amplifies rather than assuages horror on earth.

Geoffrey Chaucer extends the Theban tradition of the Council of the Gods scene in the *Knight's Tale* (ll. 2438–82 and 2663–91) and the *Merchant's Tale* (l. 2225ff.). As in the *Teseida*, his primary source for the *KT*, the gods are under new leadership, with morally and socially lesser gods of Saturn (*KT*) and Pluto (*MerT*) taking the place of Jove (1). Rather than meeting on high, these gods ascend from below to convene on earth (1) at a turning point in the human drama (3). The scenes occur toward the end of each tale, as a disordering element, to overturn a human triumph (Arcite's victory over Palaemon; May's deception of January), with gods playing favorites with humans (4). As in Boccaccio, divine agency becomes scaled down to two or three gods, with subjective aims, and limited to circumstantial, local events rather than spans of time and terrain, serving no higher purpose. In place of a coherent plan for social progress, Saturn proudly recites a personal resumé of his dark powers (ll. 2454–78) and identifies heaven as a source of "strif" (l. 2438), not wisdom. Rather than serving just ends, the gods compromise with one another (6) for compromised ends—to match Arcite's victory on the battlefield with Palaemon's reward of Emelye in the *KT*, and to enable the deception of an adulterous wife of her blind husband even while restoring his sight in the *MT* (7). As in the *Thèbes*, gods and humans share a limited vision and agency, accentuated by Chaucer's innovative setting of these councils on earth rather than in heaven. The council in the *KT*, in particular, draws upon contemporary parliamentary language. Interestingly, Chaucer omits any Council of the Gods scene in his epic *Troilus and Criseyde*, where one would most expect it, despite the manifold imitation of epic elements. Gods are invoked but never personally appear. Instead, the figure of Pandarus assumes the organizing role of the gods in devising a larger plan, early in the narrative, against a backdrop of war, and advocating for a specific player (Troilus) while achieving his goal, though long-term political ends remain elusive.

Further Reading

David Anderson, *Before the Knight's Tale: The Imitation of Classical Epic in Boccaccio's Teseida* (Philadelphia: University of Pennsylvania, 1988).

Marc S. Guidry, "The Parliaments of Gods and Men in the *Knight's Tale*," *Chaucer Review* 43 (2008): 140–70.

C.S. Lewis, "Dante's Statius," *Studies in Medieval and Renaissance Literature* (Cambridge: Cambridge University Press, 1966), 94–102.

Alistair J. Minnis, *Chaucer and Pagan Antiquity* (Cambridge: Cambridge University Press, 1982).

Brian Toohey, *Reading Epic* (London: Routledge, 1992).

Crowd of Onlookers

The crowd of faceless, anonymous, sympathetic citizens who gather around a Christian saint facing persecution before a non-Christian ruler, who holds him/her in contempt for social and/or political subversion, forming a culminating type-scene in hagiographic literature, particularly for lives of Christian martyrs undergoing torture and execution in service to faith. The scene consists of 1) a setting of persecution, featuring three "actors" of 2) a Christian saint, 3) a cruel, non-Christian ruler, and 4) a crowd of onlookers of new or potential converts, who function as a social unit in expressing 5) sympathy for the holy subject. The crowd is typically undifferentiated by measures of social class, profession, personal or familial identity, or even gender. Instead, they fulfill their importance through their numbers and their unified emotional response of pathos and empathy toward the Christian subject, thereby modeling the appropriate response to Christian suffering for the reader. Their sympathy also proves the saint's efficacy as a vehicle of God's power in the world, even against seemingly supreme earthly authority. As the saint loses his/her life, he/she wins souls for Christ, with religious conversion being the primary motivation of the scene. In its wordless prompting of the readers' emotional response, the Crowd of Onlookers operates not dissimilarly to the "laugh track" in a modern-day sitcom, though, here, in service to eternal ideals rather than disposable entertainment.

Fundamentally, the scene exposes internal weakness in the pagan ruler's kingdom and the limits of his law, when faced with the power of God, even as embodied in a lone, often low-ranking saint-citizen, whose death engenders faith within the crowd and frustration in the ruler. Ideally, the scene brings about conversion in the pagan ruler, as well. While the Crowd of Onlookers type-scene originates within hagiographic literature, it expanded into secular romance, usually in scenes involving falsely accused women, including stories involving exemplary, non-Christian women, where it proclaims the heroine's personal virtue broadly. Examples of the scene occur in many martyr passions as well as in partially hagiographically inspired works such as Chaucer's *Man of Law's Tale*, the ME *Pistel of Susanna*, the ME *Floris and Blancheflour*, *Athelston*, the ME *Erl of Toulous* (all involving persecuted heroines), and the ME *St. Erkenwald*.

The *Life of St. Cecelia* contains a conventional instance of the Crowd of Onlookers type-scene. Typical of such martyr passions, the scene forms a culminating episode in the drama—an ultimate test of the saint, now confronting a painful death (1). Having already converted many individuals, including her husband and brother-in-law, Cecelia (2) has attracted the notice of the prefect of Rome, Almachius (3), a "harsh executioner" and "wicked persecutor," intent on ending her secret proselytizing, thereby attracting a crowd of heathen witnesses (62) (4). Almachius commands the torture and death first of Cecelia's husband and brother-in-law, unwittingly causing many heathens to convert, including the executioner, Maximus. Almachius then persecutes Cecelia, as "the heathens wept that a woman so beautiful, noble, and filled with wisdom, should suffer death from tortures so young" (64). True to the scene, the crowd bears no distinguishing affiliations of rank, sex, occupation, or family, instead forming a social unit of would-be converts unified in their emotional sympathy for the holy person (5). Facing torture and death, Cecelia prevails, and "taught the unbelieving heathens for a long while, until they all said in unison, 'We believe that Christ, the Son of God, is truly God, and has accepted you as His handmaid in the world,'" resulting in "four hundred" baptisms, fulfilling the scene's purpose of conversion (64). Here, the non-Christian ruler, Almachius, is not converted, even as Cecelia survives ever-more extreme forms of torture. Nevertheless, the shared sympathy and sheer number of this outnumbered crowd of witnesses in ancient Rome highlights the saint's holiness and models for the reader the appropriate response to Christian suffering and the spiritual victory in earthly defeat.

The Crowd of Onlookers scene forms the culminating drama of the ME *Floris and Blancheflour* (ll. 1095–1230), as the young lovers face the judgment of the Emir of Babylon, following Floris' infiltration into the city to rescue Blancheflour from the ruler's harem. The young pair become the saintly figure (2), facing the Muslim Emir (3), with the dignitaries of his city forming the "crowd" (4) witnessing the suffering of the unjustly accused couple facing persecution (1). Set in the Muslim world (Spanish Almeria and Babylon), the story explores the theology and methodology of crusading, positioning the Christian Blancheflour ("white flour," evoking the Virgin Mary) as the persecuted holy subject (2). She is bartered, sold, coveted, and nearly defiled until Floris rescues her, expressing the lines of transmission of Christianity into the Holy Land and its often-precarious hold within regional circles of governance. The political underpinnings of the poem account for the scene's interesting variations: joining the accused Christian Blancheflour is Floris (2), the son of a Muslim king, whose lifelong love for the girl paves his conversion, and therefore, that of his kingdom, infusing worldly, political agency into the "holy subject" role—an element usually lacking in the saintly subject. The Emir, the non-Christian persecuting ruler, rather than losing political credibility, gains public regard when he forgives the lovers and arranges their wedding, modeling the political advantages attending Christianity. Finally, the Crowd of Onlookers in the judgment scene consist not of faceless, powerless citizens, but rather, political dignitaries of the city capable of influencing their ruler, suggesting the political as well as spiritual power of the young girl.

An ingenious variation on the scene occurs in the ME *St. Erkenwald*, featuring a pagan holy subject (2) facing scrutiny (1) under a Christian authority (3) before a diverse and differentiated sympathetic (and smart) crowd (4) (5). The incorrupt pagan body in the tomb becomes the beautiful corpse of the *inventio* scene of hagiographic tradition. Once revived, he narrates a life of service and an afterlife of suffering, "'exilid'" (l. 303) from Christ, becoming the holy protagonist of the *vita* (2). The bishop's (3) skepticism and scrutiny replace the persecution typical of the scene (1), nonetheless evoking the same tearful response in the crowd (5). Whereas the Crowd of Onlookers type-scene is typically one among many scenes, in *St. Erkenwald*, the scene spans the entire narrative, with the crowd surrounding the holy subject as the first to arrive and the last to leave in the poem (4). Instead of the anonymous, vulnerable crowd of the saint's legend, the crowd in *Erkenwald* is diverse and differentiated as masons (l, 39), diggers (l. 41), clerks (l. 55), burgers and beadles (l. 59), lads (l. 61), "werkemen" (l. 69), and "alle-kynnes so kenely mony" (l. 63), along with the sacristan (l. 66), and finally, the bishop and lords attending him (l. 138) (4). Rather than would-be converts, this crowd is already Christian, ambiguating the usual narrative aim of mass conversion. They are similarly varied in their actions, ranging beyond the typical collective swoon of hagiographic tradition to engage in digging and excavating, questioning and publicizing, researching and reporting, as well as witnessing (5). Their emotional responses are equally varied, from startled wonder to lads who "lepen þiderwardes" and "Ronnen radly in route with ryngande noyce" (ll. 61–2) to mutual curiosity (l. 93) to anguish ("pyne", l. 141) to silent attentiveness (l. 218–9) to the familiar tearful pathos of hagiographic norms (l. 310) and culminating in a complex blend of "mournynge and myrthe" (l. 350). As fully fleshed humans, this crowd commands more presence and respect, and no one in the scene stands in need of religious conversion. The sympathetic "conversion" is secular and cultural, rather than religious, and grounded in a shared faith tradition.

Chaucer gently satirizes the Crowd of Onlookers scene at the close of the *Miller's Tale*, with John the Carpenter playing the persecuted subject (2). Duped and cuckolded by (1) Alisoun and Nicholas (3), who cause his humiliating fall, John finds himself surrounded by curious villagers (4), "bothe smale and grete" (l. 3826), who stare at ("gauren," l. 3827) him. Unlike a saint, John fails to "convert" the crowd to his prophetic vision of "Nowelis flood" (l. 3834) (product of Nicholas) and his desire to save them; thus, "no man his reson herde" (l. 3844). The crowd "turned al his harm unto a jape" and "laughen at this stryf" (ll. 3842, 3849) (5), rather than empathizing with him, while his wife and lodger discredit him and steer rather than follow the emotional impulse of the crowd, preventing any sympathy. This inverse Crowd of Onlookers scene bookends the Miller's earlier drunken boast, issued "in Pilates voys" (l. 3124), that he "wol telle a legende and a lyf/Bothe of a carpenter and of his wyf" (ll. 3141–2), applying generic terminology distinctive to hagiography (*legenda* and *vita*)—in the manner of Pontius Pilate—that aligns this fabliau with the other medieval genre—the saint's life—that also often features a competent and effective woman of lesser status in a leading role. Here, the woman is the persecutor, not the saint.

Further Reading

Dominique Battles, "The Middle English *Athelston* and 1381, Part I: the Politics of Anglo-Saxon Identity," *Studies in Philology* 117 (2020): 1–39.
———, "Investigating English Sanctity in the Middle English *St. Erkenwald*," *Studies in Philology* 120 (2023): 603–57.

Dawn Song

The parting of lovers at dawn, of classical origin. Also called "aubade" after the French "*aube*" ("dawn"), or "*alba*" ("white") referring to "dawn" in Provençal. The literary scene consists of 1) clandestine lovers who 2) part sadly at 3) dawn, prompted by 4) some warning sound (e.g., a night watchman's signal, a bird singing); the lovers 5) verbally address the dawn through apostrophe. The scene idealizes and intensifies the lovers' desire for one another against a wider society hostile to their love, which necessitates their separation. Thus, the scene has a contradictory trajectory in drawing the lovers closer than ever, while foreshadowing their ultimate separation.

The late-medieval type-scene derives from the dawn-song lyric of Ovid, the French and later German troubadour poets of the twelfth and thirteenth centuries, and the scant trace of popular dawn-song lyrics from fourteenth- and fifteenth-century England and Scotland. Three strains of dawn-song emerge: the classical, the courtly, and the popular, with elements predominant to each. The classical (Ovidian) lyric dawn-song is notable for its a) personification of dawn, who b) follows a course, often in a chariot; the sun is c) chided (through apostrophe) for intruding enviously on the lovers; and d) references to classical mythology. The courtly tradition established by the Provençal poets of southern France became highly stylized and has the distinct elements of a) the watchman who warns the lovers that they must part; b) the word "*alba*" (white) to indicate "dawn"; c) the dreaded appearance of dawn; d) the occasional suggestion of a jealous husband. The Provençal poets influenced the medieval German dawn-song (the *Tagelied*), a larger and less homogenous corpus. The popular tradition of dawn-song native to England and Scotland is characterized by a) no emphasis on nature comparable to continental models; b) an ordinary house or barnyard setting; c) no night watchman, but rather, the cock-crow as the agent warning the lovers to part; d) little emotional pathos, as the lovers express no grief at parting; and e) no personification of dawn. While the classical and courtly models often characterize separation metaphorically as death, insular dawn-song lyrics sometimes literalize death; for example, featuring a ghost as one of the lovers or having the woman awaken to a lover murdered in the night by her brothers. The scenic elements of setting, characters, and action of the dawn-song lyric imply a wider love story, and thus, dawn song metamorphosed from lyric into narrative as a type-scene embedded in love stories, with first-person, masculine, lyric expression of setting and sentiment now taking the form of mutual dialogue between the lovers.

Giovanni Boccaccio includes a scene of dawn song in Book III (stanzas 41–52) of *Il Filostrato* (c. 1335), a love story set in Troy toward the end of the Trojan War. The impermanence of the love affair is mentioned at the outset of the poem, lending tragedy to the scene. The dawn scene (3) concludes the episode of Troilo and Cressida's (1) first night together and prefigures their impending separation, as Cressida will soon be sent to the Greek camp in a prisoner exchange. All three strains of dawn song (classical, courtly, and popular) infuse the scene. As in Ovidian dawn song (e.g. *Amores* I.13), day and Fortune are personified. In the type-scene, the male lover assumes the words and perspective of the masculine lyric poet; therefore, Troilo apostrophizes day as "pitiless" and accuses Fortune of depriving him of pleasure and solace (44–46) (5). Like the courtly couple, they each grieve over separation (42 and 44) (2). As in the popular tradition, cocks crowing signal separation (42 and 43) (4). Cressida speaks first in the scene, telling Troilo he must go and expressing her longing for him. Troilo first addresses her, characterizing separation as death, and then, apostrophizes day and Fortune before turning back to her. They each express their intensified love and their desire to reunite. Boccaccio's larger poetic enterprise of the *Filostrato* of transposing the epic scene into romance and prioritizing the heart over history is expressed in the scene by Troilo, who says to Cressida that if she were to hold him continually in her mind, "more dear would this be to me than the realm of Troy" (47). Troilo changes from an epic figure into a romance hero in placing her above his kingdom, and like most romance, the story prioritizes the hero's experience and perspective over hers. Thus, the scene leaves us with Troilo's elevated internal estimation of Cressida.

Chaucer employs Dawn Song in several poems, including the *Complaint of Mars* (ll. 1–12), the *Merchant's Tale* (1842–57), the *Reeve's Tale* (ll. 4233–38), as well as in *Troilus and Criseyde* (ll. 1415–1526), where he adapts and expands Boccaccio's Dawn Song scene of the *Filostrato*, echoing the scene somewhat later (ll. 1695–1715). Like Boccaccio, Chaucer blends all three strains of dawn song in the *Troilus*: he includes and expands the classical element using a range of Ovidian sources, including the *Amores*, the *Heroides*, and the *Metamorphoses*. Thus, he inserts additional references to classical mythology (e.g. Lucifer; l. 1417; Titan l. 1464; Phoebus, l. 1495) and personifies and chides the day (l. 1450ff.), incorporating Ovidian imagery of day as a bringer of labor (l. 1434–5; cf. *Amores* 1:13) (3, 5), evoking a more authentic, pre-Christian Trojan atmosphere. As in the courtly strain, the lovers express grief over separation (1, 2), and the popular element of the roosters' crowing signals separation (ll. 1415–16) (4). However, Chaucer alters the scene from the *Filostrato* by expanding the voice and agency of Criseyde to match that of Troilus, in keeping with the larger pattern of gender reversal of the couple throughout the poem (e.g. see "Teichoscopia"). Thus, the story deviates from the mainstream of continental dawn song poetry. As in Boccaccio, Chaucer's hero apostrophizes and chides the day (ll. 1450ff.), but only after Criseyde has apostrophized and chided the night (l. 1429ff.). She also speaks words normally assigned to the man in characterizing day as a bringer of labor (l. 1434). Whereas Boccaccio's hero poses rhetorical questions to abstractions like "day" and "Fortune," Chaucer's Troilus poses questions of guidance to Criseyde concerning whether to rise and go, how to survive, what to do, and how long to stay away (1474–84), enhancing her agency in the relationship. Chaucer reveals his own poetic enterprise in adapting Boccaccio's wartime love story by keeping the kingdom—and the war—in the bedroom as a determining factor in their love. Unlike Boccaccio's hero, who positions Cressida's love *above* the kingdom of Troy, thus separating them, Troilus chides the day for intruding *into* Troy (l.1452), in which their bedroom lies, merging their love and the kingdom. For Troilus and Criseyde, there can be no separation of the personal and the political, no escape from the encroachments of history, repositioning the story within its epic origins, despite its romance narrative machinery, where history shapes people, not vice versa. The later echo of this intimate dawn song scene (l. 1695ff.) underscores the couple's public and political personas in the final line, announcing the lovers as "Criseyde and ek this kynges sone of Troie" (l. 1715), never allowing us (or them) to disentangle the disparate threads of their lives. Thus, whereas Boccaccio's dawn song stresses the lovers' impending reunion, Chaucer's rendering of the scene stresses their inevitable separation.

In the fabliaux, Chaucer adheres to the popular tradition of Dawn Song, where noble sentiment has no place in the relationship. In the *Merchant's Tale*, the Dawn Song occurs on the morning after the wedding night of old January and his young wife, May (1). They are not clandestine lovers, and May willingly parts from her demanding and unimpressive husband so she can sleep (l. 1856). Aversion replaces sad longing (2). Rather than having a rooster signal them to part, January himself becomes the rooster with "slakke skyn aboute his nekke [that] shaketh" (l. 1849) as he "sang ful loude and cleere" (l. 1845) and "craketh" (l. 1850) (3) (4). The lovers' dialogue is reduced to random "jargon" ("chatter"), on his part, and equally mysterious, unspoken thoughts, on her part (l. 1851), ending with her request to leave (5). Rather than intensifying the lovers' bond and foreshadowing their future and lasting separation, the scene highlights the separate lives they will lead together into perpetuity.

In the *Reeve's Tale*, Chaucer uses Dawn Song (4233–48) at the parting of Aleyn and Malyn (1), on the morning (3) of their one and only night together. Here, Chaucer draws on popular tradition to satirize courtly tradition using a fuller range of the scene's elements. True to the scene, a cock's crow signals departure (l. 4233) (4), suitable here to the village setting. While this unmarried couple resembles the clandestine lovers of classical and courtly tradition, they are not in love and part readily (2). Like their nobler peers, they engage in dialogue (5), but mostly to discuss the logistics of the current situation: he announces he must go now, which she does not contest, and she instructs him about the stolen flour (which she helped to steal from him), and neither expresses longing for the other. Since neither feels sadness at parting (2), neither chides the day for intruding (5). Like the lovers of the *Filostrato* (III.47) and the *Troilus* (III.1493–1505), where there is a plea and a promise that the heroine hold her lover in her heart forever, Aleyn promises to remain her "awen clerk" forever (ll. 4238–9) but with no resonance on her part. The tears endemic to the classical and courtly strains of the type-scene appear here through absence, as Malyn "almoost" (l. 4248) cries when he leaves. Thus, the transience of the relationship in this popular rendition of the type-scene becomes amusing rather than tragic, by virtue of its conventionality.

Further Reading

Paul Battles, "Chaucer and the Tradition of Dawn-Song," *The Chaucer Review* 31 (1997): 317–38.

A.T. Hatto, *Eos: An Enquiry into the Theme of Lovers' Meetings and Partings at Dawn* (London: Mouton, 1965).

R.E. Kaske, "An Aube in the *Reeve's Tale*," *English Literary History* 26 (1959): 295–310.

———, "January's Aube," *Modern Language Notes* 75 (1960): 1–4.

———, "The Aube in Chaucer's *Troilus*," in Richard J. Schoeck and Jerome Taylor, eds., *Troilus and Criseyde and the Minor Poems, vol. 2 of Chaucer Criticism* (Notre Dame: University of Notre Dame Press, 1961), 167–79.

Descent into the Underworld (*katabasis*)

A beleaguered hero's solo journey into the realm of the dead for the purpose of altering his present, downward course. Of classical origin. The Descent scene generally takes one of two forms: first, the epic Descent into the Underworld of the hero, often on the advice of a seer/oracle/sage figure, to seek prophetic guidance from departed ancestors, companions, and notable leaders for completing his political mission. Distinct from the Epic Descent*, where a god descends to contact the hero in the earthly realm, the epic Descent into the Underworld scene has the hero descend to contact spirits in the world beyond. The type-scene consists of 1) a hero at a loss for options who, under the guidance of a 2) seer/sage figure, 3) journeys into the underworld, 4) separated in degrees by some natural threshold, to consult with 5) departed ancestors, mentors, or famous warrior-leaders and hears 6) a prophecy that will enable him to complete his mission. Among the dead, the hero sometimes encounters 7) a former love. The scene often forms a juncture between the first and latter half of an epic, as the hero faces near defeat and recalibrates his vision and expectations moving forward on both a practical and psychological level. The Descent forms a last-ditch attempt to salvage the mission. Despite his reduced circumstances, the hero's unscathed journey into and out of the realm of death adds to his heroic stature, while ameliorating past tragedies with the promise of a better future. In simplest terms, the Descent into the Underworld functions like a narrative trampoline, where the hero goes downwards in order to spring upwards to greater heights. Famous classical examples of this first model of the scene occur in Book XI of Homer's *Odyssey* and Book VI of Virgil's *Aeneid*. The second form of the Descent into the Underworld, also of classical origin, derives from the myth of Orpheus and Eurydice and is altogether smaller in scale, with fewer characters, more narrow aims and scope, and lacking a prophetic component, while, nonetheless, retaining the scene's recuperative narrative purpose. A popular classical example of the Orpheus myth is found in Ovid's *Metamorphoses* (Book X). In medieval tradition, the Descent into the Underworld scene cross-fertilizes with Christian visionary literature as in Dante's *Inferno* and/or Celtic tradition, as in the ME *Sir Orfeo*, and the ME *Thomas of Erceldoune*.

Medieval readers would certainly have encountered the epic Descent into the Underworld in Virgil's *Aeneid* (VI). Weary and anxious after escaping from the burning wreckage of Troy and reluctantly extricating himself from the easy comforts of Dido's new realm in Carthage, Aeneas (1) must obey the divine injunction to travel to Italy and found the empire that will becomes Rome. Two wisdom figures command him to the Underworld: toward the end of Book V, the ghost of his father Anchises (2, 5), by orders of Jove, tells Aeneas that he must soon battle in Latium and entreats Aeneas to visit him in Dis (the Roman counterpart to the Greek Hades) (3), on the guidance of the Sibyl of Cumae (2), to receive a vision (6) of his future race. After hearing a prophecy (6) of struggle and strife from the priestess, Aeneas gains passage to the Underworld, a journey partly facilitated by his own semi-divine birth from Venus, whose doves bring him the golden bough necessary for the journey. Aeneas follows the Sibyl into the gloom of Dis (3), crossing the rivers Acheron and Styx, and inquiring of the Lethe along the journey (4). Among the dead, Aeneas encounters Dido (7), a casualty of his larger political mission; his verbal remorse for her here enables him to partially right his earlier wrong of abandoning her. The shades of fallen warriors (5), some of them recent casualties from Troy, gather around Aeneas in curiosity. Moving through scenes of malefactors enduring eternal punishment, Aeneas arrives at the bucolic Elysian Fields and his father, Anchises (5), who unveils a prophetic vision (6) of the rise of Rome through the destiny of Aeneas and his illustrious descendants, culminating in Caesar Augustus, legitimizing Aeneas' coming actions in Italy. Anchises' political vision appeases past tragedies with future glory and doubles as a mirror for princes in defining the attributes for a good leader in the new age.

Dante adapts Book VI of Virgil's *Aeneid* for the *Inferno* (c.1320), modifying the timing, duration, and moral impetus of the scene. Dante nests the Underworld journey into the medieval visionary literary form of the Dream Vision, adapting this scene of classical antiquity to serve a Christian ethos. The opening scene of the narrator, "full of sleep" (l.11), aimlessly wandering in a forest landscape during an early spring morning, told in the first-person (ll. 37–41), all capture the elements of the Dream Vision (1). True to that form, the Dreamer-narrator stands in need of insight or consolation (1). However, rather than arriving at the walled garden typical of the visionary landscape of the Dream Vision, the narrator arrives at the mouth of hell along a lonely slope (4), which will substitute for the garden as the terrain of discovery and insight. In addition to repositioning the Descent scene from the middle to the beginning of the narrative, Dante extends the duration of the type-scene to encompass the entirely of the *Inferno* (3), imitating the Dream Vision "tour" of the walled garden, allegorically encoded, which forms the bulk of the narrative. The layers of the classical Underworld become superimposed on the more elaborately layered Christian schema of the Seven Deadly Sins, and the restorative beauty and birdsong typical of the Dream Vision garden gets transposed into the horrors and cries of hell. Virgil, whose genius Dante reveres and imitates, doubles as the Guide figure of a Dream Vision and the wisdom guide of classical epic (2). Similarly, Dante-the-Pilgrim blends ancient and Christian when he likens himself to Virgil's hero, Aeneas, and to the Apostle Paul by denying likeness to either (II.32). Like the beleaguered epic commander, the middle-aged Dante-the-Pilgrim (1) finds himself lost, uncertain, fearful, and essentially alone, but his predicament is personal and spiritual rather than political, and his "sleep" is more a psychic malaise. The ancient sybil who advises Aeneas becomes refashioned in Beatrice (2), the Pilgrim's spiritual guide and prompt into the Underworld. Like the epic hero, who encounters lost friends, ancestors, and mentors and gains prophetic guidance in the realm of the dead, Dante-the-Pilgrim encounters a host of old faces from his days in Florence (5) and gains spiritual insight (6) by first witnessing the sins that landed them in hell. Like the epic hero who uses his newfound insight to propel him to success, Dante-the-Pilgrim learns the lessons of hell on his journey to salvation.

The Middle English *Sir Orfeo* makes use of the second major type of the Descent into the Underworld scene in adapting the classical myth of Orpheus and Eurydice. In this instance, the classical Underworld is transposed into the Celtic Otherworld, often associated with captivity, and the hero's beloved, Heurodis, becomes the victim of a fairy abduction that traps her there. Interestingly, the poet combines elements of both the epic (Virgilian) and the Orphic (Ovidian) models of the Descent into the Underworld scene by pairing the hero's personal loss with his political losses. Like the classical epic hero, Orfeo (1) is a king and leader of his people who has suffered the loss of home and political standing once Heurodis is abducted from his kingdom. True to the type-scene, he has run out of options and ventures into the Otherworld (3), accessed through a rock (4), as an act of recuperation. The poet combines the personal restoration of his beloved wife from the Orphic tradition (7) with the political restoration of his kingdom from ancient epic tradition. Like the classical epic hero, Orfeo encounters the anguished souls of the taken, in this instance, frozen at the point of death (5), who reveal the cruelties endemic to the Fairy King's governance—a political lesson of sorts (6). While Orfeo does not solicit political advice, he accomplishes a political feat in outmaneuvering the Fairy King responsible for his losses by tricking him into a Rash Promise* and citing a king's responsibility to keep his word as leverage for regaining Heurodis. Thus, he dispenses rather than receives advice (6) that turns the tide of his fortunes going forward. The Christian element governing the Descent scene takes the form of Orfeo's ten-year self-imposed exile in the wilderness, drawn from Old English elegiac tradition, where exile forms the primary spiritual journey. The Otherworld/Underworld in *Sir Orfeo* is less a supernatural space than a negative counterpart to Orfeo's earthly kingdom.

The Celtic counterpart to the classical Descent in the Underworld scene, the journey into the fairy Otherworld, features prominently in the ME

Thomas of Erceldoune, with a similar configuration of supernatural journey, political prophecy, and visionary poetic form. The hero, Thomas, is based on the Scottish prophet (fl. 1220–1298) Thomas of Earlston (formerly "Erceldoune"), also called Thomas the Rhymer, famous for his political prophecies. The poem opens in the manner of a Dream Vision, with a lone protagonist wandering out on a May morning resounding with birdsong and lying down under a tree. Like the heroes of both of the classical underworld Descent and the Dream Vision, Thomas needs redirection (1), indicated both by his vague longing, and by the Fairy Queen (2), who corrects his misidentification of her as the Virgin Mary. She patiently consents to sexual intercourse as a first step in his re-education in the journey ahead, aligning her with both the sybil seer-guide of classical tradition and the Guide of the Dream Vision (2). Leading him into Eildon hill (4) (an actual site on the Scottish border) and through a hidden pool (4), the Fairy Queen brings him to the Otherworld, where he must follow her instructions to survive. As in *Sir Orfeo*, elegance accompanies horror. She first guides him into a bucolic garden (*locus amoenus**) typical of the Dream Vision, integrated here into the Otherworld, where he sees the alternate paths to heaven, paradise, pain and hell, in keeping with Christian allegoresis. They proceed to the fairy castle, where the Fairy King and his courtiers (5) exhibit aristocratic refinements of recreational hunting and fine music, dancing, and clothing, processing into the castle with a quarry of deer. However, the ritualistic excoriation of the quarry becomes a hellish dance of knives and blood, qualifying the admiration they elicit earlier, as in *Sir Orfeo*. Moreover, the Fairy Queen informs Thomas that three years have passed and the fiend from Hell will soon arrive and will want him, so she sends him back home, bringing the episode more fully in line with the classical Descent, as well as the Christian hell scene. Returning to Eildon tree, Thomas now possesses prophetic powers (6) of immediate political import, all the more potent, given the poem's real-life geographic setting on the Scottish border. The poem also incorporates the Loathly Lady* motif, another device of feminine guidance; the Fairy Queen transforms from beautiful mistress into an old hag at the point of rape, only to reassume her loveliness once in the Otherworld, as Thomas finalizes his education there, a feature akin to the reclamation of lost love characteristic of the Orphic tradition (7). As in *Sir Orfeo*, cultural difference informs the Descent experience, as Thomas forms a Scottish counterpart to the English prophet, Merlin.

William Shakespeare later modifies the classical Underworld journey type-scene in Act V of *Romeo and Juliet*, when Juliet (1), under the guidance of Friar Lawrence (2), follows in the footsteps of heroes when she enters the family tomb (3) (5) by undergoing a simulated death. Her prefatory monologue (IV.3.14ff.) captures the imagery of the Underworld—its loathsome smell, shrieks, darkness, and terror—where "all my buried ancestors are packed," including the recently killed Tybalt (IV.3.40) (5). Though she ventures there to save her marriage with Romeo (7), who soon joins her there, the scene marks the end, rather than a turning point, of their love; hence, the scene falls at the end of the play, and defeat replaces triumph. Nonetheless, the couple's personal demise promises a degree of conciliation between their feuding families, fulfilling the scene's political underpinnings.

Further Reading

Dominique Battles, "*Sir Orfeo* and English Identity," *Studies in Philology* 107 (2010): 179–211.

Aisling Byrne, *Otherworlds: Fantasy and History in Medieval Literature* (Oxford: Oxford University Press, 2016).

John Block Friedman, *Orpheus in the Middle Ages* (Cambridge, MA: Harvard University Press, 1970).

Howard Rollin Patch, *The Otherworld, According to Descriptions in Medieval Literature* (Cambridge, MA: Harvard University Press, 1950).

Brian Toohey, *Reading Epic* (London and New York: Routledge, 1992).

Disguise and Infiltration

A scene of political strategy, found in both Classical and Germanic traditions, involving a displaced hero (typically a nobleman, king, or prince) disguising himself as a lower-ranking figure (a beggar, pilgrim, or minstrel) to infiltrate the castle of a powerful and corrupt lord somehow involved in the hero's recent demise, forming a turning point in the hero's task of recovering his hereditary rights and/or kingdom. The impetus of the scene typically entails the covert rescue of the hero's beloved (either love interest or wife), who symbolizes the older order, now held captive, and whose reclamation presages the kingdom's restoration. The scene consists of 1) a politically displaced hero who 2) disguises himself as a lower-ranking individual who 3) infiltrates the noble residence of his enemy—and rival leader—where his 4) beloved woman is captive; the hero 5) outwits and outmaneuvers the enemy lord and 6) reclaims his former position, often breaking disguise toward the close of the scene. Medieval renditions of the scene very often associate the hero with harping. Thus, the hero adopts the lowest social status to stage his political comeback.

Homer's *Odyssey* ends with this scene, as Odysseus (1), returning home after an absence of nearly twenty years, disguises himself as a beggar (2) and infiltrates his own palace, now in the control of predatory noblemen (3) vying to marry Odysseus' wife, Penelope (4), and take control of the kingdom of Ithaka. Odysseus outmaneuvers the suitors through an archery contest involving his legendary bow (5), thus revealing his identity. In successfully overthrowing the suitors, Odysseus reclaims both Penelope and the kingdom (6). Though this story remained largely unavailable to the western medieval audience, it establishes the core structural elements that comprise the scene.

The German-speaking medieval audience would have encountered the Disguise and Infiltration type-scene in Gottfried von Strassburg's *Tristan und Isolde* (c. 1210). The scene (ll. 13,097–13,483) unfolds as an opportunistic Irish baron and long-time admirer of Isolde, Gandin (2), enters King Mark's court at Cornwall and successfully tricks Mark into granting him the Queen Isolde (4) in exchange for fulfilling Mark's request that Gandin perform for him on his small rote. When Gandin insists on knowing his reward prior to his performance, Mark unthinkingly promises him "'I will give you whatever you please!'" thus prefacing the Disguise and Infiltration scene with the Rash Promise* type-scene (5). Gandin plays for the court and requests Isolde, shaming Mark as a king potentially unworthy of his word should he not comply. It soon falls to Tristan (1) to rescue Isolde from abduction, which he does by disguising himself as a harper (and fellow Irishman) (2) and infiltrating Gandin's pavilion (2).

Using Gandin's strategy against him, Tristan agrees to Gandin's request to console the anguished Isolde with musical entertainment in exchange for taking him back to Ireland with him, the logistics of which enable Tristan to snatch Isolde back from her abductor (5), reveal himself, and return her to Mark (6). This iteration of the scene contains the core elements of disguise, infiltration, and harping against a backdrop of political rivalry, but in this case, the restoration of the woman and re-establishment of political stability does not benefit Tristan in the long term, as the brief union enjoyed by Tristan and Isolde coincides with their exile from the kingdom and ultimate separation, reversing the usual triumphal outcome of the scene.

In medieval English romance, the scene assumes particular resonance in the post-Conquest political landscape. The earliest phase of the English Outlaw tradition, itself rooted in resistance to the Norman Conquest of 1066, contains the story of the Anglo-Saxon Lincolnshire nobleman Hereward "the Wake," recorded in the early twelfth-century *Gesta Herewardi*, among other sources, who led the most sustained resistance campaign against the Norman invaders in the late 1060's and early 1070's. In the Middle Latin *Gesta Herewardi* (c. 1109–35), Hereward, a displaced Anglo-Saxon nobleman (1), comes out of hiding in Ireland after receiving a summons for help from the daughter of a Cornish prince, Alef, as she faces a forced marriage to an Irish princeling when, in fact, she loves Hereward. Joined by three companions, Hereward disguises himself by darkening his blonde hair and beard (2) and infiltrates her home on the eve of the wedding (3). Taking the lowest seat at the table, he signals his presence to the princess (4), who then circulates the room with some of her ladies (see "Lady with the Mead Cup" scene) offering drinks. When Hereward refuses a drink from one of the ladies and insists on being served by the princess herself, she slips him a ring as a sign. A harping contest ensues, and Hereward proves himself so adept at playing that the prince promises him "whatever he cared to ask, except for his wife and land" (see "Rash Promise" scene) (5). In requesting the release of the messenger of the Irish King's son, Hereward's disguise grows thin, but he manages to flee the scene with the princess, whom he marries forthwith (6). The scene contains the elements of disguise, infiltration, and harping against a backdrop of political takeover, intended to rescue a woman whose fate aligns with English political power. The story of Hereward accounts for the early English styling of the underdog heroes of these scenes in Middle English, including the element of harping in the hall, and the architectural prominence of the "enemy castle," the military architecture introduced into England by the Normans and absent in the hero's portraiture. Iterations of a similar scene from the *Gesta* appear in the ME *King Horn* and *Sir Orfeo*, with related scenes occurring in the ME *Havelok the Dane*, the *Erl of Tolouse*, and *Floris and Blancheflour*.

The earliest extant Middle English romance, *King Horn* (c. 1225) contains two scenes (ll.1,009–246; 1,465–498) that imitate the scene in the *Gesta Herwardi*. Like Hereward, Horn has taken refuge in Ireland following the invasion of his homeland, living under the assumed name "Cutberd" (cf. St. Cuthbert) (1). He receives a plea for help from his beloved, Rymenhild (4), who faces a forced marriage to King Mody of Reynes, prompting him to gather some companions, disguise himself as a pilgrim with a darkened face and neck (2), and infiltrate Mody's castle (3) on the eve of the wedding, assuming the lowest seat at the table. As in the *Gesta*, Rymenhild circulates the room, offering drink to guests. Like Hereward, Horn refuses a lesser drink, insisting on drinking from the horn while slipping a ring to her that signals his identity and enlists her aid. Like Hereward, Horn rescues both his beloved as well as a male companion (Athulf), and the three successfully escape (6). The hero repeats the strategy later, in abbreviated form, as Rymenhild (4) faces a second forced marriage, this time to Fikenhild, Horn's unfaithful friend. Disguising himself as a harper (2), Horn gathers a few companions and infiltrates Fikenhild's newly-built castle (3) during the wedding feast. He sits down, plays a song that sends Rymenhild into a swoon, and, glimpsing her ring, becomes emboldened to strike Fikenhild down with his sword and reclaim Rymenhild, the decisive step in restoring his former kingdom (5)(6). Again, disguise, infiltration, and harping, not to mention token rings of identity, become a political strategy—and turning point—in the hero's comeback, as he stoops to the lowest social level to spring back to the throne.

Sir Orfeo (c.1325) contains a similar scene of Disguise and Infiltration, again involving harping, where again, the setting of the "enemy castle" ties the story to the particular political climate of post-Conquest England, despite the story's classical and Celtic mythic roots. Orfeo (1), displaced from his kingdom following the abduction of his wife, Heurodis (4), by a Fairy King, and living the life of an exile, becomes physically unrecognizable as a king (2) after ten years of privation in the forest. This naturally acquired disguise and the "sclavyn" ("pilgrim's mantle," l. 1067) (2) he wears (the same garment worn by Horn, l. 1054) enables him to infiltrate the Fairy King's castle (3) (architecture not associated with Orfeo himself), armed only with his harp. The same exchange of musical entertainment for the woman (5) found in other texts results in Orfeo's reclamation of Heurodis (4), the first decisive step in reclaiming his kingdom (6). As in the *Gesta Herewardi* and *King Horn*, the Disguise and Infiltration scene repeats itself in the poem (ll. 497–582), and as in the *Odyssey* and *Horn*, forms the culminating, triumphal moment when Orfeo (1) again disguises himself as a beggar-harper (2), infiltrates his own hall (like Odysseus) (3) and takes the political temperature of his kingdom before revealing himself to his beloved subjects (5). Unlike Odysseus and Hereward, however, Orfeo never breaks disguise to his enemy, the Fairy King, in the earlier scene.

Related iterations of the Disguise and Infiltration type-scene occur elsewhere in English romance, though not involving harping. In the ME *Floris and Blancheflour*, a tale with numerous antecedents and variations, Floris (1), a Muslim prince, disguises himself as a merchant (2) traveling to the city of Babylon, which he infiltrates (3), first, by beating the bridge warden at a game of chess (5), and next, hiding himself in a basket of flowers (5) to rescue the Christian Blancheflour (4), forming the pivotal step to his assumption to the throne and conversion of his kingdom in Spain (6). The royal hero of *Havelok the Dane* (2) uses disguise (2) and infiltration to reclaim his kingdom in Denmark (3), now in the hands of a usurper, the prelude to his restoration of England for Goldboro, his bride (4), though Havelok's disguise as a member of the lower social orders spans most of the story, not just one episode (2). As in other English romances, the enemy of *Havelok* is associated with castle architecture, where the heroine is imprisoned. Likewise, the nobleman hero of the *Erl of Tolouse*, Bernard (1), disguises himself as a cleric (2) to infiltrate the castle of his enemy (3), the German Emperor, to rescue the Emperor's wife, Dame Beaulybon (4), whom Bernard secretly loves, from her husband's own ill-informed death sentence. Her staged "confession" (5) reveals her innocence, and Bernard and the Emperor are soon reconciled (6). Following the death of the Emperor, Bernard marries Beaulybon, consolidating her lands with his own (6).

Chaucer includes an extended narrated interlude, rather than a single scene, of Disguise and Infiltration in the *Knight's Tale*, derived from Boccaccio's *Teseida*. As elsewhere in Middle English tradition, the hero, Arcite(1), infiltrates an enemy household containing the woman he loves, Emelye (4), but to different political ends. Arcite's motive for infiltrating Athens (3), the city of his captor, is less political than amorous, for love of Emelye, the distress for which alters his physical appearance, forming a "disguise" (2). Like similar heroes, he assumes a lower social status (2) of squire, hiding his Theban royal identity, debased by the recent war. However, rather than overthrowing Theseus' court, he joins it under the assumed name "Philostrate," working for, rather than against, his recent captor (5). Likewise, the disguise *dis*empowers rather than empowers him, as he is now "so caytyf and so thral," working for "my mortal enemy" (ll. 1552-3). Arcite dies at the end, without obtaining Emelye (6). Thus, Chaucer reverses the triumphal direction normally charted by the type-scene.

Further Reading

Dominique Battles, "*Sir Orfeo* and English Identity," *Studies in Philology* 107 (2010): 179–211.

———, *Cultural Difference and Material Culture in Middle English Romance: Normans and Saxons* (New York: Routledge, 2013), 114–20, 134–35, 137–39.

Morgan Dickson, "The Image of the Knightly Harper: Symbolism and Resonance," in Nicholas Perkins, ed., *Medieval Romance and Material Culture* (Cambridge: D.S. Brewer, 2015), 199–214.

Ekphrasis

Not so much a scene but a pause within a scene to describe a significant, crafted item such as a shield, weapon, saddle, or a fine garment connected or gifted to the hero. The Greek term denotes a narrative phenomenon of diverse origin, with counterparts in classical, Germanic, and Celtic literature. A pivotal or culminating, ceremonial and transcendent scene, whereby the hero/heroine assumes an expanded identity, distilled in a precious, handmade object gifted to, or acquired by, them, possessing personal as well as collective, even cosmic, resonance. Intentionality suffuses the scene, expressed in imagery of the crafter's process, materials, and skill and in the recipient's past achievement or future goal. Stillness and meditative observation of the valuable object comprise the "action" of the scene. The scene consists of 1) a hero/ine at a 2) crossroads in their development, who 3) receives a valuable, often exotic, gift whose features and origin reflect on their emerging status, prompting 4) an extended description of the crafted object, 5) including mention of its skilled maker, that 6) speaks to the hero's broader, emergent cultural identity. In some cases, the gift marks the recipient's new, aspirational, triumphant, or empowered identity, while in others, it marks a subjugated identity imposed upon them requiring endurance. In either instance, the recipient now stands for the collective, celebrating or critiquing its larger cultural patterns and practices.

The most famous classical example of ekphrasis is the description of Achilles' shield in the *Iliad* (18.368–613). Achilles (1), having learned of Patroclus' death at the hands of Hector, decides to reenter the fight with the Trojans to reclaim the corpse of his beloved friend and exact vengeance on Hector (2). To serve this renewed purpose, Achilles' mother, Thetis, promises that Hephaestus will craft him new armor (5), including the iconic shield (3). His personal desire for supremacy over Hector coalesces with the imminent, collective Greek victory over the Trojans (6). Homer dramatizes Hephaestus' crafting of the shield, his tools, and methods, creating "a world of gorgeous immortal work" depicting the heavens and the earth and two contrasting cities: one enjoying harmony and fecundity (the victors), and the other, besieged, its sustenance endangered, and its treasures fated for spoil, clearly a metaphor of Troy itself (4). The description marks a turning point in the war and Achilles' role in it, sanctioning its outcome in favor of the Greeks through this divine amulet that will accompany the hero through the battles ahead.

Ekphrasis of a shield appears, likewise, in the ME *Sir Gawain and the Green Knight* (ll. 619–65), as Gawain arms himself (see "Arming of the Hero"), in view of the whole court, to go in search of the Green Chapel. Gawain (1), a knight of the Round Table, now assumes a larger collective and cultural identity (2, 6), as he defends the honor of Arthur and his knights against the Green Knight's earlier insult to king and court (see "Flyting"). The shield (3) he receives pronounces their collective values in its imagery of a pentangle (associated here with Solomon), the points of which correlate to interconnected Christian virtues (the five pure joys of Mary, the five wounds of Christ, the five chivalric virtues, the five senses, and five fingers) (4). Gawain's broader identification with King Arthur also accounts for the shield's interior depicting the Virgin Mary—a shield normally associated with Arthur, not Gawain. True to the scene, the shield's imagery consolidates cosmic, timeless values, as opposed to the more typical family crest or royal emblem (6). Hero and shield alike are associated with gold (ll. 620, 633); thus, it becomes a tool of both initiation and reward. Unlike other ekphrastic items, the shield's maker (human or supernatural) is never mentioned; thus, its power remains unambiguously rooted in Christian divinity (5).

Chrétien de Troyes employs ekphrasis in *Erec and Enide*, in describing the magnificent saddle Enide receives from Guivret (ll. 5287–5308). She and Erec (1) have just emerged, together, from their period of testing. She has accompanied Erec on his quest and proven her ability to act on their mutual behalf, even if it requires disobeying his command (2). Jointly, they have outmaneuvered a predatory nobleman, escaping on a single horse, with Erec seizing a shield and Enide grabbing a lance, objects symbolizing their equality and unity in the heroic project. Now facing Guivret and suspecting another ambush, Enide steps forward and seizes the reins of Guivret's horse, as Erec is weakened by his wounds. Delighted to have found Erec again, Guivret takes them in and cures Erec, and later gifts Enide a palfrey and saddle (3) upon their departure. The ekphrasis of the scene identifies Enide as a critical agent in the heroic project—feminine influence forming a cornerstone of medieval romance—and distinguishes this new genre and hero-type from the earlier, classical, heroic model of the *Aeneid* (6). On the saddle crafted of ivory, the Breton sculptor (5), working for seven years, has carved the story of Dido and Aeneas, whose love story had to end for Aeneas to achieve his destiny of founding Rome (4). As with Aeneas, Erec's private desire for his beloved threatens to subsume his public duties, but Chrétien rewrites the story. Unlike Dido, Enide is not a digression from the hero's mission, but central to it, and their love affair not a temptation to be overcome but a vital energy fueling Erec's ascension to kingship. As an object to sit upon, the saddle enables Enide to literally transcend Dido as a heroine, her victory alongside Erec contrasting with Dido's personal and political defeat and death in Carthage. As Enide, not Erec, receives the precious object, spotlighted through ekphrasis, from a foe turned ally of Erec, she assumes the position of "hero," as, together, she and Erec model not only a more balanced couple capable of governing a realm but also a new type of heroism that fuses private love with public duty (6).

Erec and Enide includes a comparable instance of ekphrasis for Erec in the culminating coronation scene (ll.6694–6911), when Erec (1) receives a splendid robe (3), crafted by four fairies (5), marking his transition to kingship (2). The timing on Christmas Day, along with the supernatural crafters of the royal robe, bespeak the cultural and cosmic import of Erec's emerging status (6). The four corners of the robe, each stitched by one of the fairies, depict the symbols of the quadrivium (Geometry, Arithmetic, Music, and Astronomy), the bases of medieval learning that unlock the secrets of the universe, symbolizing the wisdom (3, 4, 6) Erec brings to, and receives with, the throne. This wisdom is valued through the robes' rare and precious materials of gold thread, stones (chrysolite and amethyst), and the fur lining of the exotic "berbiolette" of India (4). A scepter bearing a fist-sized emerald, engraved with every type of man, animal, fish, and fowl completes Erec's cosmic garb (6). Taken as a pair, the ekphrastic items of Enide's saddle, depicting the lovers Dido and Aeneas, and Erec's coronation robes, depicting symbols of universal wisdom, join the matters of heart and head in this new royal couple.

The Middle English *Emaré* (ll. 80–168) includes another instance of ekphrasis of a precious robe, gifted by a royal father to his child but signaling her disempowerment rather than empowerment. Emaré's cloak appears early rather than late in the story, as a catalyst of suffering rather than a reward for achievement. Emaré (1), the only child of a widower emperor, the king of Sicily, grows into womanhood (2), only to invite the incestuous advances of her father. His desires are exacerbated by a precious cloth (3) he bestows on her, recently gifted to him by an eastern nobleman, whose father won it from another man. Expertly embroidered in the East by the daughter of the Emir (5), who adorned it with precious stones, the cloth spellbinds those who look upon it, notably powerful men, who suspect fairy trickery; thus, its magic is dark rather than light (as with Erec's robe). Each of the four corners of the cloth is embroidered with the images of suffering lovers whose stories prefigure Emare's: Ydoyne and Amadas; Tristan and Isolde; Floris and Blanchefleur; and the son of the Sultan of Babylon and the daughter of the Emir who made the cloth (4). Thus, the cloth, "stuffed wyth ymagerye" (l. 168), also includes the rare element of a self-portrait of its maker (5). The cloth becomes Emaré's wedding robe as she faces marriage to her father, a union approved by the Pope but refused by Emaré. Atypically, rather than signaling Emaré's initiation and acceptance into the wider culture, Emaré's cloak marks her exile from home, as her father casts her out to sea with only the cloak (6).

She navigates a life-threatening journey on the sea more typical of male heroes. Like other ekphrastic items, the cloth enlarges the heroine, who seems otherworldly in it. However, her public enhancement in the eyes of men spells her personal diminishment and objectification. As a precious, feminine object (crafted by a woman) that is won, possessed, gifted, and wielded by powerful men, the cloak represents subjugated womanhood, a larger identity Emaré assumes when she wears it (6). Like all ekphrastic items, however, the cloak becomes a tool for growth, as she later distinguishes herself in the artform of the cloak—silk embroidery—when she arrives in Wales and teaches the skill to other women, turning from victim into creator and leader of fellow women. She also begins to don the cloak voluntarily in public as she earns her social status. Eventually, she and her son are recognized through fine, embroidered garments of her own making, as she now writes her own "script" rather than living the life scripted by the cloak.

Further Reading

Paul Battles, ed., *Sir Gawain and the Green Knight* (Peterborough, ON: Broadview Press, 2012), 58–61.

Sir Israel Gollancz, ed., with Mabel Day and Mary S. Serjeantson, *Sir Gawain and the Green Knight*, EETS OS 210 (Oxford: Oxford University Press, 1940).

Norris J. Lacy and Joan Tasker Grimbert, eds., *A Companion to Chrétien de Troyes* (Woodbridge, Suffolk: D.S. Brewer, 2008).

Christine Li-Ju Tsai, "Emaré's Fabulous Robe: The Ambiguity of Power in a Late Medieval Romance," *Medieval Forum* 14 (2003).

Oliver Taplin, "The Shield of Achilles within the *Iliad*," *Greece and Rome* 27 (1980): 1–21.

Joseph S. Wittig, "The Aeneas-Dido Allusion in Chrétien's *Erec et Enide*," *Comparative Literature* 22 (1970): 237–53.

Epic Descent

Originating in classical epic, a visitation to a hesitant hero by a deity, usually Mercury, who calls the hero to fulfill a larger destiny of far-reaching consequence, usually involving a journey to another land or city. The scene marks a turning point in the narrative, where the hero has either stalled in his primary mission or must adopt a new plan of action, and the divine origin of the command lends divine favor and sanction to the hero and his mission, making him an agent of divine will. The scene consists of 1) a hesitant, stalled hero, 2) the disturbing appearance of a divine visitant who 3) usually appears in a dream and 4) who commands the hero to fulfill a larger destiny 5) involving a journey to another city, concluding with 6) the awakening of the hero 7) and his immediate resolution to obey the orders. For medieval readers, two major prototypes of the Epic Descent scene occur in Virgil's *Aeneid* and Statius' *Thebaid*. The biblical counterpart to this scene is the Annunciation, where the angel Gabriel visits Mary to announce the birth of Christ.

The iconic Epic Descent scene(s) for the medieval West occurs in Virgil's *Aeneid* (IV.352–85; 775–95) during Aeneas' sojourn in Carthage following the fall of Troy. Comfortably settled into Dido's emerging kingdom, Aeneas (1) runs the risk of channeling all his energies into the love affair and into building up Dido's seat of power while "losing sight of future towns the fates ordain," not to mention of his own descendants, a risk brought to the attention of Jupiter himself. Disappointed in the highly billed hero, Jupiter dispatches Mercury (2) to accost Aeneas, with the god's aerial journey from firmament to earth, carrying a wand that seals and unseals the sleep of death (3), inscribing the proverbial "big picture" of space and time onto the encounter. He finds Aeneas engaged in the foundations of Dido' new citadel, arrayed in gifts from her, and immediately shames the hero for effeminacy and neglect, "'wasting your days in Lybia.'" Mercury delivers Jupiter's charge (4) to depart for Italy and found Rome (5), if nothing else than to secure his son, Ascanius', heritage. He then vanishes mid-sentence. Aeneas, "shocked to the bottom of his soul" by the god (2), who has "shaken him awake" (6), immediately moves to extricate himself from Dido's amorous and political charms and readies his crew to sail for Italy (7). Not long afterwards, the scene repeats itself, in briefer form, further emboldening the hero for his final departure from Carthage.

Statius transposes the Epic Descent scene into a minor key in the *Thebaid* (II. 89–127), where the scene fuels not the creation of a new empire but the internal destruction of an old one, Thebes, through the civil war between the brothers and rival claimants to the throne, Etiocles and Polynices. The scene unfolds with Mercury descending to the underworld to summon the ghost of the Theban King Laius to arouse his grandson,

Etiocles, into confrontation with his brother Polynices, who amasses forces in the city of Argos that will march on Thebes. Indirection permeates the scene at each level. Mercury descends (2) not directly to a living hero but to the phantom of his dead grandfather, Laius, who plays the role of the divine visitant. Together, they travel not down through the crystalline firmament of the *Aeneid* but up from the vapors of the underworld, nested in a stormy, battered landscape, through the screams and wailings of the damned. Thus, Laius (2), the messenger's messenger, rises from the underworld rather than descending from the heavens to visit Etiocles (1) in a dream (3), disguising himself as the seer Tiresias, further obscuring divine presence. Claiming (falsely) he speaks on Jove's behalf, he accuses Etiocles of sloth and negligence and commands him to guard the city of Thebes against his brother's advancing forces (4). Etiocles awakens (6) and immediately resolves to seek out Polynices in vengeance (7). Thus, rather than inspiring hope leading to triumph, the scene in the *Thebaid* instills hatred, leading to ruin.

Chaucer presents a variation of the Epic Descent in the *Knight's Tale* (ll. 1380–98) that draws on the Virgilian, Statian, as well as Ovidian traditions in this sequel to the story of the Theban war. Not found in the tale's immediate source, Boccaccio's *Teseida*, the Epic Descent in the *KT* constitutes one of several ways Chaucer situates the *KT* within classical epic tradition. The Theban Arcite (1), recently released from prison in Athens, has returned to his native city of Thebes. Interpreting his new freedom as a form of exile, Arcite loses direction and motivation. Like Aeneas, Arcite has become immobilized—Aeneas by the comforts of Dido, and Arcite by his melancholy over Emelye, who remains unaware of him. After a year or two of this, Arcite is visited one night in a dream (3) by Mercury (2). With a brief command, Mercury directs him back to Athens, as "'Ther is thee shapen of thy woe an ende'" (l. 1392)(4)(5), with "shapen" evoking the element of epic destiny. Awakening with a start (6), Arcite resolves to return to Athens (7). Chaucer ironizes the Epic Descent scene by combining the Virgilian infrastructure of the scene with a Statian ethos. First, while staging Mercury's familiar visit from Virgil, unlike in the *Aeneid*, his visit in the *KT* is not prefaced by a Divine Council laying out the hero's higher political/historical destiny, instead focusing narrowly on Arcite's acute and self-absorbing lovesickness that serves no larger purpose. Second, while Mercury bears the familiar wand associated with sleep which, in the *Aeneid*, wakens the hero from his amorous stupor, the wand in the *KT* directs Arcite further *into* his amorous stupor. Moreover, Chaucer associates the wand with Argus (l. 1390), whom, according to Ovidian tradition, Mercury put to sleep and killed using the wand, presaging Arcite's untimely death in Athens. Third, while Aeneas moves forward, to a new land and purpose, Arcite moves backwards, to the city of his defeat and captivity, as a prisoner of war, thinking it will bring an end to his suffering, mimicking the futility endemic to the scene in Statius. Fourth, whereas Mercury, in the *Aeneid*, cautions the hero away from Dido, in the *KT*, which combines the mode of conflict of the Theban War (civil war) with the source of conflict from the Trojan War (a beautiful woman), Mercury directs Arcite *toward* the woman (Emelye), the source of his conflict with his kinsman Palaemon, and the boon he never attains. Thus, Chaucer transforms a scene all about guidance toward renewed purpose and new life into one of misguidance leading to pointlessness and early death without progeny.

The poet of the thirteenth-century ME *Havelok the Dane* crafts an Epic Descent scene (ll. 1, 247–352) out of a parallel scene found in earlier versions of the story of Havelok, a dispossessed Danish prince who grows up in poverty in England, eventually marries the dispossessed heir to the English throne, Goldboru, and together with her, reclaims the thrones of both Denmark and England. Earlier twelfth-century, Anglo-Norman versions of the story (Geffrei Gaimar's *L'Estoire des Engleis*, ll. 195–242, and the *Lai d'Haveloc*, ll. 397–532) contain a scene where the heroine (Argentille) has a disturbing, prophetic dream of Havelok's struggle to reclaim his kingdom in Denmark. The dream is inscrutable to her, and she relies on others for interpretation. In neither version is there a divine messenger. The English poet of *Havelok the Dane* refashions the scene to accord with the Epic Descent type-scene at this pivotal moment of the narrative, blending classical and biblical models of the scene. More importantly, he uses the scene as one of several gestures that more equally match national affairs of England with those of Denmark. As in the classical model of the scene, Havelok is a stalled hero, robbed of his kingdom, impoverished, and with no clear plan of recovery (1). The poet innovates with the scene by pairing the hero with an equally stalled royal heroine, Goldboru, similarly displaced politically and economically with no end in sight (1). The *Havelok*-poet inserts a divine messenger, an angel (2), who comes while Havelok dreams (3) yet who speaks not to the hero but to Goldboru herself, who remains awake the whole time, signaling her equal, if not greater, importance to the story. As in the biblical Annunciation scene, Goldboru imitates Mary, who is awake when the angel Gabriel appears. Since Havelok and Goldboru have not so much strayed as been thwarted, the angel (like Gabriel) pronounces, rather than commands, their glorious, joint destinies as future monarchs of both Denmark and England (4), which then redirects the couple to journey to Denmark as the first step in their political ascendance (5). Goldboru's primacy in the scene, and in the narrative as a whole, accounts not only for her being the sole (and fully awake) witness of the divine visitation, but also for how she wakes the hero (6) and interprets his prophetic dream for him in light of the angel's message, making her the arbiter of their plans. Analogous to the biblical version of the scene, Havelok is a savior figure, partly accounting for his semi-miraculous glow, only here employed in the classical vein of political salvation. True to the scene, Havelok rises with renewed determination and goes to church the next morning to seek God's assistance in reclaiming his kingdom (7). Hero and heroine, together, journey between the kingdoms and through shared adversity in this tale of political redemption.

Malory includes an Epic Descent scene in the *Morte Darthur* in the episode of Lancelot's dream (Book XIII). While on the grail quest, Lancelot (1) sees an old chapel, dismounts, and wishes to enter. Unable to enter, he lies down outside and falls asleep. He dreams (3) of a sick knight who is healed by drinking from the grail, and an accompanying squire who comments on the deadly sin that prevents the sleeping knight (Lancelot) from approaching the holy vessel (2). Upon waking (6), Lancelot hears a voice (2) that orders him away from the chapel (4). Similar to Aeneas, Lancelot realizes the error of his love affair with the queen and commits himself to a path of virtue, going in search of the grail (5)(7). Malory multiplies the voice of divine will by three (knight, squire, disembodied voice) and extends their message across sleeping and waking states. As Lancelot's private transgressions involve the king, his reform touches upon right rule and empire, much like Aeneas'. He fulfills his destiny, and God allows him to see the grail.

Further Reading

Dominique Battles, "Reconquering England for the English in *Havelok the Dane*," *The Chaucer Review* 47 (2012): 187–205.

Thomas M. Greene, *The Descent from Heaven: A Study in Epic Continuity* (New Haven, CT: Yale University Press, 1963).

Ann M. Taylor, "Epic Descent in The *Knight's Tale*," *Classical folia* 30 (1976): 40–56.

Exile

Aimless wandering of a lone protagonist, separated from his community, with no end of place or time in sight, prominent in Old English tradition. A theme often rendered as an abstract state of mind that nevertheless takes on scenic form. Though exile was a historical punishment for wrongdoers of some status, it assumed religious significance as a metaphor for the transitory nature of earthly existence and a form of living death, becoming a cornerstone of Anglo-Saxon spirituality. The scenic elements of exile consist of 1) an intimate, often first-person perspective; 2) the loss of community as imagined in a feasting hall, sometimes expressed as a catalog of lost joys—an *ubi sunt* lament; 3) the longing for the protection of a male superior in the form of a warrior-king or lord; 4) a backward-looking, nostalgic perspective; 5) a long, indefinite span of time; 6) a sense of unjust, prolonged suffering that becomes a form of heroism; and 7) a setting of a harsh, life-threatening landscape.

The protagonists of OE *The Wanderer*, *The Seafarer*, and the Last Survivor in *Beowulf* all find themselves alone in the wilderness and mourning the loss of their communities, usually emphasizing the loss of a particular male kinsman, a protecting lord whose support means inclusion in the group. The Wanderer, in a first-person lament (1), mourns the death of his *gold-wine* ("gold-friend," l. 22) (3)(4), which means that he will remain *eðle bidæled,/freomægum feor* ("cut off from my country, far from my kinsmen," ll. 20–21) (2)(5). The Seafarer (1), out at sea (7), is *winemægum bidroren* ("deprived of kinsmen," l. 16) and bereft of *hleahtor wera* ("the laughter of men," l. 21) (2). The Last Survivor of *Beowulf*, the last of his people (1), through a first-person lament, mourns that "*Ealle hie deað fornam,/ærran mælum*" (ll. 2236-2237, "death has taken away all of [my people]") (2)(4). He remains "*se an ða gen . . . se ðær longest hwearf,/ weard winegeomor*" (ll.2237-39, "that one who lived the longest, alone, a guardian mourning for his companions"), now roaming, sad and aimless, indefinitely (5). He mourns the lost joys of the hall—the harp music, the hawk flying, and the horse in the courtyard (ll. 2262-5)—and laments there is no one to carry the sword or polish the cup (2), with a barrow (a place of death) forming the setting of the lament (7). His undying loyalty to the memory of his people (4), whose treasures he tries to safeguard, becomes a tragic heroism (6).

The theme of exile survives into late medieval English literature, where it merges with the forest-quest of French chivalric tradition centering on feminine influence on the hero. The ME *Sir Orfeo* characterizes Orfeo's ten-year wandering in the forest (5) following the loss of his wife and kingdom in the poetic vein of early English exile. Rather than going in search of his stolen wife, Orfeo steps down from the throne with no goal in mind.

Alone (1) in the "wildernes" (l. 212) (7) and without a destination (5), Orfeo suffers self-imposed separation from his community and wife, the nostalgic longing (4) for which takes the form of an *ubi sunt* lament for lost joys of the hall (ll. 241–56), "Of mete & drink, of ich deynté" (l. 253) and fine bedding (l. 242)(2), all contrasted with the frozen austerity of the winter landscape he now occupies (7). As a king, Orfeo longs not for his protecting lord but for the "kni3tes of priis/Bifor him kneland" (ll. 249–50), evoking the lost circumstances of lordly protection (3). As the victim of the Fairy King's incursion into his kingdom and the abduction of his wife, Orfeo aligns with the mis-served exiled hero of earlier tradition (6), only in this instance, he emerges from exile to rescue his wife and regain his kingdom.

In *Sir Gawain and the Green Knight*, Gawain's journey into the forest of Wirral evokes the landscape of Anglo-Saxon literary tradition rather than the forest of French romance. Setting out alone (1) from Camelot into the "wyldrenesse of Wyrale" (l. 701) in the depth of winter (7), Gawain has a fixed deadline in mind for his meeting with the Green Knight but little sense of where he might find the Green Chapel, evoking the aimlessness of the type-scene (5). True to the scene, the winter landscape itself afflicts him far worse than any foes such as dragons, giants, bulls, bears, all fights which take place off stage (ll. 726 and 729) (7). Like the early English hero, Gawain sets forth not eagerly but reluctantly and assumes a retrospective, nostalgic vantage (4). He rides "Fer floten fro his frendes" (l. 714, "far adrift from his friends") and "fremedly" (l. 714, "as a stranger"), suffering nights "leudles, alone" (l. 693, "companionless, alone"), always associating aloneness with loss of community in the hall (2). While in the forest, "he fonde noght hym byfore the fare that he liked" (l. 694, "He did not find before him the food he liked") and has no one to talk to except God and his horse (l. 696), evoking the lost joys of the hall (2). His isolation comes to a head when he finds himself in the forest, "alone" (l. 735), a "mon al hym one" (l. 749, "man all by himself") on Christmas Eve, nearly frozen to death, heightening the sense of unjust suffering (6). Moreover, he has undertaken this journey not to win a woman but to defend the honor of his male lord (3), the primary relationship throughout the poem, despite the feminine seductions at castle Hautdesert, which fail to divert him from his promise to Arthur. Unlike the romance hero, who experiences the forest-quest as an opportunity for self-improvement from which he will emerge a better man, Gawain experiences the forest journey as a form of exile, likely to end in death by beheading.

In the ME *St. Erkenwald*, the resuscitated, pagan body in the tomb frames his lonely, posthumous existence of centuries (5) following his brief glimpse of Christ at the Harrowing of Hell as a form of exile. From a first-person perspective (1), the judge speaks of being "'non of þe nombre þat þou with noy boghtes/With þe blode of thi body'" (ll. 289–90), as one excluded from the community of the saved when Christ harrowed hell (7), despite a life of loyal service to his people. His soul, he says, sits "'exilid fro þat soper so, þat solempne fest,/Þer richely hit arne refetyd þat after right hungride'" (ll. 303–4), as his soul "'herken after meeles'" and "'Longe er ho þat soper se, oþer segge hyr to lathe'" (ll. 307–8), invoking the lost warmth of a hall (2), conflating the biblical imagery of the divine feast with early English communal ideals, emblematized in the image of the hall. Likewise, the narrator longs for the protection of a male superior, in this case Jesus (3), whose narrative context here within the apocryphal Harrowing of Hell characterizes him as a warrior-king, a popular image of Jesus among the Anglo-Saxons. The OE *Descent into Hell* depicts Christ as a "victorious-Son" (l. 43, "*sygebearn*") and "protector" (l. 75, "*mundbora*") infiltrating the gates of hell, where he finds hell-bound pre-Christians warriors, termed "exiles" (l. 42, "*Wraeccan*"), worthy pagans who vie with one another to catch a glimpse of Christ, expressing their nascent faith. In characterizing himself as an exile who glimpsed Christ in this heroic act and now longs for him, the dead judge of *Erkenwald* recalls pre-Conquest formulations of Christ as a beloved guardian and object of deep, nostalgic longing (4), becoming, himself, a model of honorable suffering (6).

Further Reading

Dominique Battles, "*Sir Orfeo* and English Identity," *Studies in Philology* 107 (2010): 179–211.

Christine Fell, "Perceptions of Transience," in Malcolm Godden and Michael Lapidge, eds., *Cambridge Companion to Old English Poetry* (Cambridge: Cambridge University Press, 1991), 172–89.

Gordon Mursell, *English Spirituality from Earliest Times to 1700* (Louisville: Westminster John Knox Press, 2001).

J. Burke Severs, "The Antecedents of *Sir Orfeo*," in MacEdward Leach, ed., *Studies in Medieval Literature in Honor of Professor Albert Cross Baugh* (Philadelphia: University of Pennsylvania Press, 1961), 187–207.

Flyting

A formal, public exchange of verbal insults between two warriors, usually as a prelude to combat, of both Classical and early Germanic origin. Especially prevalent in Old Icelandic tradition. Often occurring early in the narrative, the scene introduces the hero more fully to the audience and transitions him into a new phase of his heroic career by forcing him to assert his competence and resolve. The scene consists of a 1) hero faced with 2) an insult issued by a 2) warrior unfamiliar to him that requires a 4) response. Scenes of flyting occur regularly in Classical and Germanic heroic epic tradition, where the hero's worth is measured largely through martial prowess, and where the pre-Christian hero is bound by an honor code requiring a retaliatory insult. The hero, faced with a slanderous comment from a warrior he barely knows, who calls into question his record of combat, takes the insult personally and uses the occasion to profile himself by showcasing his past exploits, retorting with a comparable insult (resisting shame by shaming his opponent) and often pronouncing his intentions for future martial achievement (a.k.a. "boasting" in Germanic tradition). The scene forms one of many in epic tradition designed to garner audience respect and admiration for the hero, even amidst public humiliation, and serves the pre-Christian heroic aspiration of personal fame.

In medieval Romance, scenes of flyting differ notably in the hero's response to the insult. The challenger imitates his epic and/or pre-Christian counterpart in calling into question the hero's martial prowess and achievement, but the hero, bound by the chivalric code, itself rooted in Christian virtues of humility and service, often moderates the retaliatory response by first verbally "turning the other cheek," not taking the insult personally, and refusing to be baited by a knight exhibiting inferior character. As in epic tradition, the scene constitutes a public performance, affording the hero the opportunity to display maturity, patience, and self-control, yet suggesting a Christian heroic inclination of fighting out of necessity rather than careerism. However, his more moderate response, in fact, serves his knightly career, as the scene enables him to seem the better man and justifies his imminent martial retribution on the battlefield. In both epic and romance tradition, flyting scenes pivot on the hero's self-control, whether that be refusing humiliation through retaliation—as in heroic epic—or humbly absorbing humiliation by way of fulfilling a larger duty, as in medieval Romance.

Though not available to medieval audiences, Homer's *Odyssey* contains a valuable illustrative example of epic flyting. In *Odyssey* VIII, a scene of flyting accompanies Odysseus' transition from commander and tactician on the battle plain of Troy, back to king of peacetime Ithaca.

Odysseus is at a low point in his career. Despite his recent achievements at Troy, where his conceit of the Trojan horse effectively won the war for the Greeks, he has lost his entire crew and fleet of ships on the return journey through a combination of hubris and recklessness. He finds himself now at the mercy of the Phaeaicians, whose shores he washes up on, and whose king, Alcinoos, shelters and aids the mysterious man. Odysseus (1), "raider of cities," already a renowned war hero of mature years, finds his mettle challenged by two young men, Alcinoos' son Laodamas and Broadsea, "in looks and build the best of the Phaeaicians," (3) during a strength competition among the island's champion athletes (195). Like all flyting scenes, this one constitutes a call to growth, spurring Odysseus to reclaim his failing courage and strength for new, peacetime purposes. Therefore, rather than ushering in combat, as the scene typically does, flyting ushers in peace. The peacetime setting of the scene charts the direction of Odysseus' evolution toward civilian life, while still retaining his prowess, as noted by the two young challengers, who privately remark on Odysseus' "'big, rippling strength,'" perceiving not a loser but a man "just beaten down by one too many blows" (195). Laodamas and Broadsea take turns challenging Odysseus—the former, by inviting him into the civic games and the latter, by excluding him from the festivities as an undeserving "'skipper of profiteers'" (196) (2). Odysseus defends his honor with a simple question to Laodamas of "'why do you taunt me so with such a challenge?'" and a caustic insult to Broadsea as a "'reckless fool'" whose "mind inside is worthless'" (197)(4). In both cases, Odysseus displays a keen grasp of both social convention and human nature by refraining from offending (let alone fighting) Laodamas, his host, while publicly noting in Broadsea the mismatch between looks and brains, all insights necessary for effective kingship. Broadsea's personal insult to Odysseus' honor spurs him to grab the largest discus and throw it the furthest, discouraging any further challenge and winning the admiration of a fellow king, Alcinoos. In this sense, the scene of flyting in book VIII marks the turning point in Odysseus reclamation of his kingdom by facilitating the reclamation of his character.

A comparable scene of flyting occurs in the Old English *Beowulf*, where the hero, a guest in Hrothgar's hall, finds his reputation publicly challenged by one of the king's retainer, Unferth. The scene marks a transition, as far as we can tell, between Beowulf's status as retainer of king Hygelac to leader of his own band of retainers, albeit still under Hygelac's command. Beowulf reports how his people, knowing Beowulf's great strength, "'advised me to visit you,'" Horthgar, to offer aid against the giant endangering the kingdom, making Beowulf a budding emissary of sorts (l. 410).

Beowulf is also now old enough to reciprocate Hrothgar's past favors to his father, Ecgtheow, in his time of need, bespeaking a network of alliances, old and new, all centering on Beowulf, charting his direction as a future ruler of his own kingdom. The life-or-death scenario in Hrothgar's kingdom dictates the nature of the flyting scene, which revolves around matters of physical survival and monsters. Just prior to the insult, Beowulf presents Hrothgar with a verbal résumé of his ability, gear, and past triumphs over comparable beasts, and the flyting becomes germane to the interview process. Like Odysseus, Beowulf (1), a guest in a foreign kingdom, is insulted by a member of the king's circle, Unferth (3), who seems to enforce "quality control" in estimating Beowulf's competence. Despite Beowulf's impressive reputation, Unferth mocks him for reputedly failing a swimming contest against his friend, Breca, "'because of a foolish boast,'" only to have Breca "'swim better than you'" (ll. 508–9, 517)(2). The insult to Beowulf is personal and close to the bone, recalling the very identity the hero is moving away from—his youth. Hrothgar's silence during the scene, at odds with Anglo-Saxons customs of hospitality, suggests the vital importance of the truth before entrusting their lives to the young warrior. True to the type-scene, the insult provides Beowulf the opportunity to profile himself further, adding to his list of triumphs the sea monsters he grappled with to protect Breca, accounting for his late arrival, putting the safety of others before his own—yet another hallmark of effective kingship. Typical of the scene in epic, Beowulf insults Unferth in return, more damningly, noting how Unferth avoids such contests of strength, though "'it is true you slew your own brothers, your own close kinsmen,'" for which "'you will suffer damnation in hell'"(ll. 586–89), kin-slaying being the highest crime among the Anglo-Saxons. Unferth confesses his guilt through silence, conceding defeat. The flyting scene, through insult and response, marks Beowulf's transition from youth to manhood and from follower to leader.

The type-scene of flyting migrated from ancient epic to the emerging genre of French chivalric romance in the twelfth century, where it comes to serve the priorities of the new knightly hero. In Chrétien de Troyes' *Yvain*, for instance, two instances of flyting occur in the opening scenes of the narrative that capture and distinguish the medieval knight from his pre-Christian counterpart, notably, in terms of setting and heroic response to slander. Unlike the *Odyssey* or *Beowulf*, which feature heroes in the throes of survival, *Yvain* lacks any existential threat. Thus, the knight Calogrenant searches out adventure "'to test my courage and my strength,'" again marking the inflexion of growth accompanying flyting (299). While the story's titular hero certainly encounters dangerous foes, his greatest struggle is internal—psychological and spiritual—in nature, and therefore, deeply personal. The flyting, therefore, is casual and intimate, and the challenger, Sir Kay, is an insider to the hero's circle rather than a foreigner. In a leisured gathering, Calogrenant (1) begins to relate an attempted exploit when a fellow knight of the Round Table, Sir Kay (3), insults him for ingratiating himself to the queen through seemingly superior manners, deriding him for "'lacking in good sense'" (296) (2). Like all such challengers, Sir Kay makes the hero look good, in part, by looking bad himself, in this case even more so, as Chrétien incriminates Kay in advance as "spiteful, wicked, sharp-tongued, and abusive," setting him up as a negative example of knightly conduct, suggesting the ritualistic function of the type-scene. Chrétien duplicates the flyting within the very same courtly gathering, as Sir Kay (3) similarly insults Calogrenant's cousin, Yvain (1), for sanctimoniousness in vowing to defend his cousin's honor, further discrediting Kay's criticism through its frequency and indiscriminateness, not to mention that he criticizes fellow knights for doing the right thing, not the wrong thing. The insults themselves highlight interiority, as Kay challenges both men for pride—a matter of internal character rather than physical competence.

The response of the romance hero to insult spells the chief generic innovation to the flyting scene. If Sir Kay acts alone in slandering his fellow knights, the hero(s) have help, in the form of a woman, Queen Guinevere, who speaks first and assumes the combative tone formerly reserved for the epic hero as she returns an insult for an insult, accusing Kay of being "'tiresome and base,'" venomous, "'hated everywhere,'" and deserving the treatment of a "'lunatic'" (296 and 302) (4). In voicing the words of the epic hero, Guinevere announces the centrality of women to the genre of French chivalric romance. Indeed, Calogrenant and Yvain both respond as much to Guinevere as to Sir Kay in countering the insult, with their words merely supplementing the queen's. Both men model the Christian virtue of "turning the other cheek," by depersonalizing it and de-escalating the conflict: Calogrenant responds with the Christian virtues of non-violence ("'I'm not greatly upset by the quarrel'"), humility (Kay's insult "'will do me no harm'"; he has spoken similarly "'to braver and wiser men than I'"), and a degree of forgiveness (Kay simply cannot control his behavior, and so "'the dung heap will always smell . . . and the cad will always slander and vex others'"), depersonalizing this softest of insults (296) (4). More than that, rather than bolstering his reputation of prowess, as Odysseus or Beowulf do, Calogrenant relates his humiliating defeat with the knight of the fountain, earning dignity by confessing failure. Yvain's later response affirms the same knightly values (4). In essence, the self-effacing responses of both men in the instances of flyting in *Yvain* center around the Christian virtue of humility.

Doubling in the flyting type-scene, with two separate heroes and two separate responses, occurs also in *Sir Gawain and the Green Knight*, where two phases of flyting reflect disparate and, to some extent, competing literary and moral traditions rather than a single, shared code of conduct, as in *Yvain*. The flyting scene is a literary hybrid of epic and romance traditions. As in *Beowulf* and *Yvain*, the flyting scene occurs early in the poem, inaugurating the hero's adventure, but the poet varies the poetic formula of flyting so that it tests not a single knight but his entire kingdom. The opening setting of Arthur's Christmas feast in the poem, in which the flyting occurs, combines the life-threatening monster-in-the hall scenario, familiar from the OE *Beowulf*, with the surprise entry of a huge, green man in the dead of winter into a hall, and the festive, leisurely courtly setting familiar to the OF *Yvain*. So too, the challenger of the Green Knight is a hybrid—a blend of a Grendel-type monster and a late medieval aristocrat (see "Blason"). The challenger's dual nature extends into the contest he proposes: a Christmas "gomen" (l. 283, "game") involving a giant, deadly axe capable of beheading even a giant, combining the psychological challenge of chivalric romance and the physical threat of ancient epic. Unlike in *Beowulf*, where the noble challenger, Unferth, is not the monster, in *SGGK*, the two merge into one figure of the Green Knight (3), who insults not a single man (Arthur or Gawain) but the entire gathering, like Grendel, targeting an entire people (1), as seen in the insults: he enters uninvited; ignores the king, exclaiming "'Wher is . . ./The governour of this gyng?'" (ll. 224–5) and scanning for "Who walt ther most renoun" (l. 231); refuses Arthur's invitation to join them, using the informal "thou," as opposed to the formal "you," more appropriate to the king's status (e.g. l. 259ff.); and insults all the knights of the Round Table as "'berdles chylder'" (l. 280, "'beardless boys'") not worth a fight (2). Two men respond to the insults, contrasting epic and romance literary traditions. Like the epic hero, King Arthur rises in anger, seizing the giant axe, "And sturnely stures hit aboute, that stryke wyth hit thoght" (l. 331 "and forcefully brandishes it about, intent on striking with it"), evoking heroic epic where the leader, rather than a retainer, performs the main heroic deeds in service to an entire people. Gawain, on the other hand, models the response of the knightly hero in not getting angry, humbling himself ("'I am the wakkest, I wot, of wyt feeblest,'" 354, "'I am the weakest, I know, feeblest of sense'"), and dutifully taking up the challenge on behalf of another, his king, depersonalizing the insult. At the same time, like the epic hero, Gawain wields a giant weapon and beheads the giant, agreeing to undertake a life-or-death mission, in service to a male superior, in the winter, in search of the same monster who threatened the hall, much like Beowulf. Thus, flyting in *Sir Gawain* places old and new literary tradition side by side, not replacing one with the other but highlighting the virtue and dignity of each.

Further Reading

Carol J. Clover, "The Germanic Context of the Unferþ Episode," *Speculum* 55 (1980): 444–68.

Ward Parks, *Verbal Dueling in Heroic Narrative: The Homeric and Old English Traditions* (Princeton, NJ: Princeton University Press, 1990).

Hero on the Beach

Prevalent in Old English poetry and also surviving in other traditions, the type-scene consists of four basic constituents: 1) a hero on the beach 2) with his retainers 3) in the presence of a flashing light 4) as a journey is completed or begun. The time is generally dawn. While the elements of the hero on the beach with his men form constants of the scene, the source of the flashing light can vary between instances of the scene, from the bright, morning sun (i.e., in *Andreas*) to bright battle standards (i.e., in *Exodus*), to the gleam of bright helmets (i.e., in *Beowulf*). The scene typically prefaces a scene of carnage, and bodes the success not only of the imminent, or concluded, journey taken by the hero but also his triumph in the conflict to come. Instances of the scene also occur in the Old English poems of *Elene*, *Guthlac B*, and *Judith* as well as in the Middle English *Alliterative Morte Arthure*.

The simplest and clearest example of the type-scene occurs in the OE *Andreas* (ll. 235–47). In it, St. Andrew got up in the morning and went to the shore (*to saes faruðe*) (1) with his disciples. The Old English poet adds to his Latin source mention of the rising sun (*beacna beorhtost . . . heofoncandel blac*) and a journey about to be undertaken, providing the elements of the "flashing light" (3) and a journey (4) endemic to the type-scene in Old English poetic tradition. No sooner does St. Andrew complete the journey than carnage ensues.

An especially artful instance of the Hero on the Beach type-scene occurs in *Beowulf* (ll. 562–579a) as the hero concludes his account of his swimming contest with Breca, reporting how he ended up on the beach following his bout with sea-monsters, ready to make a feast of him "at a banquet" (*symble*) at the ocean bottom, until he attacked with his sword. Beowulf arrives back on the beach (1), and the dead sea-monsters, who lay on the sand, along the shore (*be yplafe*), provide the "retainers" (2) element, given their association with the feasting hall at the sea bottom. The morning sun, "God's bright beacon" (*Leoht eastan com*/*beorht beacen Godes*) provides the "flashing light" element" (3) that concludes the young men's journey (4) through the waves. The time is dawn. The poet's virtuosity expresses itself in the re-casting of the human retainer-allies of the hero as defeated sea-monster-foes, while retaining the triumphal tenor of the scene and setting the stage for Beowulf's imminent (and bloody) defeat over Grendel.

The scene features in the Middle English *Alliterative Morte Arthure* (c.1400) (ll. 3,724–31). Gawain has just completed a return journey to Britain (ll. 3,612–13) (4). He is on the beach (*appon þe sonde*) (1)(4), before a company of men (*þe lordes*)(2). The "flashing light" (3) element is provided twice by Gawain's flashing battle garment (*gytle wedys*; *bryghte wedys*). The scene of carnage announced by this scene soon follows in an especially bloody battle.

Further Reading

David K. Crowne, "The Hero on the Beach: An Example of Composition by Theme in Anglo-Saxon Poetry," *Neuphilologische Mitteilungen* 61 (1960): 362–72.

Alain Renoir, *A Key to Old Poems: The Oral-Formulaic Approach to the Interpretation of West Germanic Verse* (University Park: Pennsylvania State University Press, 1988), 96–102.

Inventio

The "discovery" of relic remains of a saint, precipitating the formalization of a saint's cult of hagiographic tradition. The scene proves the holiness of the reliquary remains through miraculous signs such as radiance or suspended forces of natural decay, singly or in combination. The *inventio* is generally followed by the *translatio*, or ritual transfer and enshrinement of reliquary remains, the moment at which the cult crystallizes for posterity. The discovery and translation of relics ritualistically implies a conscious and collective acknowledgement of the individual's sanctity. The type-scene belongs to a popular miracle story-type that emerges especially during periods of stress and uncertainty within monastic communities concerned for their future. Such stories address feelings of potential discontinuity and assert a community's legitimate past (through the presence of the saint), despite its precarious present. The type-scene consists of 1) the discovery of reliquary remains of a saint, (2) sometimes following a vision or miracles occurring around the gravesite of the body, which is 3) often either incorrupt and/or emitting a golden aura that elicits 4) a shared expression of wonder in the gathered community, who experience 5) a deepened faith in the holy person as an embodiment of the divine.

In the *Ecclesiastical History of the English People*, the Venerable Bede relates the *inventio* of the body of St. Cuthbert (1) eleven years after his death and burial at the Abbey at Lindisfarne. Cuthbert appeared lying in the sepulcher "whole and incorrupt as though still living" and "as if he were asleep rather than dead," with similarly undefiled garments, all of which were "not only spotless but wonderfully fresh and fair" (3), rendering the gathered monks "awestruck" (4). The monks then place the body of view for worshippers (5).

The thirteenth-century *Chronicle of Evesham Abbey*, located in the West Midlands, contains the *inventio* story of St. Credan (d. 780), Abbot of Evesham during the reign of King Offa, and St. Wigstan (Wystan; d.c. 840). The chronicler, Thomas of Marlborough, relates the post-Conquest investigation of the saint's cult, whose remains were subject to ordeals by fire in 1077 by the abbot Walter of Cerisy, "the first of the French-born" abbots, operating on the advice of Archbishop Lanfranc. Such "tests of authenticity" were imposed on some of the resident saints, who "were venerated among the English with high honor and reverence," a people who now "were vanquished and subjected to them." Thomas recounts the earlier inception of Credan's cult, when the abbot of Evesham, after a vision (2), decided to exhume Credan's remains. The abbot and those gathered discovered the saintly remains (1) "placed in the middle of two people as if amidst the purest gold" (*velut aurum purissimum*) (3), "resplendent before the eyes gathered there" (4). The chronicler contrasts this earlier translation of Credan's remains in a spirit of "the greatest devotion and reverence," with the later translation of Credan's remains performed by Abbot Walter in 1077, in the spirit of skepticism (5).

The fourteenth-century *St. Erkenwald* presents a variation of the *inventio* scene, which precipitates the entire poem. Set in the seventh century during Bishop Erkenwald's episcopacy at St. Paul's Cathedral in London, the poem opens with the discovery of an unmarked, early tomb within the foundations of a portion of the cathedral under renovation. No visions or miracles preface the discovery (2). Workers remove the lid and discover a body (1), perfectly preserved, wearing equally preserved garments hemmed "al with glisnande golde" (l. 78) and lying within a tomb "al with golde payntyde" (l. 75) (3). Though buried in consecrated space and exhibiting the posthumous signs of sanctity, the body, once miraculously revived, claims to be pre-Christian, nonetheless "'buriet in golde'" (l.248) in the manner of a saint, evoking an early cult. The discovery, rather than occurring among an established monastic community, occurs within a secular community of London citizens, who nonetheless experience sustained wonder throughout the poem (4). Rather than being followed by deepened faith, the discovery of the body is followed by skepticism (5) in the second half of the poem, thus shifting the inner orientation of the entire episode from emotion to reason, from heart to head. The citizens search, unsuccessfully, into city archives and living memory for evidence regarding the identity of the body. Questions about the body generate further questions about their own record-keeping, both oral (ll. 101–3) and written (ll. 103–4). Once the bishop revives the body, he cross-examines him on his life record and questions the body's miraculous markings by suspecting embalmment (l. 261) and doubting the state of his soul (l. 273). Unlike most scenes of *inventio*, divine intervention in the miraculously preserved body is not taken at face value but requires defense (l. 265–8). And, unlike the typical *inventio* scene, this one concludes not with the translation of reliquary remains and the formalization of a cult but with the spontaneous disintegration of the body following its inadvertent baptism by the bishop, suggesting the disappearance of such a cult. The reversal from deepened faith to doubt in this *inventio* scene, in keeping with the poem's early English setting, evokes the historic investigations into early English saints' cults in the years following the Conquest under new ecclesiastic standards that demoted some established cults.

Further Reading

Dominique Battles, "Investigating English Sanctity in the Middle English *St. Erkenwald*," *Studies in Philology* 120 (2023): 603–57.

Paul Antony Hayward, "Translation-Narratives in Post-Conquest Hagiography and English Resistance to the Norman Conquest," *Anglo-Norman Studies* 21 (1999): 67–93.

Samantha Kahn Herrick, "Introduction," in Samantha Kahn Herrick, ed., *Hagiography and the History of Latin Christendom, 500–1500* (Leiden: Brill, 2020), 1–10.

Monika Otter, "'New Werke': *St. Erkenwald*, St. Albans, and the Medieval Sense of the Past," *Journal of Medieval and Renaissance Studies* 24 (1994): 387–414.

Joy in the Hall

A scenic ornament that conjures a type-scene featuring an Old English *scop* (oral poet) entertaining his audience but occurring only in *Beowulf*. (See also "*Scop*'s Repertoire.") The scene's elements are 1) joy (*gomen*); 2) song (*sang*); 3) a harp (*gomenwudu*); and 4) a poet (*scop*). Joy in the Hall denotes the celebration of social unity or its absence and/or its endangerment. It occurs first in *Beowulf* (ll. 86–90a) when Grendel feels provoked by the joyful feasting in Heorot, from which he is excluded. Here, joy precedes the misery of his attack. The poet uses it again when Beowulf arrives in Heorot (ll.496b-98) to combat Grendel, shifting misery to hope. The poet employs it again after Beowulf defeats Grendel (ll. 1063–68), where happy relief enjoys a brief reign until the attack of Grendel's mother. Joy in the Hall does *not* occur after the hero's defeat of Grendel's mother, however, signaling the downward shift in Beowulf's fortunes from hereon. Later, the Last Survivor characterizes the loss of community using Joy in the Hall, as now "*Naes hearpan wyn,/gomen gleobeames*" (ll. 2262–3). The absence of joyful harping in the hall also marks Beowulf's reflections prior to engaging the dragon (ll. 2457–9) and the grim prospect of the Geats after his death (ll. 3018–25). Akin to the concept of Pathetic Fallacy, the Joy in the Hall scenic ornament records the interior "weather patterns" of the story.

Further Reading

John Miles Foley, "Literary Art and Oral Tradition in Old English and Serbian Poetry," *Anglo-Saxon England* 12 (1983): 183–214.

Jeff Opland, "*Beowulf* on the Poet," *Mediaeval Studies* 38 (1976): 442–67.

Lady with the Mead Cup

A type-scene depicting an ancient Germanic, domestic, and diplomatic ritual conducted by a high-ranking woman bearing a ceremonial cup, appearing in Anglo-Saxon literature and echoed in post-Conquest literary depictions of the early English past. The scene participates in the feasting culture of the ancient mead-hall and involves 1) the lord's wife entering the mead-hall with a 2) splendid cup and 3) greeting the warriors, 4) solidifying the mutual loyalty of all present. Using the cup, she serves drink first to her husband, the lord, and then each of the other warriors in descending rank. In doing so, she affirms the hierarchical structure and bond of the *comitatus* (the retainer band) under the lordship of her husband.

The scene occurs in *Beowulf* shortly after Beowulf's arrival at Heorot with the intent of offering aid against the monster Grendel, as a preface to the hero's formal boast (promise) to kill the giant (ll. 612b-624). Hrothgar's queen, Wealhtheow (1), presides. The poet identifies Wealhtheow as the most important woman in the room (*cwen, freolic wif*; "queen," "noble lady"), "mindful of etiquette" (*cynna gemyndig*) and "wise in judgement" (*mode geþungen*). Bearing a cup (*ful*) (2), she first serves the most important man in the room, her husband, identified here as "Lord of the East-Danes" (*East-Dena eþelwearde*), before serving all of the other men gathered, the greater and the lesser (3). The poet mentions the cup(s) three times (*ful*, "cup"; *sincfato*, "precious cups"; *medoful*, "mead-cup"), emphasizing the symbolic function of the cup(s) in this formal ritual of social unity conducted by this prominent woman (4). In offering the cup, finally, to Beowulf, the queen prompts him to state his mission, as he holds the ornamented cup while boasting to either work a great deed (by killing Grendel) or die, a promise that pleases Wealhtheow. The OE *Maxims I* (ll. 84–92) also references the Lady with the Mead Cup type-scene in abbreviated form, as the lady offers the mead-cup to the lord while also offering him council (*raed*), emphasizing her diplomatic role still further. While the practice of this ritual was already dying out by the time *Beowulf* was composed, the Anglo-Saxon aristocracy continued to recognize the custom and its societal value.

A variation of the Lady with the Mead Cup scene occurs in the earliest extant Middle English romance, *King Horn* (c. 1225), where it takes on a covert quality. The hero, Horn, while living in exile in Ireland under the false name Cutberd (cf. St. Cuthbert), hears word of his beloved Rymenhild's forced marriage to King Mody of Reynes, and soon, receives a message from her, pleading for rescue. Horn disguises himself as a pilgrim, dirties his face and neck, and enters Mody's castle just in time for the wedding feast. In this regard, the Lady with the Mead Cup type-scene of pre-Conquest tradition dovetails with the Disguise and Infiltration* scene prevalent in post-Conquest English literature. Just like queen Wealhtheow, Rymenhild (1), soon-to-be queen, begins circulating the room, alone, serving wine and ale to the guests (3). The poet underscores the gesture as a historical and cultural authenticating device by adding "On horn he bar anhonde,/So laȝe was in londe" (ll. 1,109–1,110, "A horn she carried in her hand, as was the custom of the land") (2), specifying the drinking horns emblematic of Anglo-Saxon society. Reaching Horn, she first mistakes him for a beggar and offers him a bowl to drink from (3), but he insists on drinking from the "'cuppe white'" (l. 1132), to drink to Horn from the horn, as he himself is Horn (ll. 1145–1146), thus disclosing his identity to her and mobilizing her rescue (4). Here, the hero's name evokes the iconic cup of the ritualistic scene. Rymenhild's call for assistance ushers in Horn's comeback as a leader of his people, fulfilling the diplomatic portrait of the Lady in this type-scene. This unusual blend of two type-scenes, the Lady with the Mead Cup, enacting social unification and harmony, and Disguise and Infiltration, rooted in social division and danger, derives from a similar scene from the thirteenth-century *Gesta Herewardi*, where Hereward "the Wake," who organized the most substantial resistance campaign against the Norman invaders in the late 1060's and early 1070's, comes out of exile in Ireland and disguises himself as a lowly minstrel to rescue to a Cornish princess from forced marriage on the eve of the wedding (see "Disguise and Infiltration"). In both these post-Conquest narratives, the Lady with the Mead Cup scene proclaims a cultural identity under assault.

Further Reading

Dominique Battles, *Cultural Difference and Material Culture in Middle English Romance: Normans and Saxons* (New York: Routledge, 2013).

Michael J. Enright, *Lady with a Mead Cup: Ritual, Prophecy and Lordship in the European Warband from La Tène to the Viking Age* (Dublin: Four Courts Press, 1996), 2–11 and 189–95.

Helen Conrad O'Briain, "Listen to the Woman: Reading Wealhtheow as Stateswoman," in Helene Scheck and Christine E. Kozikowski, eds., *New Readings on Women and Early Medieval Literature and Culture: Cross-Disciplinary Studies in Honour of Helen Damico* (Amsterdam: Arc Amsterdam University Press, 2019), 191–208.

Loathly Lady Encounter

A beautiful, young woman, enchanted to appear as a hag, saves a stranded hero by exchanging her vital wisdom for his love. Of Celtic origin in the West, traced to the Irish tradition of the sovereignty goddess, giving rise to a tale-type termed the "Loathly Lady tales." In Irish tradition, the hag appears early in the tale, sometimes to several men vying for power, and, to the one brave enough to accept her sexual advances, transforms into a beautiful young woman, offering counsel and prophecy to the rightful, would-be king. These tales form advice literature, in some cases, disguising political propaganda. English adaptations of the Loathly Lady motif usually feature a hero struggling to fulfill the chivalric ideal regarding women, and the Loathly Lady becomes an unconventional guide in his maturation. These tales are structured around two intimate type-scenes that work in tandem to catalyze and finalize the education of the hero: 1) the hero's initial meeting with the hag and 2) their wedding night. Whereas the Irish Loathly Lady tales concern the hero's political fortunes, the English tales address the hero's inner imbalance, extending the scope of the hag's influence into private affairs. Whereas the conventional romance hero's service toward women advances his knightly career, in the Loathly Lady tales, the hero's transgression involving women compromises his career, placing him on trial, under penalty of death, in a "courtroom" of powerful women. In English literary tradition, the "meeting" scene is initiated by the hag and involves 1) a recalcitrant hero trying to escape a death sentence by solving 2) a riddle or open-ended question concerning female preference, resulting in 3) a failed search, which attracts the intervention of 4) a hag who appears to him 5) in or near the forest, and who 6) bargains to exchange the answer he seeks for love/marriage. The "wedding night" scene, painful and therefore longer than in a chivalric romance, consists of a) the reluctant hero b) and his loathly bride, c) in a bedchamber, d) who offers him a conditional choice between her beauty or monstrosity and e) his relinquishment of choice to her, resulting in f) her transformation from loathly to lovely.

The Loathly Lady story-type varies the knightly quest narrative in presenting a guilty hero, who ventures alone not through a forest but among a populace for answers, who fails in his quest, and who is rescued by a woman, rather than vice versa. Rather than being a revered female protagonist, the Loathly Lady appears as a reviled secondary character—a mere aide in the hero's pursuit of a separate goal—who nevertheless assumes the prized position of the heroine by tale's end. Appropriately, she often receives a blason typically used to mark the hero's *telos*, though initially, he overlooks her significance. Such a blason, intended to describe either a beautiful woman or a monster, in fact, describes both in the Loathly Lady, who encapsulates female beauty within an exterior of physical monstrosity. Examples of the English type-scene occur in John Gower's "Tale of Florent," Chaucer's *Wife of Bath's Tale*, the ME *Thomas of Erceldoune*, and the ME *The Wedding of Sir Gawain and Dame Ragnelle* (c. 1450).

The first extended Loathly Lady tale in English is John Gower's "Tale of Florent," contained in Book One of his *Confessio Amantis* (ll. 1407–1875) and features a young knight, and nephew to the emperor, who ventures into Wales, where he unintentionally slays the son of a Welsh lord, drawing him into vengeance-driven Welsh jurisprudence at the hands of the young victim's grandmother. She disguises a death-trap as a simple test for him "on love" (l. 1479) to determine what all women most desire, a riddle (2) he takes home to his uncle's court. The emperor's wisest men fail to solve the riddle (3), and the guilty hero returns to Wales and to his death, where the "meeting" scene occurs. As he rides toward the castle, the Loathly Lady (4), cognizant of his predicament, calls to him from under a tree in the forest (l. 1528) (5), offering a bargain (6): her life-saving advice in exchange for marriage, framed as a Rash Promise* where he first blindly agrees to anything she asks (l. 1555) to save his life. He mentally plots undignified evasions—bribery, escape, abandoning her on an island—before accepting her terms, revealing his knightly deficiencies. The hero now escapes physical death only to enter a living death of marriage to the hag, embracing the chivalric tenet of honoring womanhood, despite his shame and disgust, thereby initiating his education.

The "wedding night" scene finalizes the hero's education by worsening his experience. They return to his home, and among a few loyal witnesses, the reluctant hero (a) marries his loathly bride (b) in a private chamber (c), her toiletry making a spectacle of her ugliness. Their lovemaking breaks the curse upon her, transforming her into a beautiful, young, Sicilian woman (f) who offers him a choice (d) to have her beautiful either by night or day, but not both, a decision he relinquishes to her (e), thereby gaining both. Gower's tale stress-tests the chivalric code in that Florent is challenged to apply the knightly code among people who live by a different code: Welsh native law and Sicilian custom. Both societies feature loathly women, the Welsh grandmother, "the slyheste/Of alle that men knewe" (ll. 1442–3), and the Sicilian stepmother, who enchanted her beautiful stepdaughter into a Moorish-looking hag (l. 1686), making all the women of the tale "loathly" in some way. Moreover, these women undermine one another (the hag outwits the Welsh crone (ll. 1659–62), and the stepmother curses her stepdaughter). Florent, himself a cultural outsider to the English readers, navigates these dangerous waters and abides by the chivalric code only under pain of death, internalizing the ideal of selfless service to all women by seeing the value of real women of any form. Thus, the Loathly Lady becomes the guide, savior, and reward for the knight's maturation, affirming the integrity of the chivalric code, even among cultural outsiders.

Chaucer presents a similar Loathly Lady in the tale told by the Wife of Bath, whose checkered history, strong personality, and age make her a Loathly Lady, herself, by medieval standards. Chaucer narrows the geographic range found in Gower to Arthur's Britain and directs the theoretical question of the tale to aristocratic claims on personal "gentilesse." Queen Guinevere, unlike the Welsh crone, is an icon of the chivalric ideal, an ultimate insider who justifiably imposes the penalty of the riddle-quest (2) on the knight-rapist to discern what women most desire. However, an outsider, the poor Loathly Lady, educates the hero, in the process expanding social inclusivity. Unlike in "Florent," where the knight seeks answers among aristocratic male authorities of the emperor's palace removed from ordinary female experience, in Chaucer, he goes among experiential sources—real women of diverse ranks throughout many villages and towns. Like Florent, the hero fails to solve the riddle (3) amidst competing opinions, setting the stage for the "meeting" scene with the Loathly Lady (4) "under a forest syde" (l. 990) (5). True to the scene, she apprehends him and bargains an exchange (6) via a Rash Promise*, all of it secret to the reader; she whispers the answer to him, and he blindly promises anything for his life. Both the hero and the Loathly Lady possess greater free will than in Gower, though disparately. Unlike Florent, a victim of primitive justice for an act of self-defense, the bachelor knight (1) in the WOB's tale is a guilty rapist deserving punishment. Unlike the powerless girl/hag trapped by a dark enchantment in Gower, Chaucer's Loathly Lady is a fairy with autonomous control over her form, given the early references to fairy folk of old (l. 860–1) and the concurrent vision of a fairy dance (ll. 990–6). Unlike in Gower, where the Loathly Lady and Welsh crone work to cross purposes, in Chaucer, the queen and the hag become strangely allied in reforming the knight. If the queen emphasizes external compliance to the code, the hag affects inner transformation, the women's relative official and unofficial status determining their tactics. The shared interests of both women coalesce as the hag uses the public setting of the queen's court to enforce her end of the bargain (that he marry and love her) and, unlike in Gower, his shame becomes public.

The "wedding night" scene blends the personal and political, and the bedchamber becomes a lecture hall with a third-estate lecturer: in bed, the loathly bride (b) reprimands the reluctant hero (a) for shirking his knightly duty, and his disgust at his ugly bride "'of so lough a kynde'" (l. 1101) prompts the hag's sermon on "gentilesse" (ll. 1109–1218), universalizing nobility through ideals of inner humanity in Christ, extending it beyond aristocratic bloodlines. Unlike in Gower, the hero's choice (d) of her youth or old age comes before her transformation (f) and is tied to moral issues of sexual precarity (youth) or marital fidelity (age). In deferring the choice to her (e) and reaping the reward of both, the knight simultaneously defers to a member of the third estate, who grasps the nature of inner nobility better than he does.

The fourteenth-century Middle English border narrative *Thomas of Erceldoune* draws primarily from Irish tradition in casting the Loathly Lady. The hero is neither guilty nor seeking anything, so there is no riddle for him to solve. As in the Irish tradition, the Lady appears early in the narrative as a guide to a would-be leader, Thomas the Rhymer, and prophecy is central, given his fame for his political prophecies. As she is already married, the couple never marries, and there is no "wedding night" scene. The English poet varies their initial "meeting" scene by reversing the choreography of gender, placing the hero (1), not the lady, under the tree (5) and having her ride by on a horse. Rather than apprehending him, the hero calls out to her, and she dismounts. The poet also reverses her form: the Fairy Queen first appears to him as a richly dressed woman of otherworldly beauty who incites his lust and transforms (f) into a hag (4) after sexual intercourse, having warned him of this consequence in advance, thus combining elements of the "meeting" scene and the "wedding night" scene. The hero's flawed perception (he first mistakes her for the Virgin Mary) and sexual impulsivity reveal his need for her guidance, and from this point, he becomes her captive pupil, entering the fairy Otherworld where his strict obedience to her brings wisdom. Throughout, the poem blends elements of the Loathly Lady tale and the Dream Vision, underscoring the theme of revelation. She eventually accompanies him back to the Eildon Hill, where he started, ending the relationship, highlighting the lady's primarily political function.

The web of powerful women dominating the earlier Loathly Lady tales is replaced by a network of powerful men in *The Wedding of Sir Gawain and Dame Ragnelle*, where the plot serves the bonds among men, rather than the chivalric ideal of male-female bonds, in a regional landscape of rival lords. The hero is a king (Arthur) (1), not a budding knight, and his infraction is not a transgression against a woman but a territorial trespass deep into another man's land. Sir Gromer, the landowner, takes the place of the powerful, juridical woman issuing the riddle-quest on female desire (2) on pain of death. Rather than searching alone, Arthur has a companion in his quest, Sir Gawain, a fellow man, and rather than soliciting women only, they question "every man and woman" (l. 188) for what women most desire. This male pairing persists through the two type-scenes, as Arthur participates in the "meeting" scene with the hag, while Gawain takes the "wedding night" scene. Moreover, the two scenes that, in earlier tales, catalyze and finalize the hero's education in chivalric service to women, do not, in this case, subdue the hero to the Loathly Lady, but rather, reinscribe mutual loyalties among the men. In the "meeting" scene with the hag, Arthur remains focused on his obligations to Sir Gromer and Gawain, while Gawain enters into the "wedding night" scene solely in service to Arthur, not the hag. The "meeting" scene (ll. 225–323) occurs as Arthur is concluding the riddle quest as imposed by Sir Gromer. Throughout, the poet diminishes the female preeminence characteristic of the scene by pairing it with masculine influence while still adhering to the formula of the scene. Riding through a forest (5), the Loathly Lady (4) appears unexpectedly, mounted on a fine palfrey, and is described with a blason* of ugliness, as in earlier tales. She apprehends him first, expressing awareness of his plight. From here, the internal dynamic of the scene shifts. Arthur enters the scene confident, not desperate, concerning the riddle quest, and she presents a bargain (6) that further joins Arthur to Gawain not to her: the answer to the riddle in exchange not for *his* love but for his assistance in her gaining Gawain's hand in marriage, arousing Arthur's concern for Gawain. Her request also shows her weakness as, unlike earlier Loathly Ladies, she must leverage masculine authority to obtain her goal, Gawain. Protecting Gawain's interests, Arthur delays, and her deadline now parallels Sir Gromer's deadline for the riddle quest, pairing male with female control over the hero. We later learn that Ragnelle and Sir Gromer are siblings, confirming the pattern, which also aligns her with the enemy, unlike in earlier tales. Similarly, Arthur voices his desperation (on Gawain's behalf) first to the hag (ll. 303–8) and, soon afterwards, to Sir Gawain (ll. 331–2), and both the hag and Sir Gawain promise him salvation, pairing masculine with feminine aid. Unlike in earlier Loathly Lady tales, Sir Gawain does *not* hesitate to marry the hag, but he does so only for Arthur's sake, citing Arthur's similar sacrifices for him, while speaking this promise to Arthur rather than to the hag, thus redirecting this stock promise to serve masculine over feminine interests. The pairing continues in the resolution to the riddle-quest, as Arthur offers the hag's answer to Sir Gromer only after unsuccessfully offering the answers that he and Gawain compiled earlier.

The "wedding night" scene (ll. 629–721) in *The Wedding of Sir Gawain and Dame Ragnelle* maximizes the men's support network regarding the Loathly Lady by prefacing it with an extended (and humorous) public spectacle of her hideousness, where the entire court (men and women) express the grief and disgust normally endured alone by the hero. Gawain remains unflappable. In the bedchamber (c), Gawain (a) expresses neither fear nor disgust, readily offering sexual relations with her (b) "'for

Arthours sake'" (l. 635). Like earlier knights, Gawain defers the choice of her physical form to her (e), resulting in her permanent transformation from loathly to lovely (f). However, as in "Florent," her shift discloses her victimization by another woman, her stepmother, complexifying simple chivalric notions of unqualified feminine virtue. Thus, Gawain saves both Arthur and Ragnelle, while requiring no saving himself, and gets the girl as a reward. Above all, neither Arthur nor Gawain evolve as characters under the hag's influence, and Gawain especially is never conflicted. The incident of the hag proves just another step in feudal obligations to the lord. As a kinswoman of the opposing side (Gromer), who nonetheless aids the English king, allying with him through marriage and eventually reconciling both sides, Ragnelle forges wider bonds among men. Her transformation from loathly to lovely tracks her shifting allegiance. In this way, Ragnelle's story dovetails with that of the Wise Woman* and her daughter in *Sir Degrevant*, similarly concerned with a border dispute. *Ragnelle* models the enduring value and versatility of male bonds in an unpredictable world.

Further reading

W.P. Albrecht, *The Loathly Lady in "Thomas of Erceldoune"* (Albuquerque: University of New Mexico Press, 1954).

Ananda K. Coomaraswamy, "On the Loathly Bride," *Speculum* 20 (1945): 391–404.

S. Elizabeth Passmore, "Through the Counsel of a Lady: The Irish and English Loathly Lady Tales and the 'Mirror for Princes' Genre," in S. Elizabeth Passmore and Susan Carter, eds., *The English 'Loathly Lady' Tales: Boundaries, Traditions, and Motifs* (Kalamazoo, Michigan: Medieval Institute Publications, 2007), 3–41.

Russel A. Peck, "Folklore and Powerful Women in Gower's 'Tale of Florent,'" in S. Elizabeth Passmore and Susan Carter, eds., *The English 'Loathly Lady' Tales: Boundaries, Traditions, and Motifs* (Kalamazoo, Michigan: Medieval Institute Publications, 2007), 100–45.

Glenn A. Steinberg, "Is Ugliness Only Skin Deep?: Middle English Gawain Romances and the 'Wife of Bath's Tale'," *Arthuriana* 31 (2021): 3–28.

Locus Amoenus

The "pleasant place," an earthly, garden paradise forming the central landscape setting of scenes of personal transformation through love and/or revelation. Derived from both biblical tradition (the gardens of Eden and the Song of Songs) and classical, pastoral poetry. From the late twelfth century through the thirteenth century, the *locus amoenus* features in Latin poetry, becoming formalized through the *Artes Poeticae*, or manuals for poetic composition that provided prescriptions for describing things, including idealized landscapes. The late twelfth-century *Ars Versificatoria* (I:109–111) of Matthew of Vendôme models such descriptions and advocates including them only "when we wish to convey something to the listener," making them formative rather than ornamental. The *locus amoenus* migrated into vernacular poetry, occurring intermittently in medieval romance and becoming especially prominent and allegorically encoded in the visionary landscape of the Dream Vision, the opening sequence of which forms a type-scene all its own.

Separate from the public world, the *locus amoenus* forms a safe, intimate, nurturing landscape in fostering personal love. In medieval romance, the *locus amoenus* often takes the form of a Garden of Love—a temporary, private setting where the romantic couple declares and shares their love, often sparking or solidifying mutual commitment from that point on. In the Dream Vision, the *locus amoenus*, once reached, forms the permanent setting of the lone Dreamer's education and revelation, told from a first-person perspective, facilitated by a Guide, in larger spiritual truths that bring consolation and redress of a personal impasse. The scene of the *locus amoenus* reaches its fullest expression in the Dream Vision and consists of 1) a protagonist open to, or in need of, new direction who 2) wakes and 3) wanders outside into a forest full of 4) bird song in 5) springtime; he reaches a 6) garden (sometimes walled) (the *locus amoenus*) of trees, flowers, and a spring, where he encounters a 7) Guide who provides 8) a Tour through the garden, interpreting its allegorical delights. By the end, the protagonist reaches 9) an insight that redirects his path in life. The *locus amoenus* and its imagery of earthly abundance and generativity becomes a mechanism for inner transformation, while its exclusive and pristine ideals enable a critique of the worldly status quo.

Chrétien de Troyes establishes and questions the courtly values that come to be associated with the *locus amoenus* in chivalric romance. A brief scene in *Yvain* highlights the "skill set" entailed for the romance hero. Yvain's cousin, Calogrenant, journeys, in Spring, to the castle of a vavasour, whose daughter leads him into a beautiful, enclosed meadow, where he notes her refinements of speech, manners, and demeanor, revealing those same qualities in himself—essential skills of the romance hero that Yvain will strive to master. An alternate and memorable scene of a *locus amoenus* occurs in the "Joy of the Court" episode in *Erec and Enide*, where Chrétien uses elements from the Otherworld entrapment scenes of Celtic tradition to question the courtly ideals implied by the *locus amoenus*. Toward the end of narrative, where the hero and heroine mutually negotiate an expanded, if delicate, balance of gendered agency, the couple enters a town whose central feature is a magical garden in full bloom year-round and enclosed by an invisible, dark enchantment that locks its beauties of birdsong, fruits, and herbs within. This dubious *locus amoenus* harbors an elegant couple trapped in the conventional, female-determined romance-model, exposing the potential limits of the courtly ideal, whose casualties appear vividly in the garden in the helmeted skulls on stakes, the victims of Maboagrain, the knight within. Maboagrain himself was trapped by a Rash Promise* he made to his lady, redolent of fairy-human encounters, to stay in the garden until another knight defeated him. Masculine combat between Maboagrain and Erec, within the garden, breaks the feminine spell, releasing the joy normally promised by the *locus amoenus*.

Gottfried von Strassburg's *Tristan* (c. 1210) innovates with the *locus amoenus* type-scene early in the poem upon introducing the love affair between Rivalin and Blancheflour, Tristan's parents, nesting the idyllic setting within a larger, war-torn, epic landscape. Within the scene itself, Gottfried follows the love-inspiring formula. The *locus amoenus* occurs during the spring festival at Mark's court, drawing Rivalin to Cornwall, where "charming, gentle spring had busied himself . . . with sweet assiduousness," calling forth "little wood-birds, . . . flowers, grasses, leaves, and blossoms and all that soothes the eye and gladdens noble hearts" (49), one of five such landscapes in the *Tristan*. Rivalin and Blancheflour meet and fall in love here, reflecting the core subject of romance: love. However, Gottfried juxtaposes the ideal natural setting of the May festival, and its amorous concerns, with the epic landscape of war and political conquest appearing before and after the May festival: scenes in Brittany, ravaged and pillaged by the attacks between Rivalin and Duke Morgan, preface the festival, which itself ends abruptly when Cornwall faces invasion, calling Rivalin back to the battlefield. Rivalin traverses both terrains, fighting and subduing enemies on the battle plain, and jousting recreationally at the festival, presaging the hybrid lover-warrior heroic model that culminates in Tristan. Moreover, Gottfried inserts instances of courtly jousting into the scenes of war, and conversely, interjects combative tones redolent of epic Flyting* into the first verbal exchange between Rivalin and Blancheflour, weaving the older and newer genres together. By bookending the scene of the *locus amoenus* with the harsh, life-threatening, warn-torn landscapes of Cornwall and Brittany, Gottfried elevates the subject of love with the scenic infrastructure of the older, more weighty tradition of heroic epic.

The *locus amoenus* reaches a literary zenith in the thirteenth-century *Romance of the Rose* by Guilluame de Lorris and Jean de Meun, where it opens a secular—and earthly—path to spiritual transcendence, establishing the major scenic and rhetorical standards of the Dream Vision genre. From the outset, the poem validates subjective, private authority in spiritual insight, beginning with the value of personal dreams. The protagonist (the Dreamer), a young man of twenty open to love experience (1), falls asleep and enters a dream state, in which he wakes (2) on a May morning (5) and wanders outside into a forest (3) full of birdsong (4). Spontaneous, expansive joy ("joy," "rejoicing," "enjoy(ment),") animates the journey, and he arrives unexpectedly at a garden (6), whose surrounding wall announces, pictorially, all the qualities antithetical to love, and therefore, not permitted into its pristine interior, including Hatred, Felony, Villainy, and Covetousness. Among these human sins is Pope Holiness, a symbol of religious hypocrisy depicted as a sad nun "who seems a saintly creature" in public, yet "is not afraid to commit any evil" in private, for which "the door to Paradise was forbidden" (36). The poet's critique of institutionalized piety, citing Matthew 6:16, justifies the alternate space of revelation of the *locus amoenus* beyond the wall, which embraces, rather than condemns, earthly pleasure and is unsullied by utility ("no shepherd had ever entered," 37). Inside, the garden "seemed to belong to the world of spirit" (39), and the birds (4) sang "a lovely service, [like] heavenly angels" (39), while his Guide/gatekeeper (7), Idleness, leads him (8) to a group of people who "seemed winged angels" (40), allegorical representations of Joy, Courtesy, and Diversion. The fountain of Narcissus at the center of the garden expands rather than restricts his perception, affording him a view of the entire garden, and his future love-object, rather than simply his own visage, modifying standard injunctions against introspection as an avenue of wisdom. From here, the Dreamer begins his education, by no means easy, on the nature of Love. Given the transcendent beauty of the *locus amoenus*, where the protagonist feels "I began to go out of my mind," the way for revelation opens to a private individual, in ordinary time, here on earth (9).

The late fourteenth-century Middle English *Pearl* reconfigures the visionary landscape of the *locus amoenus* to question the whole idea an earthly paradise, turning the Dream Vision landscape of joy into one of sorrow and locating the source of revelation not in this life but in the Christian concept of the afterlife. The poet accomplishes this through a series of reversals, starting with the three-part setting of house-forest-garden found in the *Romance of the Rose*, and instead, taking the dreamer from garden to forest to the heavenly city of Jerusalem, the new home of Pearl. Other reversals occur in each space. Rather than opening in the spring, the poem opens in late summer (l. 39) (5), past the season of growth. Rather than filled with exotic flowers, the garden contains common, native plants of gillyflower, wild ginger, and gromwell (l. 43), while references to season are grounded in seasonal tasks and tools (l. 39–40), rather than leisure. Rather than a young, amorous protagonist, we have a father of a young child. Rather than forming the site of joy and new love, the garden becomes the site of the loss of an existing love—of a child, whose grave forms the centerpiece of the garden (ll. 46–8) and the sole source of its beauty. Her imagery as a pearl replaces the love object imagery of the ephemeral rose of the French Dream Vision. Unlike the *Romance of the Rose*, where the protagonist awakens in a dream state and ventures through a forest and into the paradisal garden, where he encounters a Guide, in *Pearl*, the grieving protagonist (1) faints (2) while in the garden (6), and his soul soars out into a forest (3), which assumes the exoticism and emotional expansiveness normally associated with the garden in its birdsong (l. 89) (4), gemmed terrain and stream (none of it man-made) (l. 71), and its offering of a Guide (7), the image of his lost daughter, Pearl. Her wisdom concerns processing old grief rather than inviting new experience, and her lessons (8) culminate in a vision of the Heavenly City of Jerusalem, with Christ enthroned among his brides, including Pearl herself. Final insight gets minimized, with the protagonist awakening on the garden-grave somewhat consoled (9) but still grieving, underscoring the emotional realism suffusing the entire poem and denying the escapism suggested in the French Dream Vision.

Chaucer domesticates the *locus amoenus* in his Dream Visions through both setting and action. The *Book of the Duchess* modifies the setting triad of Dreamer's house-forest-garden (*locus amoenus*) by eliminating the garden altogether and relocating its elements, including birdsong, colors, and extraordinary vision, to the two other spheres. The interior of the Dreamer's house, merely implied in earlier Dream Visions, forms an important sensory space of the poem, where the Dreamer (1) wakes (2), in May (5), to birdsong heard outside his window (ll. 294–320) (4). Sun shines through the stained glass, projecting colors into the room, including images of manuscript pages on two walls, one with the story of Troy, the master narrative of ancient epic, and the other with the *Romance of the Rose*, the medieval "best-selling" romance that he imitates, capturing two sources of revelation for him as an artist (9), all of which fills him with joy (l. 325). Experientially, his room becomes the *locus amoenus*. Rather than being summoned into it, he is called out of it by a hunting horn, and rather than leaving on foot, he mounts a horse to follow a hunt, while the forest (3) he enters serves the utilitarian function as an aristocratic hunting park. The figure who should be his Guide (7) solicits guidance from the Dreamer, reversing these roles, and the inner journey of the poem concerns the lost love of the Knight, not the Dreamer, who remains fixed under a single tree of the forest, eliminating the standard Tour (8) of the landscape.

Chaucer similarly domesticates the *locus amoenus* in the *Parliament of Fowls* and the Prologue to the *Legend of Good Women*, where public and worldly concerns displace the private revelation associated with this space in the *Romance of the Rose*. In the *Parliament of Fowls*, the Dreamer (1) wakes in a dream (2) and enters a forested park (3), a functional landscape stocked with native and imported deer (l. 195) and trees identified by their practical use (ll. 176–82). Within this park lies a garden (the *locus amoenus*), itself a public domain. Chaucer greatly amplifies the element of birdsong (4) typical of the garden; however, the birds behave not like a heavenly choir but like a parliamentary session, each breed of fowl representing a social class. They debate not the nature of love but the question of who gets to talk about love in the first place, and how. Nature herself is the Guide (7) overseeing the naturalistic scene, and humorous disorder obviates any tidy revelation (9). Thus, the Dreamer's private experience in the garden concerns the public good. In the Prologue to the *LOGW*, Chaucer offers two models of the *locus amoenus*: first, we have the ordinary meadow in May fostering spontaneous joy with birdsong, sunshine, and ordinary daisies (the wild English counterpart to the French rose), which the Dreamer (1) experiences while still awake. Second, there is the garden he enters in sleep (2) that resembles a courtroom (3), where the God of Love (a Guide of sorts (7)) misinterprets and criticizes Chaucer's past writings on love. The Dreamer encounters the public eye in this otherwise private space, and while Love publicizes Chaucer's *oeuvres* by listing them, he imposes an onerous commission, the tales of the *LOGW*, turning his mood from expansiveness to defensiveness, and the landscape of understanding and leisure into one of misunderstanding and more work. Similarly crowded and/or troubled gardens appear in the *Knight's Tale* (where the garden adjoins a prison), the *Franklin's Tale*, the *Merchant's Tale*, and Book II of *Troilus and Criseyde*.

Further Reading

Rod Barnett, "Serpent of Pleasure: Emergence and Difference in the Medieval Garden of Love," *Landscape Journal* 28 (2009): 137–50.

Dominique Battles, "The Heroic Voice in Gottfried von Strassburg's *Tristan*," *Tristania* 25 (2009): 1–24.

Ernst Robert Curtius, *European Literature and the Latin Middle Ages*, trans. Willard R. Trask (Princeton, NJ: Princeton University Press, 1953), 195–200.

Laura Howes, *Chaucer's Gardens and the Language of Convention* (Gainesville: University Press of Florida, 1997).
William Sayers, "*La Joie de la Cort* (*Érec et Énide*), Mabon, and Early Irish *síd* [peace; Otherworld]," *Arthuriana* 17 (2007): 10–17.
A.C. Spearing, *Medieval Dream Poetry* (Cambridge: Cambridge University Press, 1976).
Frederic C. Tubach, "The *Locus Amoenus* in the *Tristan* of Gottfried von Straszburg," *Neophilologus* 43 (1959): 37–42.

Magic Ring

A private exchange of a magical, protective ring gifted by a woman to the hero as an amulet against future physical harm. Prevalent in medieval romance. This brief scene involves 1) the hero; 2) a prominent woman, usually the love interest or a woman connected with her; 3) an intimate setting; 4) a magic ring; 5) her verbal explanation of the ring's magical powers; 6) the hero's acceptance of the ring. Later scenes invariably follow that prove the ring's efficacy in either combat or similar life-or-death scenarios. The scene generally occurs early in the narrative as the hero first pledges his love for the heroine and launches himself into challenges that will prove him worthy of her love. The Magic Ring scene makes the woman a primary agent in the hero's success, "arming" him for future martial confrontation, often on her behalf, and illustrates a core feature of the genre of romance in tying combat to love, with the woman as the prize. The ring doubles as a love token as well as a protective amulet.

Chrétien de Troyes' *Yvain* contains two scenes where the hero is gifted a protective ring by a woman, both of them marking the hero's transition from the familiar mission of defeating Esclados the Red (to avenge Calogrenant's earlier humiliating defeat) into the unfamiliar world of Laudine's castle and the love experience awaiting him, whereby he sheds his former intentions. The first scene occurs as the hero finds himself trapped and alone in the barbican of the castle (3), having chased the wounded Esclados through the gates. Lunete, Laudine's lady-in-waiting (2), enters and secretly offers him a Magic Ring (4) that, she says (5), will render him invisible from the eyes and swords of castle security, who are looking for the slayer of Esclados. Yvain accepts the ring (6), and we soon see it shield him as castle knights ransack the room where Lunete hid him. The fact that Lunete requests a return of the ring once the danger passes indicates that she will not be his love interest—a place reserved for Laudine. Nevertheless, she serves Laudine, and during the tumultuous search for her husband's killer, Yvain first spies the heroine and immediately falls in love with her, so that the magic ring coincides with feminine influence and love. A second Magic Ring scene occurs shortly after Yvain's marriage to Laudine (2), when she privately (3) grants the hero (1) a ring (4) with a stone that she says (5) will protect him from imprisonment, loss of blood, or any ill, which he willingly accepts (6). Her centrality to the hero's development from hereon in is emblematized in the ring, which "'will be your shield and hauberk,'" arming him better than plate armor and which comes with the condition that he return to her within a year. The ring apparently works through months of tournaments, joining martial activity with love. When he overstays his absence and has the ring revoked, he loses its protective powers and disintegrates into madness, illustrating his dependence on her. From this point, all of his martial activity occurs in service to women, enabling him to re-earn the woman he loves, Laudine.

Two variations of the Magic Ring scene occur in some of the earliest Middle English romances: *King Horn* (c. 1225) and *Floris and Blancheflour* (c. 1250). In both cases, the English poet retains the basic elements of the scene, and yet, ties the ring's power primarily to larger political interests and only secondarily to love. In *King Horn* (MS C, l. 523ff.), the heroine and love interest, Rymenhild (2), gifts Horn a ring (1)(4) as he visits privately with her in her bower (3) shortly after her father has knighted him, at her bequest. She explains to him how the stones have such power that he will never have to fear the blows of battle or feel distraction on the battlefield (5); he need only look at the ring and think of her and he will prevail. Horn accepts the ring (6). While the ring doubles as a love token and a protective amulet, as in the French tradition, even bearing an inscription of her name, Rymenhild's ring does not hold explicit magical powers. Instead, it relies on the hero's mental focus and fortitude for it to work in battle, so that it never affords the hero any unfair, magical advantage on the battlefield that could compromise his own mettle. Also, the English poet honors early English bonds among men, despite the romantic element, by having Rymenhild promptly offer a second, similar ring to Athulf, Horn's close companion, essentially combining elements of French and English literary tradition. This blended tradition also manifests in how the ring later works as promised on the battlefield, emboldening Horn to defeat his enemies, and thus, tying Rymenhild to his success, as in French tradition. Yet, Horn never fights exclusively "for the girl," or on behalf women, as Yvain usually does, instead using the ring as a tool to avenge political wrongs, including in a Disguise and Infiltration* scene, where he defeats a political traitor and personal rival for Rymenhild, illustrating the English tendency to pair (if not prioritize) the public and political with the personal and amorous.

The political also overshadows the personal and amorous in the Magic Ring scene in *Floris and Blancheflour*. The tale centers on the youthful love between the Muslim prince, Floris, and a Christian girl, Blancheflour, but the Magic Ring scene does not involve the lovers themselves. Instead, the magic ring (4) is gifted to Floris (1) by his mother rather than his love (2), announcing the primacy of *her* influence and the political and religious ramifications of her actions in the hero's success. As a Muslim queen working to rescue the Christian girl and future queen of the kingdom, she serves a mission that is as much political and spiritual as amorous. The public nature of his actions accounts for the more public setting (3) of the ring-exchange, and its protective powers, as explained by the queen (5) extend beyond the battlefield to include burning and drowning, as well as guaranteeing whatever he may wish for as long as he possesses the ring. Floris accepts the ring (6). The ring later features not on the battlefield, but during the final trial of the young lovers, now hostage and sentenced to death in Babylon, where Floris, then Blancheflour, publicly and lovingly insist on the other using the ring for its protective powers, which are never actually put to the test. Here, the magic ring, instead, becomes a tool of religious and cultural conversion, as the Muslim Emir and his councilors are moved to tears by the selfless love of the young pair, the first step in the spread of Christianity that ends the poem, again prioritizing the political over the personal in this English romance. (For further discussion of this scene, see Part III).

The *Gawain*-poet utilizes the Magic Ring scene in *Sir Gawain and the Green Knight* (Fitt III, l. 1733ff.), modifying each of its narrative components so that it *in*validates rather than validates feminine influence in the hero's success. Like Yvain, Gawain (1) finds himself in an unfamiliar castle, where he encounters an alluring married woman (2), the wife of his host, Lord Bertilak, evoking the transformative setting of French romance. But the similarities end there. Rather than occurring at the beginning of the narrative, launching the hero on his mission, the Magic Ring scene in *SGGK* occurs toward the end of his journey to the Green Chapel, where he will encounter the Green Knight, and as a final attempt of Lady Bertilak to influence Gawain's mission. Rather than being an object of love and devotion, Lady Bertilak is a temptress—an agent of her husband—threatening to derail the hero from his mission. In the last of three intimate bedroom scenes (3), the Lady offers Gawain a precious ring (4) with a glittering stone, easily construed as a love token, but rather than accepting it, the hero refuses the offer (6), suggesting this hero's noncompliance with the familiar romance formula. His refusal shows his abiding orientation to other men (Arthur; Bertilak) rather than a shift in orientation to women, as in French romance. Not dissuaded, the Lady promptly offers him a silk girdle, whose magical, protective powers, described by the Lady (5), mimic those typically assigned to the ring in this type-scene. Gawain accepts the girdle purely for its strategic martial advantage rather than for its emotive qualities (6). Finally, rather than emboldening the hero in the physical challenge ahead, the ring-substitute shames the hero, causing him to lose confidence and conceive of himself as a coward. Rather than keeping the amulet as a continuing source of strength, the hero wears the green girdle as a reminder of his weakness. As it happens, the seemingly private bedroom (3) was quite known to Bertilak, who masterminded the temptation. Thus, the poet uses yet undermines the purpose of the Magic Ring type-scene within French romance, exploring the potential dangers, rather than benefits, of feminine influence in the heroic project.

Further Reading

Corinne Saunders, *Magic and the Supernatural in Medieval English Romance* (Cambridge: D.S. Brewer, 2010), 125–30.

Open Heavens

The righteous are led up to the bright opening of heaven of Old English tradition, illustrating the Christian concept that those who live virtuously, persisting through present struggles, can draw hope from the knowledge that their place in heaven is guaranteed. The scene guides readers, rhetorically, toward a life of Christian virtue. This brief scene consists of 1) the righteous being summoned and/or led up to heaven, which 2) shines brightly in glory, a reward that 3) requires being mindful of virtue and Christ's teachings here on earth, which ushers in 4) an afterlife far more excellent than life of earth. The scene occurs in four OE poems: two each in *Christ and Satan* (ll. 549–56 and 588–96), *Andreas* (ll. 102b-6 and 1609–12), and *Guthlac A* (ll. 6–10 and 484–87) and once in *Solomon and Saturn I* (ll. 36–42). Unlike other type-scenes, which unfold in real time through characters and familiar choreography, the Open Heavens scene is hypothetical—a scene projected imaginatively into the future, either by the narrator to the audience, or within the narrative by God (or his disciples) to a character. The scene is a consoling visualization exercise of a future reward contingent on present actions.

The fullest instance of the Open Heavens occurs in *Christ and Satan*, first as a visualized promise (ll. 1609–12) spoken by the narrator to the righteous (1), where God led them out of captivity to their "native land" (*eðle*) in heaven, whose bright light of glory stands open to those mindful of virtue (2) (3). Later, the scene (ll. 588–96) takes more specific form, imagined with a divine invitation, God's healing power, a seat alongside God and his angels—a "holy retinue" (l. 591, *halig eardað*)—where bright splendor stands open (4).

Guthlac A offers two vivid variations of the Open Heavens scene. In its first instance (ll. 6–9), an angel comes to lead the hero now to the holy homeland, saying "'you are now a traveler'" (*Eart nu tidfara* l. 9) (1), bringing future glory promised in the scene into immediate proximity to the present (4). In the second instance (ll. 484–87), the journey actually happens, but the hero is led by demons (1), rather than heavenly entities, to a place near but not in the open heavens, where he sees earthly depravity (2)(3), eliciting Guthlac's anger rather than joy at coming so tantalizingly close to heaven. Despite the unusual demon-guides, the Open Heavens scene fulfills its rhetorical purpose of making heaven irresistibly appealing (4).

Further Reading

Paul Battles, "Christian Traditional Themes and the Cynewulfian Sociolect in Old English Verse," *Studies in Philology* 119 (2022): 555–78.

Outlaw Gathering

A gathering of outlaws at the edge of a forest, of English origin, Middle English period. This brief type-scene uses 1) a single verbal formula, some version of "under the leafy boughs," to announce 2) a secret gathering of dispossessed and/or incriminated men, including noblemen 3), under forest cover 4), often as a prelude to covert activity. The verbal formula is common, though not exclusive, to the English outlaw tradition and became a stock phrase in the Robin Hood tradition.

The phrase occurs in the very first extant Middle English romance, *King Horn* (c.1225). Horn, dispossessed of his kingdom, living in exile, and struggling to regain his rightful place, infiltrates the castle of Fikenhild, a friend-turned-traitor, in an attempt to rescue his beloved Rymenhild, now forced into marriage with Fikenhild. Disguised as a pilgrim, Horn enters Fikenhild's hall and secretly reveals his identity to Rymenhild, who promptly slips out of the hall to tell the imprisoned Athulf, Horn's closest friend, that Horn and his companions (including many knights) are gathered in the nearby forest "'vnder wude boȝe'" ("'under wood bough,'" 1227) (1) (2) (3). Not long afterwards, Horn and his companions, disguised as harpers, infiltrate the wedding feast (4), and Horn strikes Fikenhild down with his sword, one of the final steps in Horn reclaiming his kingdom and throne. The themes of conquest, exile, and reclamation in *King Horn*, whose hero captures the Anglo-Saxon experience at the time of the Norman Conquest of 1066, and whose name alludes to the iconic Anglo-Saxon drinking vessel, introduces the association of embattled Anglo-Saxon identity and forest refuge that forms a meaningful thread in the later outlaw tradition.

The phrase "under the leafy bough" occurs with far greater frequency—and under similar circumstances of disenfranchisement—in the fourteenth-century *Tale of Gamelyn*, where the hero, Gamelyn, has been swindled out of his rightful inheritance. His older brother, Johan, ignores their father's wish to divide his property among each of his sons, a pre-Conquest model of inheritance that the poet sets in direct opposition to the post-Conquest system of primogeniture, which would serve Johan better. Humiliated and cheated by his brother, Gamelyn and his servant, Adam, flee into the forest (3), and "Adam lokede tho vnder woode-bowȝ" (l. 633) (1), where he spies the band of outlaws living (2). Gamelyn asks if he might join them in exile "vnder woode-lynde" (676) (1) and eventually becoming their leader "vnder woode-schawes" (l. 696) (1), living well among "his mery men vnder woode-bough" (l. 774), these being just some of the instances of this image in poem, always in connection with the forest-dwelling outlaws. *Gamelyn* also introduces into the outlaw tradition the criminal activity of poaching deer in the king's forests, which the tale's outlaws clearly do for sustenance (l. 674), a crime carrying severe punishment. In the pivotal final scene of the poem, Gamelyn and his companions, armed with bows, secretly "cam . . . fro vnder woode-rys" to infiltrate and undermine the trial proceedings that would ensure Johan's final possession of Gamelyn's property, thus restoring Gamelyn to his rightful place in the community (4). Thus, *The Tale of Gamelyn* distills and encodes many of the associations of the phrase "under the leafy bough" with righteous outlawry, poaching, and guerilla warfare waged by loosely organized, dispossessed men of few resources against the greedy, exploitative powers that be.

This same imagery of outlaws meeting "under the leafy bough" becomes a stock phrase in the later, fifteenth-century Robin Hood tales, where Robin and his men (2) live in the forest (3) in perpetual resistance to corrupt authority. For example, in *A Gest of Robyn Hode*, phrases such as "Under this grene-wode tre" (ll. 316, 704, 948, 1189), "Under the grene-wode shawe" (l. 1136), and "Under a mantel of grene" (ll. 844)(1) serve to identify the outlaws by the forest space they typically occupy, while Robin invites guests to meet "Under my trystell-tree" (ll. 1096,1190), a locus of Robin's authority that suggests an alternate social system outside the law (4).

We find variations of "under the leafy bough" in the sixteenth-century outlaw tale *Adam Bell, Clim of the Clough, and William of Cloudesley* (ll. 1–4, 189–90, 380, 405) (1). Imagery of the leafy cover of the forest (3), where the outlaws live (2), indicates protected space for the tale's heroes, whose criminal activity begins with poaching and escalates to killing the king's officials in self-defense (ll. 13, 564) (4), driving them to take up permanent residence in the forest, away from their family members living in the nearby town.

A more unusual instance of the phrase "under the leafy boughs" occurs in the late fourteenth-century *Athelston*, a poem not classified as an outlaw tale and featuring a hero who never takes up residence in the forest with a band of merry men wielding bows. Nevertheless, the poetic gesture toward the outlaw tradition in *Athelston* accords with the poem's post-Conquest setting, in which Anglo-Saxon identity became powerfully associated with outlaws. Upon introducing the group of the four men of the poem (2), all of them messengers, the poet tells us how "By a forest gan þey mete/Wiþ a cros, stood in a strete/Be leff vndyr a lynde . . . (ll. 16–18)(1)(3). These men have no familial relationship and no prior acquaintance, and we never find out who they work for, yet they quickly enter into sworn brotherhood, suggesting some undisclosed common purpose (4). The scene forms a prelude to their swift and disturbing rise to political power, with one of them, Athelston, assuming the throne and providing titles and estates for the others. Thus, the variant of the phrase "under the leafy bough" again coincides with covert activity by the less powerful against existing power structures. Their pact of sworn brotherhood soon deteriorates into rumor and rivalry, destabilizing the entire realm. The central conflict of the poem unfolds as a legal drama, contrasting a judicial ordeal, attributed to pre-Conquest legal procedure, with the post-Conquest legal practice of the "playne parliament" and concludes with Athelston recognizing the errors of his ways. The pattern at play in the poem of political ascendance followed by legal and political instability, carried out by men introduced as outlaws and bearing Anglo-Saxon names, accords with late-fourteenth-century peasant fantasy of a better age under the Anglo-Saxon kings, including the tenth-century King Athelstan, that found violent expression in the peasant uprising of 1381, which began as a groundswell of resistance pursued through the nation's courts and concluded with the massive execution of the rebels, officially deemed outlaws. The case of *Athelston* suggests how a poet, so inclined, might employ the phrase "under the leafy bough" for negative cultural profiling.

Further Reading

Dominique Battles, "The Middle English *Athelston* and 1381, Part I: the Politics of Anglo-Saxon Identity," *Studies in Philology* 117 (2020): 1–39.

Nancy Mason Bradbury, "*The Tale of Gamelyn* as a Greenwood Outlaw Talking," *Southern Folklore* 53 (1996): 207–23.

Laura A. Hibbard, "*Athelston*, a Westminster Legend," *Publications of the Modern Language Association* 36 (1921): 223–44.

Timothy S. Jones, *Outlawry in Medieval Literature* (New York: Palgrave Macmillan, 2010).

Paraclausithyron

A lament to a closed door, of Classical origin. The scene occurs within the framework of a love story and involves 1) an excluded lover (*exclusus amator*) facing 2) the closed door of his beloved (now absent), with the door symbolizing an obstacle in the course of the love affair, which the lover 3) laments. The lover (often the man) finds himself alone on the threshold of his lover's house, a place holding fond memories associated with the early days of the affair. The impassive door separating the man from his beloved becomes a stand-in for the absent lady, apostrophized, praised, kissed, and castigated in a verbal monologue by the frustrated man. Instances appear in the works of the Greek poets Aristophanes, Asclepiades, Meleager of Gadara, and Callimachus, as well as the Roman poets Horace, Tibullus, Catullus, Martial, and others, in both formal and comedic forms.

A representative example and variation occurs in Ovid's *Amores* (I.6), where the lover (1), holding vigil by night at his beloved's door (2), addresses not the door but the watchful porter at the door barring entry—one who holds "the bolt that could finish me off" (3). He attempts to bargain with the man, alternately prevailing on him for return favors and begging him for pity, urgently and repeatedly insisting "The night is passing: slide that door bolt free!," all messages equally intended for the lady, Corinna. He then blends the porter and the door itself, likening them to "oak-battened defenses" suitable for a military siege, who treat him like a hostile invader, when "no army marches behind me," only to switch tones and threaten "I've a sword and a torch, I'm ready to storm this standoffish/Mansion by frontal assault," distilling the Ovidian paradigm of the lover as a fighter. Surrendering, he leaves a garland on her threshold and departs.

Chaucer presents a variation of the *paraclausithyron* type-scene in Book V of *Troilus and Criseyde*, toward the end of the love affair between the Trojan prince, Troilus, and the noblewoman, Criseyde. The specific episode forms part of a larger tour Troilus makes of all the former sites within Troy he associates mentally with Criseyde—material, some of which, he found in the Proem of Boccaccio's *Filostrato*. Chaucer draws the specific scene at Criseyde's palace from a briefer, parallel version of this scene found in the *Filostrato* (V. 52–53). Troilus (1) approaches the house of Criseyde, now empty after her departure for the Greek camp (2). The scene employs the stock elements of the frustrated male lover at the closed door of his beloved lady who apostrophizes the inanimate building with praise and longing, her house forming the site of their early, secret courtship and love affair. True to the poetic formula, the impassive door signals the seemingly insurmountable obstacle in their love affair. At the same time,

Chaucer varies the scene in ways that speak to larger themes in the poem, rendering this normally intimate and apolitical scene altogether more public and political. For example, Troilus goes to her house not alone but with Pandarus (1), replicating the bonds among men—these two men in particular—seen throughout the poem, which places it within the literary tradition of Classical heroic epic, whence the story of Troy originated. Furthermore, the figurative language of siege warfare in Ovid's *Amores* becomes a political reality in the *Troilus*, where the circumstances of siege warfare literally divide the lovers, despite their best efforts. Thus, unlike the home of Corinna, whose porter suggests occupants, Criseyde's house stands truly empty, "her dores spered alle" (V.531, "her doors all barred") (2), and "shet was every window of the place" (V.534, "every window of the place was shut"), showing no light within, as a result of her recent departure. Unlike the metaphorical "enemy" lover of Ovid's verse, Troilus and Criseyde now occupy opposing sides of the Trojan conflict following her exchange to the Greek camp. Troilus' lament captures the public scale of the conflict threatening their intimate relationship, as he addresses the entire, public façade of the palace ("'O paleys desolate,'" V.540) (3) with many doors and windows, rather than a single door (2), and issuing this lament in the morning light (V.519), rather than in the darkness of night, locating darkness inside rather than outside the house itself (V.543–4), as is more typical of the scene. Similarly, calling her house the "'crowne of houses alle'" ("'crown of all houses,'" (V. 546 and 541) (3), Troilus situates Criseyde's house within the wider social order of Troy, the very thing that forced them into secrecy and prevented their long-term union. Rather than blaming the locked house, as lovers typically do in *paraclausithyron*, Troilus identifies with it, suggesting it should fall down, just as he should die, shifting the blame away from the building (and Criseyde herself) and onto the situation that left both of them "cold." The public nature of this normally intimate type-scene culminates when Troilus laments that he dare not kiss the doors of her house in front of "'this route'" ("'this crowd,'" V.552), suggesting watchful eyes making him self-conscious. Thus, Troilus' lament voices not a frustration with the house itself, a symbol of Criseyde, for whom he reserves only praise, likening her to the sun, a ruby, and a saint, but rather, with the circumstantial reality beyond their control that inevitably shaped the trajectory of their love. The tour through the now-deserted city sites in both the Proem of the *Filostrato* and the *Troilus* bear some resemblance to the biblical tradition of the destruction of Jerusalem, further grounding the scene in public and historical forces encroaching upon individuals. In all, the instance of *paraclausithyron* in Chaucer's *Troilus* emphasizes the public and political, rather than private and personal, determinants in the love affair.

Further Reading

Lawrence Besserman, "A Note on the Sources of Chaucer's *Troilus* V, 540–613," *The Chaucer Review* 24 (1990): 306–8.

Morton W. Bloomfield, "Troilus' Paraclausithyron and its Setting," *Neuphilologische Mitteilungen* 73 (1972): 15–24.

H.V. Canter, "The Paraclausithyron as a Literary Theme," *The American Journal of Philology* 41 (1920): 355–68.

Rash Promise

A blind promise, made in the interest of gain or advantage, possibly of eastern origin. In some cases, the Rash Promise responds to a formal request for a promise, and in other cases, the promise is made voluntarily and spontaneously. Two main types of Rash Promise emerge from textual tradition: one, the 1) promise made between 2) a man and a woman, generally in a 3) private setting, and usually made by the man in response to 4) the woman's formal request of a promise, where the promise is later 5) inadvertently broken; second, the a) promise made between b) two men, generally in a c) public setting, which is d) sometimes solicited and e) kept on the basis of social codes surrounding verbal honor. As a pattern, the Rash Promise is a tool for a weaker character to gain advantage over a more powerful character (either intentionally and surreptitiously or fortuitously), whether it be a woman over a man, or a lower-ranking/disadvantaged man over a higher-ranking man. The Rash Promise is common, though by no means exclusive, to the genre of the Breton Lai, where the promise occurs between a fairy person (with magical advantages) and a human.

We find the first type of Rash Promise in the *Lais* of Marie de France (c.1180), between a magical being and a human. For example, in *Lanval*, the Fairy Princess, in the sumptuous privacy of her pavilion (3), offers the hero respite from financial woes imposed by Arthur's court, so that "henceforth he could wish for nothing which he could not have . . . however generously he gave or spent" (74–5) (2). In exchange for her riches, not to mention her love, she demands "'I admonish, order, and beg you not to reveal this secret to anyone! . . . [as] you would lose me forever if this love were to become known'" (75)(4). Lanval readily agrees that he "would do what she commanded" (75)(1). What seems like an uncomplicated stroke of good fortune, however, soon sours when Queen Guinevere propositions Lanval, meeting his resistance with contrived accusations of his homosexuality, prompting the hero to disclose his love of the Fairy Princess, whose lowest servant, he says, "'is worth more than you, my lady the Queen, in body, face and beauty, wisdom and goodness'" (77)(5). True to the bargain, Lanval loses the fairy's gifts, while his situation at court worsens as the queen opens a formal case against him on false charges of inappropriate conduct toward her. In the long run, the fairy restores her relationship with Lanval, and they depart together for her realm. In the short term, however, the Rash Promise, with its seemingly effortless terms, teaches the hero the fragility of his wondrous fortune, impressing upon him the need for greater self-control, vigilance, and appreciation in deserving the gifts of this powerful, however compassionate, magical woman.

A comparable bargain between a fairy and a human, this time between two men, occurs in the Middle English *Sir Orfeo* (c.1325); only, in this case, the fairy person becomes the author of, rather than the antidote to, the hero's woes. After a Fairy King abducts Orfeo's queen, Heurodis, King Orfeo retreats from his kingdom into the forest in self-imposed exile. Wandering in the wilderness for ten years, Orfeo reflects on his former fortune of worldly riches and the comforts of companionship. One day, he spies a fairy hunt in the forest, whose gathering includes his wife, with whom he makes eye contact. Following the fairies into their realm, Orfeo enters their castle under the guise of a "pouer menstrel" (l. 430, "poor minstrel"). He soon serenades the Fairy King and his court (b) (c) with his renowned harp-playing, eventually luring him into making a rash promise (d), whereby the Fairy King offers him whatever he likes in exchange for more music (a). Thus, unlike in Marie's *Lanval*, where the fairy procures a promise from the human, thereby gaining certain leverage over him, in *Sir Orfeo*, the human procures the promise from the fairy by way of gaining leverage. Seizing upon the situation, Orfeo demands the release of Heurodis, which the Fairy King initially refuses, until Orfeo appeals to the social code and kingly duty to keep one's word, therefore not allowing the Fairy King to break his promise as Lanval does (e), an argument facilitated by the public setting of the promise (c). In this instance, we see the less powerful human—lacking both magic and home-turf advantage, while also suffering from diminished royal status—prevail over the more powerful, magical person by means of a Rash Promise, which becomes a tool of the hero's empowerment rather than disempowerment, as in *Lanval*.

An earlier—and far less honorable—version of this very scene in *Sir Orfeo* occurs in Gottfried von Strassburg's *Tristan* (c.1210), when Gandin, a young Irish knight from Isolde's native kingdom in Ireland, arrives at Mark's court in Cornwall (b), intent on winning Isolde through trickery. Bearing a rote into the court, the knight waits for the king to request a performance to then demand a reward (d), in advance. Mark casually offers "'anything of mine'" (215) (a) and is struck when Gandin requests Queen Isolde. When Mark resists, Gandin capitalizes on the public setting (c) and stands on the principle of a king honoring his word, threatening him with both legal and martial recourse should Mark fail to comply, indicating a formal and binding social code surrounding verbal oaths (e). In this way, Gandin gains Isolde. Upon returning from a day of hunting, Tristan learns of the trickery, promptly grabs his harp and heads to the pavilion, where Gandin (b) attempts to comfort the weeping queen. Tristan, like Gandin, passes himself off as a musician, and through trickery, snatches Isolde back, though this sequel scene of trickery does not involve a formal Rash Promise. Gottfried uses the Rash Promise, therefore, as a tool of trickery wielded by a less powerful nobleman against a king, and, true to the Rash Promise between men, the promise is kept (e), against all reason, on the basis of verbal honor. In the *Tristan*, as in *Sir Orfeo*, the Rash Promise scene revolves around the queen and her tenuous position among competing men, where promises are made—and kept—about her but not by her.

Chaucer's *Franklin's Tale* contains a famous example of a Rash Promise, when the heroine, Dorigen, entreated by Aurelius to return his affections (2) (4), flippantly promises to grant him his wish on the condition that he make the rocks along the coast of the harbor disappear (1). Interestingly, Chaucer combines elements of both types of Rash Promise—that made between a man and a woman (often broken) and that made between men (usually kept)—in the scenario that follows. On the one hand, while Aurelius (a would-be lover) is not magical, he secures the pseudo-magical aid of the Clerk or Orleans, evoking the fairy lover plot of certain Breton lais. On the other hand, when Dorigen later wishes to break the promise, her husband, Arveragus, learns of the bargain and insists, behind the scenes, that she keep her word, replicating the Rash Promise between men in emphasizing verbal honor, upholding the social code between men through her (b) (e). (By contrast, in the source text for the *Franklin's Tale*, Boccaccio's *Decameron* 10.5, the lady's husband permits her to keep her promise in part out of fear of the magician's vengeance, should she renege.) Varying the type-scene further, Chaucer reverses the usual gender roles of the man-woman promise, where generally, the man makes the promise to the woman; here, Dorigen makes the Rash Promise to a man. Furthermore, Arveragus' subsequent appeal to codes of verbal honor occurs not in a public but in a private setting (3)(c), in their home. In the end, masculine honor prevails, as Aurelius releases Dorigen from her obligation of romantic union purely on the basis of his admiration for Arveragus. Thus, the promise is both kept and broken, effectively combining both types of Rash Promise scenarios.

Chaucer incorporates a Rash Promise into the *Wife of Bath's Tale*, his rendition of the Loathly Lady* story-type. As a promise made by a man to a fairy woman (2), in private (3), the promise aligns with other Rash Promises involving a man and a woman, resembling Marie's *Lanval* insofar as the fairy requests a promise in exchange for rectifying the knight's standing at Arthur's court (4). In this case, however, the knight has invited his own distress, having raped a young woman, earning a sentence, issued by the queen, involving a life-or-death quest for the answer to "what thyng is it that wommen moost desiren" (l. 905). The knight's mandatory submission to the queen parallels his later subservience to the fairy, disguised as an old hag, who surreptitiously imposes her own sentence upon him to marry her in exchange for the answer to the riddle. Where other versions of this bargain between a knight and a Loathly Lady, such as Gower's "Tale of Florent," afford the knight fair disclosure of the terms in advance of the promise, Chaucer casts it as a blind promise whereby the knight agrees (1) to the fairy's request to "'Plight me thy trouthe heere in myn hand'" (l. 1009, "'Pledge me your promise here in my hand'") without knowing the conditions of the bargain (4), setting the knight up for further punishment in an already hopeless sentence. In this sense, unlike other Loathly Lady tales such as the "Tale of Florent" or the fifteenth-century *Weddynge of Syr Gawen and Dame Ragnell*, where the hag and the queen work to cross purposes, in the *WOB*'s tale, the two women collude in the rehabilitation of the hero. Consistent with the Rash Promise between a man and a woman, the promise proves fragile, as the knight, suddenly faced with the prospect of marrying the old hag, quickly backtracks, begging for "'a newe requeste!'" (l. 1060 "'new request'") in order to avoid "'my dampnacioun!'" (l. 1067, "'my damnation'") (5). In the end, he marries her in deed only, choosing this form of death over the queen's literal death sentence. In fact, the public nature of the hag's disclosure of the full terms of the bargain, before the queen and her court (3), refashions this Rash Promise according to the type involving two men, where the social code enforcing the verbal oath ultimately binds the knight into compliance, again blending elements of both types of Rash Promise, as in the *Franklin's Tale*.

Further Reading

Richard Firth Green, "Rash Promises," in *A Crisis of Truth: Literature and Law in Ricardian England* (Philadelphia: University of Pennsylvania Press, 2002), 293–335.

Scop's Repertoire

A recently identified, traditional theme of pre-literate Germanic origin, prevalent in Anglo-Saxon poetry, denoting the live, poetic performance of a *scop* (a poet-performer, generally a harper) in a mead-hall, reciting verse tales, partly spoken and partly sung with instrumental accompaniment, as a core expression of the communal life of the Anglo-Saxons. The *Scop*'s Repertoire has less to do with plot than with narration itself, its sources, and its transmission, drawing the connection between events and the interpretation of those events as a tool of meaning-making in forging a collective identity. It stages the making of verse, both the transmission of known stories as well as the creation of new stories, and involves three elements: 1) copiousness (denoting the extent of the poet's repertoire of songs and poems, which also implies his ability to create and perform new material); 2) orality (indicating spoken, not written, words shared publicly); and 3) antiquity (emphasizing the power of tradition as embodied in old, and therefore venerable, subject matter and stories). The scene takes two main forms: 1) the "tradition" model, indicating the poet's accumulation of ancient songs and learning that qualifies him to create his own, a model that contains all three elements of "copiousness," "orality," and "antiquity"; and 2) the "inspiration" model, stressing the poet as a vessel of unmediated divine inspiration, even when his subject matter derives from ancient (Christian) narratives, themselves understood to be divinely inspired, in which case the element of "antiquity" recedes or is replaced. The *Scop*'s Repertoire appears, among other places, in the Old English *Andreas*, *Beowulf* and *Widsith* (the "tradition" model) and in *Christ II* and *Gifts of Men* ("inspiration" model). The "tradition" model also finds counterparts in the Middle High German *Nibelungenlied* (c.1200) and Old Saxon *Heliand* (9th century).

The *Scop*'s Repertoire ("tradition" model) appears in *Beowulf* (ll. 867b-76a), immediately following the hero's victory over Grendel, and underscores Beowulf's greatness in successfully breaking the deadly, twelve-year cycle of Grendel's nightly onslaught (ll. 867–876). Many of Hrothgar's retainers, old and young, praise Beowulf as the greatest hero alive. Then, one of Hrothgar's thanes, "well-supplied with words of praise and knowledge in songs—one who recalled an abundance of old tales," begins to "artfully recite the exploit of Beowulf" by composing "new words, correctly linked," and aligning Beowulf's deeds with those of an earlier hero, Sigemund the Waelsing. The element of the "copiousness" of the poet-performer's repertoire is invoked by the adjective "mindful" (*gemyndig*) and verb "to remember" (*gemunan*) (ll. 868 and 870) (1), while "antiquity" and "orality" are expressed in the compound term "old tales" (*ealdgesege*; *gesege* literally denoting something that is spoken) (l. 869) (2) (3). True to the scene, the performer both relates old stories and composes new stories, nevertheless fitting the new into the old by means of poetic form, or "correctly linked" (*soðe gebunden*) words (l. 871). The scene dramatizes Beowulf's passage into greatness as he now becomes the subject of song, seamlessly integrated into earlier songs, highlighting the value of fame in Anglo-Saxon heroic tradition. The passage is also explicitly metapoetic in that the *Beowulf*-poet portrays the very process of poetic composition and transmission that he himself is engaged in, not only telling us of Beowulf's deeds but also of the *original* telling of those same deeds, deriving his own artistic authority, in large measure, from his predecessor(s) of the past and the seemingly unbroken chain of transmission from one generation to the next. As a scene of poetic transmission, the *Scop*'s Repertoire announces the import and worthiness of the story to follow, in the case of *Beowulf*, of the deed the hero just performed that earned the highest honor of song. The scene also calls as much attention to the harper in the mead-hall as to the hero he celebrates, as the honor of both becomes intertwined in their service to the community.

In more explicitly Christian Old English poetry, such as *Christ II* (ll. 659–667a) and *Gifts of Men* (ll. 35b-36a, 49–59, 91–94a), employing the "inspiration" model of the scene, the poet-harper of the *Scop*'s Repertoire scene becomes elevated further as an arbiter of divine inspiration and wisdom, as poetry itself becomes one of the "gifts of men" bestowed by God on humankind. Here, the poet becomes not so much (or merely) a bearer of tradition but inspired directly by God. "Copiousness" and "orality" (1) (2) remain core elements of the scene, but "antiquity" becomes more inclusive and expansive, incorporating not only the shared history of the local people but also the wisdom stories of the Bible recording the deeds of a different ancient people (3), greatly expanding the variety of the *scop*'s repertoire and further enhancing the figure of the poet-performer. The range of the type-scene is illustrated by the Venerable Bede's well-known portrait of Caedmon, a native poet divinely inspired to honor God in the form of an Old English "hymn" appearing within the larger Latin *Ecclesiastical History of the English People*.

Further Reading

Paul Battles and Charles D. Wright, "*Eall-feala Ealde Saege*: Poetic Performance and 'The *Scop*'s Repertoire' in Old English Verse," *Oral Tradition* 32(1) (2018): 3–26.

Sleeping After the Feast

Distinctive to Old English poetry, the scene participates in hall-based culture, where feasting (referring to drink rather than food) solidifies and celebrates social bonds. Set in a hall, the scene involves three components: 1) feasting, followed by 2) sleeping (*swefan aefter symble*) as a prelude to 3) danger, often from external attack, thereby threatening social disruption or disintegration. The basic triad divides into six elements: a) feasts, b) sleep, c) unawareness of impending doom, d) the approach of an aggressor to the hall, e) the aggressor enters and looks at the victim(s), and f) the aggressor attacks or threatens. The scene occurs, often in multiples, in a number of Old English poems, including *Beowulf*, *Daniel*, *Genesis A*, *Judith*, and *Andreas*.

Akin to similar fatal feast scenes in classical and medieval narrative, such as Agamemnon's murderous homecoming celebration, the scene affects an abrupt shift from a major to a minor key, from joy to sorrow, security to danger, life to death, hope to despair. However, the scene does not always result in doom, as poets sometimes offset the danger with hopeful solutions.

The *Beowulf*-poet employs the Sleeping After the Feast scene five times. The most famous instances of the scene, containing the deadly triangle of feasting, sleeping, and danger, preface the monster attacks of Grendel and Grendel's mother. For a full discussion of this type-scene in *Beowulf*, see Part II of this volume.

This type-scene of pre-Christian, native poetic tradition comes to serve the Christian message, as in the OE *Daniel* (ll. 108–19), where physical danger from external attack gets transmuted into spiritual danger producing spiritual despair. Thus, the story of King Nebuchadnezzar's terrifying dream, sent by God, of all worldly joys coming to an end, related in a single line of the biblical Book of Daniel, 2.1, assumes the form of the Sleeping After the Feast type-scene, using five of the six typical elements. In this instance, the poet ushers in the type-scene with feasting, sleeping, and unawareness of fate (a, b, and c) but transposes the physical "approach" (d) into a mental approach—"there came moving into his mind" (*com on sefan hwurfan*), while the physical danger manifests as spiritual danger—"the disturbing dream" (*swefnes woma*) (f). True to the formula, the king awakens distressed, as "his mood was not joyful, sorrow came to him" (*Naes him bliðe hige,/ac him sorh astah*). The biblical source passage makes no mention of the king's drinking, yet the OE poet adds that the king "had earlier slept drunk with wine" (*se aer wingal swaef*), reshaping the biblical account to conform to the type-scene, proving its resilience in early English poetics.

Further Reading

Paul Battles, "Dying for a Drink: 'Sleeping After the Feast' Scenes in *Beowulf, Andreas*, and the Old English Poetic Tradition," *Modern Philology* 112(3) (2015): 435–57.

Harry E. Kavros, "*Swefan Æfter Symble*: The Feast-Sleep theme in *Beowulf*," *Neophilologus* 65 (1981): 120–28.

Teichoscopia (Teichoscopy)

A viewing from the wall, of Classical origin. The scene typically occurs within the context of armed conflict, marking a pause in the action where a 1) woman, with ties to both opposing armies, 2) views the battle plain from atop the 3) city walls and 4) laments the destruction she has caused because of the beauty of 5) her face.

The most famous example in western literary tradition, which formed the blueprint for subsequent iterations of the scene, occurs in Homer's *Iliad* 3.121–244, where Helen, the Greek woman whose abduction by the Trojan prince, Paris, precipitated the Trojan War, mounts the walls of Troy and identifies for King Priam a series of Greek warriors on the battle plain surrounding the city defenses. An armed challenge of single-combat between the young, effete Paris and Helen's husband, the seasoned Greek commander and king, Menelaus, is imminent. The scene encapsulates the full span of the war, now in its tenth year, while contrasting the personal and private origins of the war as a dispute between two men over a woman, with the grand scale it assumed in terms of geographic scope, military investment, and timeframe. The scene marks a pause in the conflict where Helen (1), summoned to the walls (3) by the messenger-goddess Iris, in the guise of Hector's sister, feels some nostalgia for her old home in Greece and rushes to the walls in tears in order to view (2) the Greek army on the battle plain outside the city. A gathering of Trojan elders atop the walls laments about the "'years of agony all for her, for such a woman. Beauty, terrible beauty!'" (4) (5), a refrain that inspired Christopher's Marlow's famous metaphor of Helen as "the face that launched a thousand ships" in *Doctor Faustus* (1604). Helen amplifies their lament with her own, as she expresses to Priam her regret over "'forsaking my marriage bed, my kinsmen, my child, my favorite, now full grown,'" identifying herself as "'whore that I am'" (4). Her own diminished faith in what her new life in Troy has become correspondingly diminishes the import of the war itself, now reduced to a single-combat between Paris and Menelaus that, held at the outset, could have prevented the entire conflict. Helen's regret finds expression in her admiration for a series of Greek warriors she identifies for Priam, including Agamemnon, Odysseus, Ajax, and Idomeneus. Her illustrious praise of the Greek host simultaneously highlights Trojan folly in sacrificing so much for this single, changeable woman, while prefiguring the imminent Greek victory.

Medieval audiences would have encountered this scene, unavailable in Homer's original Greek, in a variety of sources, including the fifth-century, Latin, supposedly eye-witness accounts of Dares Phrygius and Dictys Cretensis and Guido delle Colonne's *Historia Destructionis Troiae* (1287), an adaptation into Latin of Benoit de St. Mauré's OF *Roman de Troie*, which, itself, often circulated in abbreviated prose redactions as part of the *Histoire ancienne*.

Guido (*Historia*, XV), a source for both Giovanni Boccaccio and Geoffrey Chaucer, has Hellen (1), trembling and full of "fear and doubt," mount the walls of Troy (3) accompanied by a group of Priam's daughters, with no mention of Priam and his fellow advisors. Rather than a series of verbal profiles through Helen's eyes (2), we see the Greek commanders, from the narrator's perspective, assembling their forces, foregrounding masculine cooperation within and between Greek units. Helen's presence and voice, in this instance of *teichoscopia*, is altogether diminished, in keeping with Guido's overall disparaging characterization of Helen as lustful and selfish.

In his *Teseida* (1339–41), set in the intervening period between the end of the Theban war and the beginning of the Trojan War, Giovanni Boccaccio creates a fictional antecedent of Helen's later *teichoscopia* at Troy. Within this hitherto undeveloped period of history in chronical accounts of the time, Boccaccio fashions a similar conflict in Athens over a woman, Emilia, an Amazon captive from Scythia, fought between two Theban kinsmen, Palamone and Arcita, whose impassioned dispute extends the Theban propensity for civil strife into yet another generation. Boccaccio previews Helen's experience at Troy in the figure of Emilia (1) as she observes the combat between Arcita and Palamone, whose ranks include young Greeks (including Helen's brother Pollux) and Trojans who will later fight at Troy. Emilia's *teichoscopia* (8.98–110), a private monologue, anticipates Helen's sentiments while observing the Trojan War from atop the walls of Troy. Like Helen, Emilia is "'sought by two with the forces of many'" and laments the "'wicked and ruthless conflict waged here only because of my face!'" (4) (5). And, like Helen, she imagines "'how many mothers, fathers, friends, brothers, sons, and others will curse me'" (4). Boccaccio amplifies the scene's function to critique and question the cause of this conflict and its Trojan successor, first, by reducing Emilia's power in the political equation, as a war captive herself rather than a queen, standing alone on the walls (2) (3) and lamenting her lot in life. The poet also greatly reduces her emotional investment in either side of the conflict as equally undesirable options, while, in turn, grounding the men's desire for her in purely subjective idealizations of her from afar. Boccaccio thus reduces the conflicts of Athens—and, by extension, Troy—to nothing more than *cupiditas* over an indifferent young woman—"such a small thing" (7.5).

Boccaccio briefly gestures toward the scene of *teichoscopia* in the *Filostrato* (c. 1335) (V.70–1), referencing yet modifying many of its elements. Technically, Troilo (1) does not mount the city walls, yet, over several scenes, he views the enemy camp (2), looking for Cressida, imitating the "viewing" of the enemy camp. The scene occurs after Cressida has stayed in the Greek camp well beyond her promised date of return to Troy, changing the choreography of the scene entirely. For instance, rather than having a woman observe the enemy camp in broad daylight to look down at the warriors on the battle plain below, Boccaccio has Troilo view the Greek camp by night, after the day's fighting is over, to look upon the Greek tents. Rather than feeling disturbed by the Greek army below, "now they were gazed at with delight," and rather than referencing the woman's (Cressida's) face, Boccaccio calls attention to Troilo' face (5) as he imagines the breezes coming from the plain as conveying her "sighs." Like Emilia in the *Teseida*, Troilo laments privately to himself (4), though his friend Pandaro appears close by. Feelings of guilty regret over the political ramifications of one's actions, typical of the scene, are replaced by simpler feelings of personal longing on Troilo's part, and his later regrets remain personal rather than political in scale. Nonetheless, the scene captures the sense of futility and powerlessness endemic to *teichoscopia* in that Cressida never returns to Troilo.

In his adaptation of Boccaccio's *Teseida* for the *Knight's Tale*, Chaucer eliminates Emelye's *teichoscopia*, along with nearly all the other Trojan material that preoccupied Boccaccio. However, Chaucer formalizes the scene of *teichoscopia* in his adaptation of the scene from the *Filostrato* in *Troilus and Criseyde* (c.1387) (V.666–86). While keeping all of Boccaccio's innovations of gender, timing, perspective, and sentiment, Chaucer expands the element of *teichoscopia* in the story by having Troilus (1) actually mount the city walls (l. 666) (3) and making a habit of it (l. "ek wolde he walke," l. 666), formalizing the scene as a "viewing from the walls." Troilus laments to himself (4) not of destruction he caused but of pain he suffers in Criseyde's absence, due to the circumstances of the war (ll. 679–79). True to the scene, Chaucer infuses facial imagery, as Troilus imagines the wind that "encresseth in my face" (l. 674) come from Criseyde's sighs (5). Chaucer adds a further instance of the type-scene later, as Troilus and Pandarus together (1) climb the walls over the city gate "To loke if they kan sen aught of Criseyde" (ll. 1113) (2) (3) among the people passing below, pairing the two men in the endeavor of love here, as in numerous other scenes of the poem. However, whereas Helen recognizes and identifies for Priam various Greek warriors below, Troilus struggles and fails to find the face of Criseyde in the crowd (4), heightening the type-scene's tell-tale sense of futility. Nor is he looking down on former kinsmen as Helen does, but rather, on enemies who now possess the object of his love. As in the *Filostrato*, the futility in this instance is not martial and political, as is typical of the scene, but personal and emotional, as Troilus' hopes remain "byjaped" ("deluded," l. 1119) and "aboute naught" ("for nothing," l. 1120).

Further Reading

Brian Toohey, *Reading Epic: An Introduction to Ancient Narratives* (London: Routledge, 1992).

Traveler Recognizes His Goal

A moment at the end of a long journey, where a traveler-protagonist first spies his destination with an air of wonder, anticipation, and/or relief, marking his arrival at an important threshold of a locus where he will be tested. The scene is prevalent in Old English and Old Saxon poetry, utilizing conventional poetic schemes and vocabulary. The relatively compact scene contains eight elements: 1) departure (often eager) for travel; 2) a reference to sustained or completed motion toward a goal; 3) a milestone in travel marked by "until" and often referencing time; 4) vocabulary of sight and perception; 5) a description of the goal, 6) emphasizing its height and 7) brightness; 8) a comment concerning arrival. In most instances, the destination constitutes a man-made fortress or a hall. Centering more on perception than action, the scene marks a pause in action, inviting the audience to appreciate visually the magnitude of the destination through the eyes of the traveler-protagonist, with the scale of the place signaling the scale of the challenge awaiting him. The scene occurs in the Old English *Beowulf*, *Genesis A*, *Solomon and Saturn*, *Andreas*, *Judith*, and the Old-Saxon *Heliand*, among other works.

The familiar scene in *Beowulf* (ll. 217–24a) of Beowulf's arrival in Denmark, having traveled over the sea from his homeland, accords with the Traveler Recognizes his Goal: Beowulf's ship departs (*gewat*) (1), "urged on by the wind" (*winde gefysed*), suggesting eagerness; it "journeyed so far (*gewaden haefde*) (2) "until" (*oð þaet*), by the beginning of the third day (3), "the sailors saw land" (*gesawon*) (4), "land . . . slopes . . . headlands" (*land . . . brimclifu . . . beorgas*) (5), which are "steep" and "great" (*steape . . . side*) (6), and which are "shining," at which point (*blican* [infinitive]) (7); "the voyage had ended" (*þa waer sund liden*) (8). This instance of the scene signals the threshold of place where the hero will soon be tested in his fights with Grendel and Grendel's mother. In all, *Beowulf* contains five instances of this scene, including his arrival back in Geat-land, with the first, third, and fifth marking sea voyages, *Beowulf* being the only poem containing this scene to apply it to sea voyages, as opposed to land journeys. Moreover, these three sea-voyage scenes, along with one instance of the scene in *Genesis A* (ll. 2870–79), are the only ones where the traveler's destination is a natural landmark rather than a man-made fortress or a hall.

In explicitly Christian texts, the Traveler Recognizes His Goal scene marks the protagonist's arrival at a place of spiritual testing or reward. In the OE *Solomon and Saturn* (ll. 234–37a), the scene pertains to the arrival at the heavenly city of Jerusalem, a shining city bathed in light. In *Genesis A* (ll. 1816b–22a), the scene marks Abraham and Sarah's departure for and arrival at Egypt in search of a new life, where they find a tall, shining fortress—the threshold of the place where they will undergo many trials and tribulations while under God's protection. In *Andreas* (ll. 837b-45a), the saint recognizes that he has arrived at the city gates of Mermedonia (having been conveyed while sleeping)—a city of tile-adorned buildings and towers surrounded by steep hillsides—a place where he will endure great suffering to rescue Matthew and convert the Mermedonians. The "Traveler" scene occurs similarly in the Old Saxon *Heliand*, first (ll. 649b-668a) to characterize the magi's journey to and arrival at (1) the manger (5) of the Christ-child; they recognize the "shining stars" (*huuîton sterron*) in "high heaven" (*them hôhon himile*) (6) (7) as a sign from God leading them to Bethlehem (5), where they then recognize the star over the house/inn with the holy child, whom they recognize upon arriving at the manger (4), with the bright stars providing the elements of light and height endemic to the scene, and the successive "recognitions" creating the reflective pauses in action signaling the magnitude of their final approach at their goal, in this case, a place of spiritual reward rather than testing (8). Later, the *Heliand*-poet employs the scene to mark Christ's arrival at Jerusalem (ll. 3671–87a)—that "renowned fortress" (*mârean burg*) where he saw "glittering the fortress wall" (*blican thene burges uual*) of the place where he will be tested. In this way, the Traveler scene in the *Heliand* characterizes Christ as a spiritual reward (a goal) for others and a protagonist who will undergo and model spiritual testing.

Further Reading

Paul Battles, "Old Saxon-Old English Intertextuality and the 'Traveler Recognizes His Goal' Theme in the *Heliand*," in Larry J. Swain, ed., *Old English and Continental Germanic Literature in Comparative Perspectives* (New York: Peter Lang, 2019), 5–37.

George Clark, "The Traveler Recognizes His Goal: A Theme in Anglo-Saxon Poetry," *Journal of English and Germanic Philology* 64 (1965): 645–59.

Wise Woman

A negative portrait of a foreign ruler by means of his wiser wife, originating in crusading literature. This type-scene is used primarily to discredit a male-ruler, specifically, one whose cultural and/or religious affiliations differ from those of the audience of poem. The scene consists of 1) a domestic setting within a foreign land governed by 2) an emotionally volatile ruler pursuing an extreme and destructive course of action that violates the rights of others. Encountering a setback in his plan, the ruler retreats to his home, where he broods in frustration. His 3) wife enters, patiently questions his motives, and suggests an alternative course of action, revealing her superior grasp of political realities. In general, her advice fails to divert him from his foolish path, but her verbal diagnosis of the problem catalyzes political change in ways that accord with the political ambitions of the audience of the story. In some cases, the couple has 4) an only child, who is, him/herself, directly threatened by the ruler's plans and policies, in which case, the child works in tandem with his/her mother to steer the political crisis in the direction of "progress." The ruler, it seems, cannot even control his own household, as his wife and child become infiltrators unwittingly acting on behalf of his enemies. It becomes a stock scene designed to highlight the shortcomings in the husband as a leader, as, in each case, his inability to control his emotions of anger and jealousy overwhelms his capacity to make effective decisions, and his wife sounds more like a patient mother than a spouse.

While the figure of the Wise Woman finds precedent in early biblical and ancient Sumerian tradition, with figures such as the biblical Wise Woman of Tekoa (2 Samuel 14) and Siduri in the *Epic of Gilgamesh*, both of whom confront and guide powerful male rulers, the Wise Woman type-scene becomes formalized as a literary device within the context of medieval crusade literature, with western European poets drawing upon negative cultural stereotypes of the emotive, impulsive, sensuous, and irrational Middle Eastern male temperament in their depictions of the foreign rulers against whom they warred. Such depictions feminize these rulers, disqualifying them for governance. The Wise Woman scene draws upon this gender dynamic—first, by employing a domestic rather than public setting, and second, by reversing the gender roles between husband and wife, with the ruler exhibiting the emotive and ultimately submissive role typically assigned to the woman, and the wife, assuming the role of the cool-headed political advisor.

An early instance of the Wise Woman type-scene occurs in the twelfth-century OF *Roman de Thèbes*, which overlays the ancient story of the civil war between the sons of Oedipus at Thebes with the moral and political ecology of the crusades, drawing upon the chronicle accounts of the

First Crusade; Pollinicés and his allies headquartered in Argos take on the aspect of crusaders overcoming the forces of Thebes, a city under the rule of Ethïoclés, whose ranks include various eastern peoples generally classified as infidels, including Persians, Turks, Achopars, Pechenegs, Syrians, and Moors. In a pivotal scene marking the beginning of the end of Ethïoclés' rule over Thebes, as the king rages over the recently disclosed treasonous dealings of one of his top advisors (2), Daire le Roux, the king's mother, Jocaste (3), draws Ethïoclés (1) to one side and advises him to avoid further political risk by sparing Daire's life, pointing out the militarily disadvantaged state they now suffer (Constans, ed., ll. 8409–22). Her daughter, Antigone (4), ultimately diffuses Ethïoclés' anger by introducing Daire's young, beautiful daughter, Salamander, whose romantic appeal to Ethïoclés inspires him to spare her father's life. While this early instance of the Wise Woman scene involves a larger crowd of witnesses to the king's appeasement, nonetheless, it contains what will become the core elements of the type-scene: an enraged foreign tyrant insisting upon an extreme course of action, a motherly female advisor (in this case his mother) dispensing political advice to the ruler, a foreign setting within the ruler's household, and a child (Jocaste's daughter, Antigone) who takes practical steps to realize her mother's goals, which align with the "enemy" side of Pollinicés and his army of veteran crusaders.

The earliest Middle English romance, *Floris and Blancheflour* (c.1250), contains three iterations of the Wise Woman scene, set in a similarly eastern landscape of Muslim Spain, that punctuate the opening sequence of the story. King Felice of Almeria proves to be a failed ruler, husband, and father. His wife, in charting her son's reunion with his beloved Christian Blancheflour, unwittingly paves the way for her kingdom's conversion to Christianity. While the Wise Woman scene seems to originate in literary depictions of the crusading landscape, the portrait of the emotive, ineffectual ruler proved remarkable versatile for medieval poets depicting other "foreign" cultures, including Scotland (*Sir Degrevant*) and early English society (*Athelston*), to equally damning effect. For a fuller discussion of all three of these Middle English romances, see Part III of this volume. The scene also occurs in the *Erl of Tolouse*, negatively depicting the German emperor.

The early fourteenth-century, Middle English *King of Tars* (c.1330) contains a variation of the Wise Woman scene (ll. 217–77), set within the characteristic eastern, crusading landscape, within the household of the "foreign" king of Tars (i.e., Tartary, the eastern Mongol empire of central Asia), whose kingdom is now Christian (1). Thus, the portrait of this Mongol ruler is favorable rather than discriminatory, initiating the assimilationist agenda of the tale through a positive rather than negative example. The scene occurs as the king has just fled the battlefield trying to defend his kingdom against the forces of the Sultan of Damas (Damascus), who attacks in revenge for being denied the king's beautiful daughter as a bride. The king fights defensively, not offensively, as the victim, not perpetrator, of political overreach. The king, overwhelmed and out of ideas, sits, brooding, in his hall (2) alongside some of his knights, but his emotionalism expresses selfless sorrow (l. 217) for his countless fallen knights rather than frustrated greed. His daughter, rather than his wife, enters (4), and offers an alternative plan, that she marry the sultan to spare the lives of their worthy knights, expressing her faithful idealism rather than political savvy. Rather than questioning his authority, the daughter affirms it by kneeling before her father (l. 221) and asking permission to serve the sultan. Rather than showing internal familial division, the scene develops an exemplary portrait of family unity. The king readily considers his daughter's plan rather than asserting rank over her, revealing a loving father, not a tyrant. The mother enters (3) and initially refuses consent to the plan, preserving rather than threatening cultural (and Christian) tradition, expressing loyalty rather than nascent treason. That the daughter assumes the role normally filled by her mother in this scene prefigures her future role as the wise wife to the sultan, whom she will convert. Both parents respect their daughter's wish to settle peace through marriage, and the three of them, together (l. 277), resolve on the plan that eventually leads to the "progress" of conversion of the sultan's kingdom. Unity, loyalty, and love—not internal division—drive the scene. Thus, this instance of the Wise Woman scene illustrates the benefits of assimilation rather than the costs of backwardness by showing the progress of a "foreign," Mongol ruler who embraces Christianity.

Further Reading

Dominique Battles, *The Medieval Tradition of Thebes: History and Narrative in the* OF Roman de Thèbes, *Boccaccio, Chaucer, and Lydgate* (New York: Routledge, 2004).

Mary Housum Ellzey, "The Advice of Wives in Three Middle English Romances: *The King of Tars, Sir Cleges*, and *Athelston*," *Medieval Perspectives* 7 (1992): 44–52.

Lillan Herlands Hornstein, "The Historical Background of the *King of Tars*," *Speculum* 16 (1941): 404–14.

Sierra Lomuto, "The Mongol Princess of Tars: Global Relations and Racial Formation in *The King of Tars* (c.1330)," *Exemplaria* 31 (2019): 171–92.

Part II

Type-Scene Sequences within Single Works

I Sequencing for Chronology
Boccaccio's Use of the Epic Type-Scene in the *Teseida*

In addition to orienting and guiding reader attention and interpretation through their own internal workings, type-scenes do these same things in combination, as medieval writers sequence such stock scenes to various purposes. Perhaps the most fundamental arrangement of type-scenes serves chronological design, moving the narrative from a natural starting point to an equally natural ending. We all recognize the standard type-scenes of the average romantic comedy: boy meets girl; they fall in love; the first kiss; a brief period of harmony; the first argument; the purported break up; the final reunion and happy ending. While the standard formula can become formulaic, nevertheless, it also enables more inventive writers to engender surprise through simple variations on the formula, including rearrangement.

Similar chronological configurations of type-scenes govern classical epic, and medieval authors could innovate with these scenes through simple changes in placement, thereby changing the scene's original function and meaning. Thus, in the *Knight's Tale*, Chaucer varies the Council of the Gods scene. Typically, this scene of divine council falls at the beginning of an epic as an ordering device, conveying divine oversight and providing the "big picture" and the "long view" of the characters and narrative to follow. Chaucer, however, uses this type-scene of order to foster a sense of *dis*order by placing it unexpectedly in the middle of the tale, in the thick of the conflict, not to mention populating the scene with dubious deities like Saturn. One of Chaucer's inspirations as a writer in the Theban tradition was the Italian poet of the previous generation, Giovanni Boccaccio, whose *Teseida* marks an especially new direction in the medieval tradition of Thebes, and in epic in general, in part through its unusual styling and arrangement of epic type-scenes, which literally forge a new direction.

In 1339, Giovanni Boccaccio began writing what he claimed to be the first epic in the Italian language.[1] He chose as his subject matter the events between the end of the Theban war and the beginning of the Trojan war, an uncharted chapter in ancient history indicated only by signposts in both

DOI: 10.4324/9781003369592-3

the literary and historical accounts of ancient history available to him. Approaching this period as a transitional moment in history, Boccaccio created his *Teseida* as a fusion of elements from the Theban and Trojan wars: he borrows characters, episodes, and narrative circumstances from the Theban conflict, as recorded by Statius, as well as from the Trojan conflict, as preserved in a variety of classical and medieval sources; he designs the main action of the poem (a conflict between two kinsmen over possession of a woman) in such a way that it combines the mode of conflict at Thebes (civil strife) with the source of conflict at Troy (a woman), so that it becomes both a repeat of the Theban conflict and a rehearsal for the Trojan conflict; he populates the armies of the opposing sides with personnel from both the Theban and Trojan wars; and he manipulates epic type-scenes to guide the narrative out of one conflict and into another. The result is what I call a "transitional epic," designed to both substantiate the rather nebulous period between the Theban and Trojan wars and to construct a precise relationship between these two conflicts.

One way Boccaccio affects the narrative transition from the end of the Theban war into the start of the Trojan war involves chronological structure. Organized into twelve books, in imitation of the major classical epics of the *Thebaid* and the *Aeneid*, which take up the matters of Thebes and Troy in twelve books respectively, the *Teseida* divides itself roughly into halves, with the first half tracking the main action of the *Thebaid*. In his study of the *Teseida* against Statius' *Thebaid*, David Anderson highlights the analogous conflict of Etiocles and Polynices over possession of the city of Thebes in books 1–4 of the *Thebaid* and the similar trajectory of conflict between Arcita and Palamone over possession of Emila in books 3–6 in the *Teseida*, the latter text progressing alongside the former.[2] In this way, Boccaccio continues the Theban conflict beyond the end of the Theban war by imitating the narrative progression of that war in the next generation of Theban kinsmen. However, the story's conflict over the heroine, Emilia, resolves as of Book Eight, leaving four books to go. From here, Boccaccio redirects the poem away from the Theban conflict and toward the Trojan war, and he signals that narrative turn by reversing the normal chronological sequence of certain epic type-scenes, effectively backing out of the Theban conflict in the second half of the poem in order to deliver us to the next chapter in history: Troy.

Trojan history helps to make sense of much of the seemingly static quality of the second half of the *Teseida*, perhaps the most frustrating segment of the poem for the modern reader. With the battle over Emilia having ended in Book Eight, the battery of the plot has expired. From this point, the narrative shifts into a series of ceremonies (an awards ceremony, a funeral, funeral games, and a wedding) in which, as one scholar says, "quasi-epic heroism seems continually on the point of being wholly subsumed by courtly ritual."[3] The narrative seems to continue to no end. It is also at this point in the poem that the correspondences in the main action between the *Teseida* and the *Thebaid*, documented by Anderson, begin to break down (although Boccaccio continues to borrow material from Statius). The apparent formlessness of the poem from Book Eight on has led more than a few scholars to feel that Boccaccio somehow lost control over his material at this point, leading to the poem's reputation as a "failed epic."[4] If, however, we approach the second half of the poem as a preview for the Trojan war, it becomes clear that Boccaccio maintains his original intent for the poem as an epic and that he exercises very tight control over his material.

Boccaccio structures the second half of the *Teseida*, from the battle of Book Eight to the ending in Book Twelve, around a series of epic type-scenes, characteristic of Latin epic, each of which echo Thebes and anticipate Troy and that function collectively in the narrative as a transition device between the two conflicts. The scenes are as follows: 1) the formal description of a woman, or blason (not a feature of ancient epic but a standard rhetorical device in medieval epic and romance), 2) funeral games, 3) the arming of the hero, and 4) battle. I will discuss them in the order that they appear in the *Teseida*.

The battle of Book Eight of the *Teseida* has been characterized as more of a medieval tournament than an epic battle, despite Boccaccio's avowed intentions of writing the first Italian epic.[5] After all, it operates along explicit rules, with each side being assigned exactly one hundred combatants, is presided over by a judge, Teseo, who refers to the battle as "giuoco a Marte" (7.13, "games for Mars"), and takes place in an amphitheater before an audience. Moreover, unlike Latin epics, the *Teseida* confines the battle neatly to a single book and a single battle. Thus, despite his conscious imitation of classical epic models, Boccaccio appears to diminish the most central activity of ancient epic: war. The battle of Book Eight, therefore, seems to have less in common with epic battle and more in common with epic (and medieval) martial games. This is because, as Anderson has revealed, Boccaccio modeled the battle of Book Eight on the funeral games of *Thebaid* VI, the games commemorating the death of Archemorus (known to Boccaccio as Opheltes).[6] The result is what Anderson calls a "simulated war"; not a war but a rehearsal for war. More importantly for our purposes, games in ancient epic serve a proleptic function in that they preview the course and outcome of the war to come. Statius' games are no exception, and he announces the games in *Thebaid* VI as an exercise by which "praesudare paret seseque accendere virtus" (6.3–4, "martial spirits may prepare to catch fire and may have a foretaste of the sweat of war").

Boccaccio appropriates this proleptic function of the epic games by using his battle/games as a foretaste of war; in this case, the Trojan war. Indeed, most of the combatants in the battle will later fight at Troy, and Boccaccio evaluates their performance in battle (both in the catalog of Book Six and during the battle itself) not in terms of this war but in terms of the Trojan war. For example, Agamemnon assumes the same leadership role here that he will later have at Troy; Pollux shows that he "per Elena a Troia/al grande Ettor donata molta noia" (8.25, "would have given great Hector considerable trouble at Troy for the sake of Helen"); Ulysses and Diomedes share the same close association in Athens that will surface at Troy in their embassy to Priam, while Diomedes acts with the characteristic impetuousness that he will later display at Troy. So, too, we have the cameo appearance of Dictys (8.34), the name of the Greek chronicler who followed Idomeneus and Meriones to Troy and who left what medieval readers considered an eye-witness account of the Trojan war from the Greek perspective. Appropriately, Boccaccio shows him in this single instance attempting to rescue Minos, who, according to Dictys' own account, bequeathed the rule of his cities and lands to none other than Idomeneus and Meriones.[7] Finally, Boccaccio interrupts the battle with Emilia's Helenesque lament from atop the walls (8.94ff.), an example of the epic type-scene *teichoscopia* so famously performed by Helen atop the walls of Troy. (No such scene occurs in the *Thebaid*; certainly not during the funeral games.) Boccaccio appears to have modeled his battle on Statius' games not simply because the games better suit the style and scale of a medieval tournament but also because games in Latin epic typically function as a preview of war.[8]

A ceremony follows the battle in which Emilia grants prizes to the winner, Palamone. In Book Nine, Teseo presents Palamone to Emilia to do with as she pleases. She decides to set him free and bestows on him a series of gifts which, for the most part, include battle gear: a sword, a quiver, arrows, a Scythian bow (recalling her own epic origins as an Amazon), a charger, a lance, and armor crafted by Vulcan. This scene in Book Nine has not generally been recognized as an "arming of the hero" scene for the rather obvious reason that the battle is now over. After all, the occasion for the splendid armor has passed, and the armor now seems superfluous.

However, several elements in the scene indicate that Boccaccio had in mind the epic type-scene of the Arming of the Hero. First, there is no other formal arming of a hero—either Arcita or Palamone—anywhere else in the *Teseida*. There is a brief mention of the heroes having spurs placed on them just prior to battle, but there is no catalog of the armor used by either man. This scene in Book Nine comes the closest to such a catalog. Second, armor crafted by Vulcan, the Roman blacksmith god, is a very powerful signal for the epic hero going into battle. Vulcan's armor, in particular, which has a magical and prophetic quality in classical epic, is typically bestowed upon the hero before, not after, battle and generally guarantees the hero's triumph. Aeneas, for example, receives armor made by Vulcan just before going into battle with Turnus. In fact (and this is my third point), Emilia's words upon bestowing the battle gear on Palamone echo Venus' words as she bestows Vulcan's armor on Aeneas:

> ". . . perciò che tu dei vie più a Marte
> che a Cupido dimorar suggetto,
> ti dono queste, acciò che, se in parte
> avvien che ti bisogni, con effetto
> adoperar le puoi; esse con arte
> son fabricate, che sanza sospetto
> le puoi portar: forse l'adoperrai
> dove vie più che me n'acquisterai.—"
> (Tes. 9.75)

> [". . . since you must remain more the subject of Mars than of Cupid, I give you these gifts, so that should it chance that you need them, you can use them to advantage. They have been made with skill, so you may bear them without qualm. Perhaps you will make use of them where you will gain much more than me."][9]

As a recipient of Vulcan's armor and as "più a Marte che a Cupido dimorar suggetto" ("more the subject of Mars than of Cupid"), Palamone clearly follows in the footsteps of the ancient epic hero.[10]

However, what distinguishes Boccaccio's arming of the hero from previous examples in classical epic is the placement of this scene within the larger narrative. It would seem that Boccaccio intends this scene of the arming of the hero to anticipate a war other than the one in Teseo's Athens, and, in fact, Emilia's own words point to a future battle when she says, "'forse l'adoperrai dove vie più che me n'acquisterai'" (9.75, "'Perhaps you will make use of them where you will gain much more than me'"). Since there is no further armed conflict in the *Teseida* after Book Eight, Boccaccio primes the reader in this scene, as elsewhere, for a future conflict beyond the scope of his own poem; and, in the chronology of ancient history, that can only mean the Trojan war—a war which will also revolve around the possession of a beautiful woman.[11]

Boccaccio follows up this episode with another epic type-scene: the funeral games of Book Eleven.[12] Very briefly, funeral games occur in ancient epic when a prominent figure dies, and sports competitions are held in his honor for which prizes are given (e.g., Anchises of the *Aeneid*). In this case, the games are held in honor of Arcita (11.18–29), whose funeral just prior to the games contains numerous echoes of Archemorus' funeral in *Thebaid* VI. At first, however the funeral games in Book Eleven seem to suffer from the same purposelessness as the Arming of the Hero scene did before it, for the simple reason that the battle has already taken place in the *Teseida*; and thus, the funeral games would seem to have lost their function as a preview of the war.

However, the funeral games of the *Teseida* do anticipate war, the Trojan war, and we can see this by looking through the roster of winners, all of whom have some connection with Troy and its aftermath[13]: Idas (11.59) (who sailed with Jason and the Argonauts in the expedition that sparked the first destruction of Troy—an event related by Dares and Dictys and by Guido delle Colonne), Theseus (11.62) (who abducted Helen prior to her more famous abduction by Paris), Castor and Pollux (11.59 and 64) (the brothers of Helen of Troy), Agamemnon (11.68) (the famous Greek general on the battlefield of Troy), Evander (11.66) (later allied with Aeneas and the one who guides Aeneas around the area that will later become Rome). Thus, through these winners, Boccaccio previews the Trojan conflict in all its stages: 1) "First sack of Troy" indicated by Idas, whereby the young Priam's sister Hesione was abducted, 2) "Abduction of Helen" indicated first by Theseus, whose earlier abduction of Helen is alluded to in the games, and second by Castor and Pollux, for after the first attack on Troy, Paris abducts their sister, Helen (allegedly in revenge for the abduction of Hesione), 3) "Siege of Troy" indicated by Agamemnon, who commanded the Greek forces on the Trojan plain, and 4) "Fruition of Troy" indicated by Evander, who was instrumental in Aeneas' enterprises as recounted in the *Aeneid*. Thus, the winners of the games of Book Eleven represent each phase of the Trojan conflict, from its inception to its fruition.

Boccaccio employs a final type-scene in the last book of the *Teseida*, Book Twelve: a blason, or a catalog of female beauty, in this case Emilia's. While the blason belongs to the romance tradition rather than to the tradition of ancient epic, we do find them in medieval adaptations of ancient history, such as Guido delle Colonne's *Historia Destructionis Troiae*; thus, it is by no means unusual for Boccaccio to employ one in his own adaptation of classical Latin epic.[14] Book Twelve presents a peaceable resolution to the conflict of the *Teseida*. Mourners cease their grieving for Arcita, Palamone marries Emilia, and the numerous kings and nobles who participated in the conflict return home. In every way, this seems a happy ending, as the optimism of romance appears to triumph over the destructive threat of epic—of Theban history. As part of his description of the wedding festivities of Palamone and Emilia, Boccaccio pauses in the main action of the episode to describe Emilia in a formal blason (12.52ff.), comparing her various features to fruits and flowers, praising each for its good proportion.

The content of the blason of Emilia is unremarkable, a textbook example of *descriptio* applied to female beauty, proceeding from head to toe, focusing mostly on the face and skipping over indescribable parts (12.63). Such descriptions of female beauty constitute a rhetorical commonplace in medieval romance and in the poetic handbooks of the twelfth century.[15] Of course, there are numerous and wonderful variants of this device throughout the Middle Ages (especially in the works of Chaucer), but this blason of Emilia is not one of them. Yet the various critical discussions of this particular blason all focus on its rather ordinary content while overlooking its extraordinary function within the larger narrative of the *Teseida*.[16]

One constant in the tradition of the blason, certainly for narrative, is that it occurs early in the story, generally when the woman first appears or shortly thereafter. There is a simple reason for this: beautiful women generate narrative. Conflicts and quests so often revolve around them. Thus, for instance, Guido delle Colonne describes Helen from head to toe early in Book Seven of his *Historia*.[17] Emilia would appear to prove no exception to this rule since without her there would be no *Teseida*. Why, then, would Boccaccio wait until the end of the poem to describe her beauty (the very source of the conflict)? Why end his narrative with a device that normally launches a narrative?

By focusing, instead, on its placement at the end of the *Teseida*, it appears that Boccaccio introduces the blason of Emilia as a narrative hinge joining both the end of his narrative and the beginning of the story of Troy and the wars of Thebes and Troy at the opposite ends of the *Teseida*. First, Boccaccio, quite self-consciously, calls attention to his strategic placement (or misplacement) of the blason through a formal rubric: "Disegna l'autore la forma e la bellezza di Emilia, e prima invoca l'aiuto delle Muse" (12.51, "The author describes the appearance and beauty of Emilia, and he first invokes the help of the muses"). He marshals the rhetorical tradition of such formal descriptions, a tradition that would normally place it at the beginning of a narrative, not at the end. Secondly, Boccaccio bookends the blason with images of Thebes on one end and Troy on the other, and specifically, the sources of those conflicts: at the beginning of the blason, he invokes those muses "la quale Anfioni/astate a chiuder Tebe" (12.52, "who helped Amphion enclose Thebes"), recalling the beginning of Theban history, the construction of the city which became the source of conflict; at the end of the blason, Boccaccio depicts Menelao gazing upon Emilia and comparing her to Helen (12.67), the source of the Trojan conflict. The reference to Helen situates the ending of the *Teseida* at the very beginning of the Trojan war (Menelaus and Helen are still together at this point). Finally, Boccaccio situates the blason in the epic, not romance, tradition in the stanza that follows: the wedding celebrations include musicians as skilled as the "Anfion tebeo" ("Theban Amphion") and songs so well-written that "sarebbero stati/belli a Caliopè" ("they would have been lovely to Calliope,") the muse of epic poetry (12.72). Thus, despite the closure of conflict promised by this "romance ending," the celebrations themselves announce a continuation of epic concerns—of war—and the only war on the horizon at the end of the *Teseida* is the Trojan war.

Perhaps the most ingenious way that Boccaccio manipulates epic type-scenes as a structuring device for his epic involves his placement of them as a group, for when we chart the sequence of these scenes as they occur in the *Teseida*, we see that they occur in precisely the reverse of the order in which they would normally appear in classical Latin epic (and much of medieval romance). Examined within the exclusive parameters of the poem itself, these four episodes seem to lock the narrative into a series of false starts whereby the hero receives his armor after the battle is over, and where the funeral games showcase warrior talent that will serve no greater challenge, and where the heroine is admired only after her fate has been sealed through marriage. Since the outcome of the Athenian affair has been resolved by Book Eight, episodes which typically generate narrative become stripped of their potential to foster mystery and suspense. Thus, the second half of the *Teseida* seems to turn into one never-ending state function.

However, by approaching the *Teseida* as a transitional epic that attempts to fill the temporal gap in ancient history between the sieges of Thebes and Troy, it becomes clear that Boccaccio enacts on the level of narrative structure the same transition that he is trying to achieve on the chronological level. The following chart compares the arrangement of these scenes in two Roman epics with their arrangement in the *Teseida*:

Order of Type-Scenes

	Statius' Thebaid	*Virgil's Aeneid*	*Boccaccio's Teseida*
Blason	—	—	Book 12
Funeral Games	Book 6	Book 5	Book 11
Arming of Hero	—	Book 8	Book 9
Battle	Books 7ff.	Books 9ff.	Book 8

In the first half of the *Teseida* (excluding Book One), Boccaccio mirrors the narrative sequence of the first half of Statius' *Thebaid*, moving from the beginning of the conflict between two Theban kinsmen to the tournament (which corresponds to Statius' funeral games of *Thebaid* VI). At this point, he reveals the outcome of the struggle at Athens but does not end the poem here. In the second half of the *Teseida*, Boccaccio continues to borrow from Statius but abandons the narrative structure of the *Thebaid*. In its place, he substitutes a series of type-scenes common to Latin epic but unfolds each of them in reverse order, so that the poem ends the way most classical and medieval narratives begin.[18] Taken as a sequence, the four epic type-scenes punctuating the second half of the *Teseida* (the Battle, the Arming of the Hero, the Funeral Games and the Blason) move the narrative from the end of one conflict to the beginning of another. In the meantime, Boccaccio fills these episodes with Trojan personnel and allusions to the Trojan war, thus affecting a narrative transition into the siege of Troy. Boccaccio's highly imaginative use of epic type-scenes in the second half of the *Teseida* has gone largely unnoticed precisely because it defies the narrative logic of ancient epic, but we see that the poem in its entirety is thoroughly grounded in that tradition, from beginning to end.

Notes

1 Boccaccio composed the *Teseida* somewhere between 1339 and 1341. He seems to have begun the work while living in Naples, and he completed it after he had moved back to Florence. See Vittore Branca, *Boccaccio: The Man and His Works*, trans. Richard Monges (New York: New York University Press, 1976), 49; David Anderson, *Before the* Knight's Tale: *Imitation of Classical Epic in Boccaccio's* Teseida (Philadelphia: University of Pennsylvania Press, 1988), 7. On the *Teseida* as the first epic in the Italian language, Boccaccio addresses his work as "*primo a lor cantare/di Marte*" (12.84)["the first to sing of Mars"]. Many scholars feel that Boccaccio alludes to Dante's list of subjects suitable for vernacular poetry which includes (along with love and moral rectitude) "arms" (*arma*). See Dante Alighieri, *De vulgare eloquentia*, ed. P.V. Mengaldo, in *Opere minori*, 2 vols (Milan and Naples: Ricciardi, 1979), 152.
2 See Anderson's chart comparing the plot structure of the *Teseida* and the *Thebaid* in *Before the* Knight's Tale, 79.
3 Winthrop Wetherbee, "History and Romance in Boccaccio's *Teseida*," *Studia sul Boccaccio* 20 (1991–92): 173–84, 174.
4 For a concise history of the critical bias toward the *Teseida* as a failed epic, see Anderson, *Before the* Knight's Tale, 1–37. Even a critic like Piero Boitani, who has devoted much of his career to Boccaccio's works, including the *Teseida*, accuses Boccaccio of "often losing sight of the main thread of his story and thus diluting the compactness and consequentiality of his theme." See "Style, Iconography and Narrative: The Lesson of the *Teseida*," *Chaucer and the Italian Trecento* (Cambridge: Cambridge University Press, 1983), 185–99, 187.
5 Rita Librandi, "Corte e cavalleria della Napoli Angioina nel *Teseida* del Boccaccio," *Medioevo romanzo* 4 (1977): 53–72.
6 Anderson, *Before the* Knight's Tale, 97–119.
7 *The Trojan War: The Chronicles of Dictys and Crete and Dares the Phrygian*, trans. R.M. Frazer, Jr. (Bloomington and London: Indiana University Press, 1966), 23.

8 For further discussion of the Trojan elements in the catalog of warriors, see James H. McGregor, *The Shades of Aeneas: The Imitation of Vergil and the History of Paganism in Boccaccio's* Filostrato, Filocolo, *and the* Teseida (Athens and London: University of Georgia Press, 1991), 64–66.

9 Venus' comparable lines in the *Aeneid* read:

"en perfecta mei promissa coniugis arte
munera. ne mox aut Laurentis, nate, superbos,
aut acrem dubites in proelia poscere Turnum." (8.612–14)
["Here are the gifts I promised, Forged to perfection by my husband's craft, So that you need not hesitate to challenge Arrogant Laurentines or savage Turnus, However soon, in battle."]

R.A.B. Mynors, ed., *P. Vergili Maronis Opera* (Oxford: Clarendon Press, 1969); *The Aeneid*, trans. Robert Fitzgerald (New York: Vintage Books, 1981). In both scenes, the armor is the work of Vulcan and is bestowed on the hero by a female figure as a gift (i.e., not actually placed on the hero but granted to him). Both women indicate that the armor can be used with confidence (without qualm or hesitation).

10 Thideüs of the OF *Roman de Thèbes* carries a sword crafted by Vulcan, a detail that emerges well before the battle begins. Constans, ed., *Roman de Thèbes*, 2 vols., (Paris: Librairie de Firmin Didot et Cie, 1890), ll.1561–62.

11 There is some incongruity here in that Palamone does not fight at Troy, since, after all, Boccaccio created him as a fictional character and thus he does not appear in the accounts of Troy.

12 For a discussion of the games in Book Eleven as Boccaccio's attempt to create an atmosphere of pagan authenticity in the theater at Athens, see James H. McGregor, *The Image of Antiquity in Boccaccio's* Filocolo, Filostrato *and* Teseida (New York: Peter Lang, 1991), 150–59.

13 Although Boccaccio claims that many others participated in the games (11.67), these are the only winners named for the event.

14 See, for example, Guido's descriptions of Helen (VII.171ff.), Andromache (VIII.264–67), Cassandra (VIII.268–72), Polyxena (VIII.273–81), and Briseida (VIII.191–99).

15 Geoffrey of Vinsauf's *Poetria Nova*, for instance, devotes an entire section to describing female beauty, proceeding from head to toe and likening a woman's features to fruits and flowers. See *The Poetria Nova of Geoffrey of Vinsauf*, trans. Margaret F. Nims (Toronto: Pontifical Institute of Medieval Studies, 1967), ll. 550–620.

16 Robert Hollander suggests that this very sensuous description participates in the submission of the Terrestrial Venus to the Celestial Venus that marks the ending of the poem, a view shared by Victoria Kirkham. Hollander, *Boccaccio's Two Venuses* (New York: Columbia University Press, 1977); Kirkham, *The Sign of Reason in Boccaccio's Fiction* (Florence: Leo S. Olschki Editore, 1993), 203. Hope Weissman, for example, views the catalogue as a "masterful performance of . . . vacant and vacating detail." See "Aphrodite/Artemis// Emila/Alison," *Exemplaria* 2 (1990): 89–125, 106. Disa Gambera accounts for the late description of Emilia within the context of other formal descriptions in the poem, suggesting that Emilia memorializes "virginal sexuality." Her body becomes a monument, and as such, it "walls up the troubling chapters of Theban History." See "Disarming Women: Gender and Poetic Authority from the *Thebaid* to the *Knight's Tale*," Dissertation Cornell University, 1995,

208. Carla Freccero concurs that the blason provides one last instance where "courtly romance, as genre, is deployed to resolve the conflict set up in the epic presentation of the heroines" (notably, their Amazon origins). See "From Amazon to Court Lady: Generic Hybridization in Boccaccio's *Teseida*," *Comparative Literature Studies* 32 (1995): 226–43, 239.

17 *Historia*, VII.171–230.

18 James H. McGregor argues that the second half of the *Teseida* is a "partially disguised version of the second half of the *Aeneid*" (47). He sees Theseus as "a kind of Aeneas" (49), the conflict between Palamone and Arcita as modeled on that of Aeneas and Turnus (47), and Emilia as "a Dido figure" (65). While he has done much to bring the epic machinery of the second half of the *Teseida* to the forefront, his larger reading is not in keeping with the chronological framework that Boccaccio works so hard to abide by. See *The Shades of Aeneas*, 44–103.

II Sequencing Type-Scenes for Characterization
Anglo-Saxon as Other in the Middle English *Athelston*

Certain type-scenes come pre-loaded with suspicion. The scene strikes a minor key through tell-tale cues—of setting, choreography, or circumstance—that prime the reader to distrust central characters, even before they say anything. Three such type-scenes are the Outlaw Gathering, the Wise Woman, and the Crowd of Onlookers. The outlaw of the first scene, the foreign ruler of the second scene, and the heathen despot of the final scene all fall outside respectable social norms for the medieval audience and single-handedly make trouble that consumes the entire narrative. As a rule, these type-scenes announce distinct and mutually exclusive story types: the Outlaw Gathering signals the English Outlaw tradition; the Wise Woman belongs to narratives of cultural and/or territorial expansionism; and the Crowd of Onlookers dramatizes martyrdom in a saint's legend. Though each of these scenes is designed to incriminate, the specific criminals involved occupy different worlds, and therefore, different story-types. In the Middle English *Athelston*, however, these worlds collide when these three iconic type-scenes converge within a single narrative, featuring a ruler who checks all the boxes of the "bad guy" implied in each type-scene. The poem charges Athelston with multiple crimes, committed in multiple settings. The poem becomes a case study of Athelston's problem personality by piling on negative stereotypes from three literary domains, which all frame the root of his problem in his cultural identity.

The late-fourteenth-century Middle English *Athelston* features an English king, on English soil, presiding over English subjects. While many scholars agree that his volatile, eruptive behavior, which targets innocent children and pregnant women, including his own wife, sets a negative example of kingly conduct and differentiates him from most other early English kings elsewhere in the corpus of Middle English romance, none have examined his Anglo-Saxon cultural identity as a culprit in his crimes. After all, other Anglo-Saxon, or Anglo-Saxon-styled kings of English romance, figures like Murry of *King Horn*, Athelwold of *Havelok the Dane*, or Orfeo of *Sir Orfeo*, present a benevolent and beloved, if endangered, portrait of early

DOI: 10.4324/9781003369592-4

English monarchy. Athelston, however, in his disconnection from his people and amateurish handling of governmental procedure, seems, in every way, foreign to the task of governing. The poem, in fact, casts him in the role of a racial and cultural foreigner—an Other—by means of three type-scenes whose language suggests racial and cultural difference.

The poem opens with the Outlaw Gathering type-scene through the language of poetic convention, invoking the English Outlaw tradition, a tradition rooted in Anglo-Saxon resistance to the Norman Conquest, immediately incriminating this English king. Later in the narrative, the poet employs the Wise Woman type-scene, designed to portray incompetent foreign rulers. Athelston's emotive body language conforms to that of similarly styled, foreign, and non-Christian rulers, therefore disqualifying him from the highest office of the realm. Finally, the poem ends with the Crowd of Onlookers type-scene of hagiographic tradition. As Athelston insists on subjecting his pregnant sister, Edith, to the judicial ordeal by fire, Edith's language while standing on the hot ploughshares echoes the language of a tortured saint of a saint's life, ironically casting Athelston as a heathen despot persecuting Christians. Thus, the poem's various forms of conventional language in these type-scenes, expressed by the poet, the protagonist, and his victim alike, function to frame the Anglo-Saxon Athelston not simply as a villain but as a foreigner, despite his English nationality.

The first type-scene employed in the poem that serves to marginalize Athelston as an Anglo-Saxon participates in the English Outlaw Tradition. The Outlaw Gathering scene occurs in the very opening of the poem, where four messengers meet randomly on the side of the road. The men are perfect strangers, and yet, they quickly enter into a pact of sworn brotherhood. The poet announces "Off foure weddyd breþeryn I wole ʒow tel" (l. 10). He then tells us "By a forest gan þey mete/Wiþ a cros, stood in a strete/Be leff vndyr a lynde . . . (ll. 16–18). Several scholars have traced this image of meeting at the edge of a forest under the leafy boughs as a verbal formula distinctive to the English Outlaw Tradition.[1] For example, in the outlaw narrative *The Tale of Gamelyn*, when Gamelyn and his servant Adam flee into the forest, "Adam lokede tho vnder woode-bowʒ" (l. 633), where he spies the band of outlaws living. Gamelyn asks if he might join them in exile "vnder woode-lynde" (676), and eventually becoming their leader "vnder woode-schawes" (l. 696), living well among "his mery men vnder woode-bough" (l. 774), these being just some of the instances of this image in poem, always in connection with the forest-dwelling outlaws.[2] This same imagery of outlaws meeting under the leafy boughs becomes a stock phrase in the later, fifteenth-century Robin Hood tales, where Robin and his men live in the forest in perpetual resistance to corrupt authority.[3] While the verbal echoes between the opening lines of *Athelston* and similar phrases in other tales certainly establish its connection with the English

Outlaw tradition, its plot does not. Gamelyn and Robin Hood never become kings like Athelston, and Athelston never takes up residence in the forest with a band of merry men wielding bows like other outlaws. Nor is *Athelston* typically classified among the outlaw narratives, like *Gamelyn* or the Robin Hood tales.[4] Nevertheless, the poetic gesture toward the Outlaw Tradition in *Athelston* accords with the poem's post-Conquest dating, in which Anglo-Saxon identity became powerfully associated with outlaws.

The outlaw context of the opening lines in the ME *Athelstan* is part and parcel of the poem's Anglo-Saxon milieu, as configured in the post-Conquest period. The English Outlaw Tradition, by several accounts, has its roots in Anglo-Saxon resistance to the Norman Conquest, where dispossessed Anglo-Saxon noblemen, stripped of their titles and estates, took refuge in the forests where they waged a guerilla war against the Normans, becoming known as the *silvatici*, ("forest-dwellers" or "wild men"). The most famous leader of this resistance, the Lincolnshire nobleman Hereward "the Wake," whose efforts to reverse the Conquest spanned the late 1060's and early 1070's, forms what Maurice Keen calls "the lineal ancestor of the later English outlaws," including Gamelyn and Robin Hood.[5] Numerous episodes in the story of Hereward inspired similar scenes in a host of Middle English poems, including *King Horn, Havelok the Dane, Sir Orfeo*, and *The Tale of Gamelyn*, all stories featuring dispossessed heroes attempting to restore what is rightfully theirs.[6] Thus, the peculiar scenario in *Athelston* of four men in servile occupations (messengers), all of them perfect strangers, bearing Anglo-Saxon names, one of them holding royal lineage, who enter into a sworn pact of mutual cooperation and suddenly rise into major positions of authority, begins to make more sense within the context of the English Outlaw Tradition of the post-Conquest period, whose abiding fantasies of political overthrow and restoration of a lost Anglo-Saxon past become miraculously realized in the lives of Athelston and his three "breþeryn" (l. 23). In this instance, however, Athelston's affinities with the other outlaws of Middle English literature does not make him into an underdog hero who commands our sympathies. Rather, the evocation of the Outlaw Tradition in the very opening lines of *Athelston* predisposes us to see him as a troublemaker, an unreliable custodian of the realm at odds with its normal functioning, a suspicion soon borne out by his blunt and cruel handling of judicial procedure.

In addition to framing Athelston as an outlaw, the poem introduces a second type-scene that further profiles and incriminates Athelston as an Anglo-Saxon ruler, this one occurring amidst the central "courtroom drama" of the poem. As King Athelston succumbs to the rumor of Egelond's treason, a rivalry ensues in the poem between the older, pre-Conquest judicial ordeal preferred by Athelston and contemporary, post-Conquest legal practice for such criminal cases, including those involving treason, when Athelston's queen suggests that the case be handled, alternatively, "be comoun sent/In þe playne parlement" (l. 265–6). Her suggestion gains further affirmation later from Archbishop Alryke (l. 448). The term "playne parlement" refers to a collaborative, judicial body of the king's court, consisting of peers of the realm who gather to preside over a specific case, as opposed to the general Parliament tasked with debating new policies and procedures.[7] Essentially, the queen and Alryke refer to the great innovation of post-Conquest English law: the jury system, whereby legal cases were determined by a jury of peers who have examined the evidence of the case.[8] While by no means immune from abuse in practice, the jury system promised to mitigate against arbitrary and potentially unfair applications of justice, such as we see in the poem.[9] As Helen Young has noted, this contrast of pre- and post-Conquest legal practice in the poem also contrasts private and public approaches to justice, implying greater objectivity afforded by the "playne parlement," which involved a public hearing of the evidence and a shared verdict, as opposed to Athelston's highly subjective handling of the case without any legal counsel, a practice forbidden even to the king by late-fourteenth-century English law.[10] The poem never delivers a live contest between the "playne parlement" and the ordeal by fire, as Athelston forbids any further mention of the parliamentary tool. Nevertheless, by placing these two options of justice side by side, the poet invites a comparison of the two, pitting a model of pre-Conquest justice in direct opposition to post-Conquest legal practice, and in doing so, calling into question the validity of the ordeal as a mechanism for determining truth.

Amidst this contest of past and present legal systems, the *Athelston*-poet inserts a type-scene, the Wise Woman scene, used elsewhere in Middle English romance to delineate foreign (and inferior) cultural status in a leader, by way of discrediting Athelston and his choices of justice. The queen, hearing of the arrest of the innocent Egelond, his wife Edith, and their children, enters into the hall where Athelston sits, pondering his decision. Deferring to him as "Sere kyng" (l. 259) as well the father of their unborn child (l. 260), she appeals to him to handle the matter by "playne parlement" (l. 266) rather than via the ordeal, a request he rejects outright, saying "þy bone schal nouȝt igrauntyd be" (l. 268). When she falls to her knees in tears to pray for all of them, the king grows angrier and more defiant, accusing her of disobedience. His verbal rejection extends into physical rejection when "Wiþ hys foot. . . He slowȝ þe chyld ryȝt in here wombe" (ll. 282–3), resulting in the miscarriage of their male baby, his future heir. Understandably, the king's violent gesture against his pregnant wife has consumed the field of vision in scholarly discussions of this scene, focusing us squarely on the queen. Scholars have explored this well-known scene of "the kick" for its unusual depiction of woman's superior political wisdom and the horrendous price she pays for speaking up, discussions that focus primarily on the queen herself.[11]

However, the scene is equally distinctive for what it tells us about the king, Athelston. Drawing upon wider literary tradition, the scene constitutes an example of a type-scene used primarily to discredit a male-ruler—specifically, one of *foreign descent*. The scene originated in the literature of the crusades for characterizing the eastern Other, and spread from there. The scene consists of a domestic setting involving an emotionally volatile ruler pursuing an extreme and destructive course of action that violates the rights of others. Encountering a setback in his plan, the ruler retreats to his home, where he broods in frustration. His wife enters, patiently questions his motives, and suggests an alternative course of action, revealing her superior grasp of political realities. Almost without exception, her advice fails to divert him from his foolish path. It becomes a stock scene clearly intended to expose the husband's shortcomings as a leader, as in each case, his inability to control his violent emotions overwhelms his capacity to reason and govern, and his wife sounds more like a patient mother than a spouse.[12] We find this scene in poems like *Sir Degrevant*, *Floris and Blancheflour*, and *The Erl of Toulouse*, among others, all poems sharing a non-English setting, whether it be Scotland, Muslim Spain, or lands of the Holy Roman Empire. The occurrence of this stock scene between emotive husband and his more sensible wife in other Middle English poems of the period, where the ruler in question is culturally Other, contextualizes this same scene in *Athelston* by signaling his cultural otherness, which, in this case, derives from his Anglo-Saxon identity. In this sense, the poet distinguishes between competing versions of Englishness, whereby to be Anglo-Saxon is to be foreign and inferior, despite one's "English" nationality.

We find the Wise Woman type-scene in the Middle English poems *Sir Degrevant*, the *Erl of Tolouse*, and *Floris and Blancheflour*, all poems featuring a foreign ruler. In brief, in *Sir Degrevant*, the aggressive earl of the poem is styled on Scottish earls and border lords who vied with one another—and with English landholders of the region—for dominance. The earl of the poem features in the Wise Woman scene.[13] After waging unprovoked raids on his neighbor's lands, he escapes back to his castle "wonded to scham" (l. 374) and "lam" (l. 375).[14] Approaching him in his broken state, his wife, the countess, asks him "'Haue ye nat parkus and chas?'" (l. 378), wearily implying that he should cease his raids. Like a naughty schoolboy, he apologizes and makes an (empty) promise to stop raiding (ll. 382–4). The Wise Woman scene also occurs in the *Erl of Tolouse*, where the emperor "in Almayn" (l. 13, "in Germany"), "full woo" (l. 133), finds himself similarly taken to task for raiding his neighbor's lands by his wife,

Dame Beaulybon, who boldly concludes "'Ye haue the wronge and he the ryght'" (l. 154), again, to no avail.[15] Likewise, the Muslim parents of young Floris in *Floris and Blancheflour* engage in two similar domestic conversations (ll. 41–79 and 131–53), where they debate ways of separating their son, Floris, from the Christian girl he loves, Blancheflour. In both cases, the emir's wife refutes his suggestion to kill the girl, with the somewhat less violent solutions of, first, sending Floris away for a while, and, when that fails, selling Blancheflour to merchants. In the second domestic scene, we again have the tell-tale combination of an emotive, foreign male leader motivated by "wreth/wraþ" ("anger," ll. 137, 139) being advised by a wife with better sense, who, in this case, prevails.[16] The ubiquity of the Wise Woman scene in tales with foreign settings and featuring foreign rulers helps to account for its occurrence with Athelston, where the king bears a family resemblance to these other ineffectual and dangerous rulers.

If *Athelston* opens like an Outlaw narrative, it ends in the manner of a saint's life, and the shift in genre ushers in our last type-scene—the Crowd of Onlookers scene—in which Athelston is framed not just as an outlaw and a foreigner, but as a heathen despot. As I mentioned, the judicial ordeal tests the innocence not just of Egelond, the friend suspected of treason, but also of his wife, Edith. Like the queen, Edith is in advanced pregnancy, and the ordeal poses a direct threat to her unborn baby, making her yet another obvious innocent victim of the king's myopic understanding of the crisis at hand. She and the baby survive the ordeal unharmed, and the scene closes with the miraculous birth of St. Edmund, already pre-canonized. As in the earlier type-scene involving the queen, the pregnant woman and baby have naturally consumed the scholarly field of vision, given the cruelty imposed on them, and given the surprise appearance of St. Edmund, a pre-Conquest English saint.[17] However, the scene achieves its greatest innovation in its depiction not so much of Edith but of Athelston himself.

Edith's trial highlights cultural difference in ways that cannot be overstated, and in ways that have direct bearing on our understanding of this judicial ordeal as an expression of Anglo-Saxon culture. Her trial forms a type-scene within the hagiographic tradition involving an innocent Christian subject standing accused before a heathen despot, often in a foreign land, surrounded by a crowd of sympathetic onlookers, who model the appropriate emotional response to Christian suffering. For example, in the *Life of St. Cecilia*, the heroine, an early Christian in ancient Rome, faces a similar trial by fire in the form of boiling, on the order of the Roman executioner, Almachius, and, like Edith, her body remains unharmed. In fact, she "lay for more than a day and night, in the bath above the burning fire, as though she were in cold water."[18] Her house in Rome forms the site of her torture as well as the recent site of four hundred baptisms among her followers and sympathizers. Likewise, in Chaucer's *Man of Law's Tale* (ll. 610–93), Constance finds herself standing trial on false charges of murder, and while she does not suffer physical torture like Cecilia, the trial includes the same elements of innocent Christian (female) subject, heathen king/judge Alla, and a crowd of sympathetic onlookers who model the proper emotional response for the reader. Moreover, in her case, religious difference coincides with cultural difference, as she remains an outsider in a foreign land. In *Athelston*, Edith follows in the footsteps of the innocent saintly subject undergoing persecution when she enters into the fire "And callyd it merye and bryȝt" (l. 635), emerging "vnblemeschyd foot and hand" (l.642), in clear vindication for her innocent suffering. Her children, too, pass over the hot ploughshares unharmed, and even echo Celicia's experience in calling the fire "cold inowȝ" (l. 610). In how it follows the pattern of the trial type-scene from hagiographic tradition, the scene is unremarkable. What does differentiate this scene from others of its kind, however, concerns Athelston himself, who is neither heathen nor foreign but Christian and English. His "difference," rather, consists, once again, of his Anglo-Saxon identity within the larger English cultural landscape. As the type-scene invariably frames the king/judge as an unjust victimizer of the innocent, the poem therefore frames Anglo-Saxon identity, or at least his version of it, as a force to be overcome.

But what about St. Edmund, the miracle baby born at the end of the narrative? Is not he, too, Anglo-Saxon? In the larger project in which I explore the two kings of the poem, I identify Athelston and Edmund as competing versions of Anglo-Saxon identity that came to dominate the political landscape of the late fourteenth century, cutting along class lines.[19] In this regard, I feel it is critical that, unlike the pre-Conquest kings we find elsewhere in ME romance, who are purely fictional and do not align, in name or otherwise, with any historical Anglo-Saxon kings, both Athelston and Edmund do, in fact, correlate to historical kings: the tenth-century King Athelston (924–939) and King Edmund the Martyr (855–869). In other words, we are dealing with real kings, representing real policies that could affect the policies of the present. Athelston, as I have explored, seems to embody a confrontational model of Anglo-Saxon identity, rooted in political resistance and championed by the servile classes of late medieval English society. These artisans, peasants, and lesser political leaders worked through the nation's court system, waging numerous lawsuits aimed at defending their rights against the encroachments of heavy-handed landlords intent on freezing wages and restricting economic advancement. In these court cases, peasant plaintiffs referenced a number of pre-Conquest kings, including Athelston, for legal precedent in their claims. This political vision comes under sharp censure in the poem, *Athelston*, where we get a worst-case scenario of Anglo-Saxon legal precedent applied in late fourteenth-century London. The poem, I feel, challenges the peasant nostalgia for the "good old days" under the Anglo-Saxon kings. To counter this seemingly misplaced nostalgia, the poet posits a more acceptable, non-confrontational model of Anglo-Saxon identity in the figure of St. Edmund, a model rooted in a shared faith tradition and long championed by English monarchs of the post-Conquest period. In watching Athelston defer to baby St. Edmund at the end of the poem, bequeathing his realm to Edmund, we see a capitulation of the more rebellious, politically subversive uses of Anglo-Saxon identity, in preference of a state-sanctioned Anglo-Saxon figure representing the status quo.

Thus, while Athelston joins the ranks of pre-Conquest kings appearing in post Conquest Middle English romance, he stands apart from figures like King Murry, King Athelwold, and other kings who are modeled, at least in part, on Anglo-Saxon monarchs, in his glaring unfitness to rule. The three type-scenes structuring the poem uphold a sustained critique of King Athelston, placing him outside the law, outside of medieval English culture, and even outside of the Christian faith, despite his legitimate membership in all three. The unrelentingly corrosive portraiture of Athelston by means of these stock scenes, drawn from wider Middle English literary tradition, ultimately frames him as unreliable, even dangerous, and they do so by calling into question his cultural identity as an Anglo-Saxon, evoking it only to incriminate it. Rather than a nostalgic portrait of a pre-Conquest ruler, such as we see elsewhere, we get a caricature of an early English monarchy in the figure of Athelston, an irrational autocrat bearing the name of a famous Anglo-Saxon king.

Notes

1 Laura A. Hibbard, "*Athelston*, a Westminster Legend," *Publications of the Modern Language Association* 36 (1921): 223–44, 231–32; also Nancy Mason Bradbury, "The *Tale of Gamelyn* as a Greenwood Outlaw Talking," *Southern Folklore* 53 (1996): 207–23, 216.
2 Other forms of this image in *The Tale of Gamelyn* occur on ll. 638, 771 and 803. See W.W. Skeat, ed., *The Tale of Gamelyn* (Oxford: Clarendon Press, 1893).
3 For similar language and imagery of meeting under greenery, sometimes involving oaths, in the Robin Hood tradition, see *Adam Bell, Clim of the Clough, and William of Cloudesley* (ll. 1–4, 189–90, 380–81, 405), and *A Gest of Robyn Hode* (ll. 316, 704, 844, 948, 1096, 1136, 1189–92, ff.). Both are collected in Stephen Knight and Thomas Ohlgren, eds., *Robin Hood and Other Outlaw Tales* (Kalamazoo, MI: Medieval Institute Publications, 2000), 235–67 and 80–168. See also Bradbury, "The *Tale of Gamelyn* as a Greenwood Outlaw Talking," 221, n.17.

4 *Athelston* is most commonly classified under "The Matter of England" romances, despite the fact that it has no known source. Charles W. Dunn categorizes it under "Romances Derived from English Legends," in J. Burke Severs, ed., *A Manual of Writings in Middle English* (New Haven: Connecticut Academy of Arts and Sciences, 1967), 2–37, 33–34; also Rosalind Field, "Romance as History, History as Romance," in Maldwyn Mills, Jennifer Fellows and Carol M. Meale, eds., *Romance in England* (Woodbridge, Suffolk: D. S. Brewer, 1991), 163–73. Dieter Mehl categorizes it under "Homiletic Romances," in *The Middle English Romances of the Thirteenth and Fourteenth Centuries* (London: Routledge and Kegan Paul, 1968; reprint 2011), 148–52. Within the general heading of "Matter of England" romances, W.R.J. Barron includes *Athelston*, tentatively, under the sub-heading "Romances of Greenwood," as a precursor, of sorts, to the later Robin Hood tales. See *English Medieval Romance* (London: Longman, 1987), 63–88, 81.

5 See Maurice Keen, *The Outlaws of Medieval Legend*, 2nd ed., (London: Routledge, 2000), 11 and 23. Keen devotes two chapters to the legend of Hereward, 9–38. Concurring with Keen's assertion that this tradition emerged out of the political conflicts of the Norman Conquest, Thomas Ohlgren identifies the story of Earl Godwin, whose conflicts with a French advisor of Edward the Confessor are preserved in the anonymous *Vita Ædwardi Regis* (c.1065–1067), as the "earliest extended account of outlawry in English literature." See Thomas H. Ohlgren, ed., *Medieval Outlaws*: *Ten Tales in Modern English* (Stroud: Gloucester: Sutton Publishing,1998), "General Introduction," xvii, and Timothy S. Jones' introduction to the *Vita*, 1–4.

6 See Dominique Battles, *Cultural Difference and Material Culture in Middle English Romance: Normans and Saxons* (New York: Routledge, 2013), 107–45.

7 See Helen Cam, *Law-Finders and Law-Makers in Medieval England* (London: Merlin Press, 1962), 17; Geraldine Barnes, *Council and Strategy in Middle English Romance* (Cambridge: D.S. Brewer, 1993), 55–56; Robert Allen Rouse, *The Idea of Anglo-Saxon England in Middle English Romance* (Cambridge: D.S. Brewer, 2005), 131.

8 On the development of the jury system in medieval England, see Doris M. Stenton, *English Justice Between the Norman Conquest and the Great Charter 1066–1215* (Philadelphia: The American Philosophical Society, 1964), 13–17; Alan Harding, *The Law Courts of Medieval England* (London: George Allen & Unwin, Ltd., 1973), 32–63.

9 The Middle English *Tale of Gamelyn* dramatizes abuses of the jury system in late fourteenth-century society. See Richard W. Kaeuper, "An Historian's Reading of 'The Tale of Gamelyn'," *Medium Aevum* 52 (1983): 51–62; also Edgar F. Shannon, "Mediaeval Law in *The Tale of Gamelyn*," *Speculum* 26 (1951): 458–64. On how the legal practice of the poem also traces lines of pre and post-Conquest cultural identity. See Battles, *Cultural Identity and Material Culture in Middle English Romance*, 52–55.

10 See "*Athelston* and English Law: Plantagenet Practice and Anglo-Saxon Precedent," *Parergon* 22 (2005): 95–118, 114.

11 See Nancy Mason Bradbury, "Beyond the Kick: Women's Agency in *Athelston*," in Corinne Saunders, ed., *Cultural Encounters in the Romance of Medieval England* (Cambridge: D.S. Brewer, 2005), 149–58, 150–51; Mary Housum Ellzey, "The Advice of Wives in Three Middle English Romances: *The King of Tars, Sir Cleges,* and *Athelston*," *Medieval Perspectives* 7 (1992): 44–52,

50; Elizabeth Ashman Rowe, "The Female Body Politic and the Miscarriage of Justice in *Athelston*," *Studies in the Age of Chaucer* 17 (1995): 79–98, 82–83; John Carmi Parsons, "The Pregnant Queen as Counsellor and the Medieval Construction of Motherhood," in John Carmi Parsons and Bonnie Wheeler, eds., *Medieval Mothering* (New York: Garland Publishing, Inc., 1996), 31–61, 43–51.

12 See Ellzey, "The Advice of Wives in Three Middle English Romances: *The King of Tars, Sir Cleges,* and *Athelston*," 48–51; Parsons, "The Pregnant Queen as Counsellor and the Medieval Construction of Motherhood," 51.

13 See Dominique Battles, "The Middle English *Sir Degrevant* and the Scottish Border," *Studies in Philology* 113 (2016): 501–45; also "The Middle English *Sir Degrevant* and the Architecture of the Border," *English Studies* 96 (2015): 853–72, and "Behind Enemy Lines: The German Connection in the Middle English *Sir Degrevant*," *Neophilologus* 100 (2016): 1–13.

14 All citations to *Sir Degrevant* are from L.F. Casson, *The Romance of Sir Degrevant* EETS, o.s. 221 (London: Oxford University Press for the Early English Text Society, 1949).

15 All citations to the *The Erl of Tolouse* are from Walter Hoyt French and Charles B. Hale, eds., *Middle English Metrical Romances* (New York: Russell and Russell, 1964), 283–419.

16 See A. B. Taylor, ed., *'Floris and Blancheflour': A Middle English Romance* (ed. from Trentham and Auchinleck MSS.) (Oxford: Clarendon Press, 1927).

17 See Rosalind Field, "*Athelston* or the Middle English *Nativity of St. Edmund*," in Rosalind Field, Phillipa Hardman, and Michelle Sweeney, eds., *Christianity and Romance in Medieval England* (Woodbridge, Suffolk: Boydell and Brewer, 2010), 139–49; Rowe, "The Female Body Politic and the Miscarriage of Justice in *Athelston*," 96–97.

18 See Leslie A. Donovan, ed. and trans., *Women Saints' Lives in Old English Prose* (Cambridge: D.S. Brewer,1999), 57–65, 65.

19 "The Middle English *Athelston* and 1381: The Politics of Anglo-Saxon Identity," *Studies in Philology* 117 (2020): 1–39.

III Sequencing for Virtuosity
The "Sleeping After the Feast" Type-Scene in *Beowulf*

Generally, a single type-scene will occur infrequently, often only once, in a narrative. After all, the important thresholds of a narrative, where type-scenes cluster, tend to be crossed only once. The blason of the beautiful love interest of a romance will occur once, when she first appears in the story, to signal her centrality to the heroic project. A formal arming-of-the-hero scene will often occur once, just prior to the pivotal heroic challenge of the tale. The epic descent scene will occur once, as a divine intercessor redirects a stalled hero back onto his mission. The crowd-of-onlookers scene will occur once, toward the end of a saint's life, at the martyrdom of the saint. That certain scenes (e.g., a blason) tend to double as chronological markers of the story accounts for their singularity, as things happen at the beginning of the story that will not happen later. The OE *Beowulf* presents a compelling exception to this general pattern by punctuating the story with the same type-scene, Sleeping After the Feast, again and again. We get six instances of the type-scene in the poem proper and the intimation of many, many more that have taken place during the twelve years that Grendel has been attacking Heorot, amounting to countless instances of this same scene. However, the repetition of the scene never gets repetitive. Quite the opposite. In the discussion that follows, we see how the Old English poet varies the core elements of the scene (six in all) with each new iteration. By emphasizing one of the elements over the others and varying which elements he favors, the *Beowulf*-poet demonstrates the stunning variety he can affect with a single type-scene within a long poetic tradition.

In Old English poetry, feast-scenes are the quintessential expression of joy and well-being.[1] For those partaking of them as well as for those who sadly recall them in less happy times, feasts define the good life. The image of warriors at their mead-cups, served by attendants moving busily among the benches, is invariably accompanied by descriptions of happiness—*gleo, dream, wynn, bliss, sæl*.[2] Feasts are also the occasion for establishing and reaffirming ties that bind the community together: the lord dispenses gifts, while the retainers, in turn, pledge their loyalty. Ritual gestures punctuate the whole. Yet, an ominous current of potential strife often moves just below the surface of harmony and happiness. If many Old English poems equate the feast with "bliss," as when the *Dream of the Rood* depicts heaven as the place "where the Lord's people are seated at the feast" (*þær is dryhtnes folc geseted to symle*, 140b-41a), others depict it as the occasion for dissension and violence, giving rise to the type-scene of "Sleeping After the Feast," a version of the "fatal feast" found throughout ancient and medieval poetry, whose particular styling makes it distinctive to Old English literary tradition.

A variety of factors may have contributed to the frequent "fatal feast" images in Old English poetry. Perhaps the most obvious is that feasting involves letting down one's guard, and therefore, creates an opportunity for violence, both from within (as in, for example, the drunken flyting described by *Juliana*) and from without (as when the Assyrians are routed in *Judith*). Moreover, if feasting symbolizes the good life and expresses social harmony, it is a short step to articulating the transience of happiness and the breakdown of order through the disruption of a feast. Finally, Old English poetic diction often associates "sleep" with "death." Several traditional compounds, especially those that equate graves with beds, associate "sleep" and "death": *wælbedd* ("bed for carrion"), *wælrest* ("resting place for carrion"), *morðorbedd* ("bed for the murdered"), *neobed* ("bed for corpses"), *hildbedd* ("bed for [those slain in] battle"). One of the poetic synonyms for "to kill" is "to put [someone] to sleep," *swebban, aswebban, aswefan*.[3] A gnome in *Solomon and Saturn* makes the connection between sleep and death explicitly: *slæp bið deaðe gelicost* (l. 313, "sleep is most like death"). Thus, feasting, conventionally being followed by sleeping, is connected figuratively with a death-like state.

This is precisely the combination of elements present in the "Sleeping after the Feast" type-scene: "feasting," "sleeping," and "death" (or the threat of death, that is, "danger"). It is so strong, in fact, that, in Old English poetry, a mention of feasting and sleeping is inevitably followed by a powerful threat. This seems to be an Anglo-Saxon version of Chekov's loaded gun: it is never *not* fired. Whenever an Old English feast-scene is followed by sleeping, danger—usually outright carnage—is automatic. The basic triad further divides into six elements: 1) feasting, 2) sleep, 3) unawareness of impending doom, 4) the approach of an aggressor to the hall, 5) the aggressor enters and looks at the victim(s), and 6) the aggressor attacks or threatens.

These six elements organize themselves in two types of "Sleeping after the Feast" passages, distinguished by time of day, each having somewhat different structures, contexts, and associated elements. The first and more common variant of the theme is "Night-Attack," which has the following pattern: the victims feast and go to sleep in the hall; they do not realize that they are fated to die; the aggressor approaches and penetrates the hall; he looks at the sleeping victims and then attacks. The "Night-Attack" is a stealth operation: it takes place at night and inside the victims' safe-haven—the hall. The second variant of the theme, "Morning attack," lacks the elements leading up to the assault (feasting, approach of night, aggressor's approach, and so on). Instead, it launches straight into a description of hung-over victims being attacked. Rather than playing up the victims' ignorance of their approaching doom, these scenes focus on fatal-feast metaphors (likening deadly sword-blows to drinks being served at a feast).

This chapter explores the Sleeping After the Feast type-scene in the OE *Beowulf*, demonstrating not only the centrality of this scene to Old English poetry, but also how poets could display poetic virtuosity in varying their use of the scene, even in the same work, interjecting surprise into the predictable formula.[4] The basic matrix of feasting-sleeping-danger allows poets considerable freedom in elaborating the theme, despite quite a bit of verbal repetition; therefore, no two instances of the theme in an individual poem are exactly alike, even as they share the same underlying pattern. For instance, the three attacks of the Grendel-kin on Heorot are obviously very similar, but the *Beowulf*-poet varies the scenes enough to keep them from becoming rote. Even so, the key phrase *swefan æfter symble* ("sleeping after the feast") occurs in three of the five "Sleeping after the Feast" passages in *Beowulf*.

Instance 1

One could argue that the Sleeping After the Feast type-scene predicates the whole of *Beowulf* in forming the central—and recurring—nature of conflict necessitating Beowulf's arrival. After Hrothgar has Heorot built, he holds a feast. The hall reverberates with the joy of feasting and with the *scop*'s song of creation (88–90a), and this, after an unspecified time, provokes Grendel's nocturnal raid. This is the first "Sleeping after the Feast" passage in the poem (with the above motifs indicated):

(4) Gewat ða neosian syðþan niht becom,
hean huses, hu hit Hring-Dene
(1) æfter beorþege gebun hæfdon.
(5) Fand þa ðær inne æþelinga gedriht
(2) swefan (1) æfter symble; (3) sorge ne cuðon,
wonsceaft wera. Wiht unhælo,
grim ond grædig, gearo sona wæs,
reoc ond reþe, ond (2) on ræste (6) genam
þritig þegna, þanon eft gewat

huðe hremig to ham faran,
mid þære wælfylle wica neosan.
[115–25, (4) "Then, after night arrived, Grendel departed to seek out the high hall, to see how the Ring-Danes had arrayed it (1) after the beer-drinking. (5) There he found, inside, the company of noblemen (2) sleeping (1) after the feast; (3) they did not know grief, the misery of humankind. The unholy creature, grim and fierce, soon made himself ready, savage and cruel; he (6) took thirty thanes, (2) asleep, and then departed to journey back to his home, exulting in his booty; with that fill of carrion he sought out his dwelling."]

The type-scene is signaled most clearly when the poet mentions that the Danes are *swefan æfter symle*, "sleeping after the feast," 119a. This is a formula that the poet also uses in the gnomic passage cited previously (1008a, *swefeþ æfter symle*). Other mentions of "feasting" and "sleeping" in this passage, or in close proximity, include *æfter beorþege* 117a ("after beer-drinking"), and *on ræste* 122b ("reclining," "sleeping"). These serve as cues to alert the audience to the peril of the situation—danger follows feasting and sleeping—and indeed, Grendel quickly kills thirty of Hrothgar's retainers. This early instance of the scene includes all six elements of the type-scene: feasting, sleeping, unawareness of impending danger, the approach of an aggressor (Grendel), the aggressor entering and looking at the victim(s), and his fatal attack. This single attack soon becomes habitual, as Grendel attacks for twelve years.

Given that Grendel has been attacking Heorot for so long, always following the same pattern, the poet establishes an infinite loop of Sleeping After the Feast scenes, disrupted only by the arrival of Beowulf. This rut of countless repetitions of the same scene, *without* variation, therefore, is itself a variation on the type-scene.

Instance 2

A playful example of the "morning-attack" version of the Sleeping after the Feast type-scene occurs in *Beowulf* as he recounts his earlier deeds against monsters to King Hrothgar and his thanes. In this instance, the poet innovates with element 6 of the type-scene ("the aggressor attacks and threatens"), with Beowulf, not the monsters, as the aggressor. Beowulf casts his struggle against sea-monsters (559–67a), using language of the fatal feast:

Swa mec gelome laðgeteonan
(6) þreatedon þearle. Ic him þenode

deoran sweorde, swa hit gedefe wæs.
(3) Næs hie ðære fylle gefean hæfdon,
manfordædlan, (1) þæt hie me þegon,
(1) symbel ymbsæton sægrunde neah;
ac on mergenne mecum wunde
be yðlafe uppe lægon,
(2) sweordum aswefede, þæt syðþan na
ymb brontne ford brimliðende
lade ne letton.
["In this way, spiteful enemies often (6) pressed me hard. I served them with my precious sword, as was proper. (3) They had no joy from that plenty, the evildoers who (1) meant to eat me, sitting about (1) feasting near the bottom of the sea; instead, in the morning, (2) they were lying up along the shore, put to sleep by my sword, so that thereafter they did not hinder the passage of ocean-travelers through the broad passage."]

The theme's three defining elements are clearly present: feasting (the monsters *symbel ymbsæton*); sleeping (they are *aswefede*); and death ("putting them to sleep with the sword" means killing them). Beowulf, with further irony, compares himself to an attendant "serving" (*þegnian*) the monsters with his sword. He serves up a kind of "plenty" or "feast" (*fyllo*) very different from what the sea-creatures desire.[5] Immediately after these verses, the poet describes the sun rising, giving the scene a morning-setting: *leoht eastan com,/beorht beacen Godes* (559b-60a, "daylight, God's bright beacon, came in the East"). The humor of this instance of the Sleeping After the Feast scene clearly derives from how the monsters, not Beowulf, are on the receiving end of this fatal feast.

Instance 3

The Sleeping After the Feast type-scene occasions the hero's first great feat of the poem. While all six elements of the type-scene are at play, the poet innovates especially with elements 4 ("the approach of the aggressor") and 5 ("the aggressor looks at his victims") by giving us the perspectives of the hero and the monster alike. Beowulf's arrival at Heorot is celebrated with a feast, followed by a voluntary repetition of the fatal feast sequence in order to end the deadly cycle. The poet has the Geats fall asleep because that is the usual pattern: feasting—sleeping—danger. Sleeping, as noted previously, is intimately linked with death, not only by the *Beowulf*-poet, but within the tradition as a whole. Preceding Grendel's approach, both "feasting" and "sleeping" are described in great detail: the ending of the feast is described from lines 642–687; the following lines, 688–709, repeatedly mention sleeping (especially 688–96a, 703b-05a, 708–09). Then, Grendel approaches (710–19). This scene is remarkably similar to the first night-attack, but much more elaborately developed: elements 1 and 2 (the onset of night, the feast's end, and sleeping) are developed in lines 642–709; 4, the aggressor's approach, is described in 710–19; and 5 and 6, the aggressor's entry and attack, occur in 720–36a. An excerpt from the latter part of this "Sleeping after the Feast" passage shows the poet's innovation, as it differs from the first instance of the theme:

(4) Com þa to recede rinc siðian,
dreamum bedæled. Duru sona onarn,
fyrbendum fæst, syþðan he hire folmum æthran;
onbræd þa bealohydig, ða he gebolgen wæs,
recedes muþan. (4) Raþe æfter þon
on fagne flor feond treddode,
eode yrremod; him of eagum stod
ligge gelicost leoht unfæger.
(5) Geseah he in recede rinca manige,
(2) swefan sibbegedriht samod ætgædere,
magorinca heap. Þa his mod ahlog . . .
[720–30a, "(4) Then came the warrior, deprived of joy, approaching the hall. The door, though reinforced with metal, quickly sprang open when he touched it with his hands, for he was angry; intent on killing, he tore open the hall's mouth. (4) After that the adversary quickly stepped on the variegated floor; he walked along, spoiling for a fight. An ugly light, most like a flame, shone in his eyes. (5) He saw many warriors, a band of kinsmen, (2) sleeping near each other in the hall. Then he rejoiced in his heart . . ."]

This passage puts great emphasis on Grendel's gaze. His eyes are described in horrid detail, and then, the perspective shifts so that we are looking through these very eyes: we see "many warriors, a band of kinsmen, sleeping near each other in the hall." His joy, of course, soon turns to fear. In an interesting reversal of a motif often associated with "Sleeping after the Feast," it is the *aggressor* who does not know that he is "fated": *Ne wæs þæt wyrd þa gen,/þæt he ma moste manna cynnes/þicgean ofer þa niht* (734b-36a, "But it was not fated that he should eat any more men that night").

Appreciating the force of this association also helps to make sense of what is surely one of the strangest moments in *Beowulf*. The Geats guarding Heorot against Grendel promptly *fall asleep*. Everyone knows that the monster will attack; Hrothgar deputizes Beowulf and makes a hasty exit, for he *wiste þæm ahlæcan/to þæm heahsele hilde geþinged* (646b-47, "knew that battle was intended against the hall by the demon"). After the Danes leave, one would expect Beowulf and his men to prepare for battle. So, how do the Geats prepare? Do they decide on a strategy? Do they post guards to warn them of Grendel's approach? Do they polish their swords and keep their shields close at hand? No. They all go to sleep! Moreover, they fall asleep fully expecting to die, as the poet explains at length (691–96a). The poet qualifies this by adding, rather vaguely, that they knew that Grendel could not kill them if "the Lord did not wish it." (This, however, is no consolation to Hondscioh! Nor do the other Geats know if "the Lord did not wish" their deaths.) Before his departure, Hrothgar explicitly and publicly warns Beowulf to remain awake: *waca wið wraþum* (660a, "wake for the foe"). Yet, they do not. However, the poet varies the Sleeping After the Feast type-scene by keeping one man awake—Beowulf: *sceotend swæfon,/þa þæt hornreced healdan scoldon,/ealle buton anum* ("the warriors who were to guard the hall slept, all but one," 703b-05a). True to the type-scene, the men go to sleep and thereby invite danger, but the variation of Beowulf's *not*-sleeping tips the balance of danger away from the monster and toward the hero himself, and that makes all the difference.[6]

Instance 4

Yet another variation of the Sleeping After the Feast type-scene in *Beowulf* occurs immediately following Grendel's wounded retreat from Heorot. In this instance, the poet innovates on the type-scene through element 2 ("sleep") by making it metaphorical, rather than literal, to mean death. True to the type-scene, we have the predictable triad of sleeping, feasting, and danger. After Grendel has fled from Heorot, the poet states (1002b-1008a):

No þæt yðe byð
to befleonne—fremme se þe wille—,
ac gesecan sceal sawlberendra,
nyde genydde, niþða bearna,
grundbuendra gearwe stowe,
þær his lichoma legerbedde fæst
(1) swefeþ (2) æfter symle.
["It is not easy to flee from this, whoever may try it! Compelled by necessity, each of those endowed with souls, each of the earth-dwelling sons of men, must seek out the prepared place where his body will (1) sleep securely (2) after the feast, on his resting bed."]

Here, *swefan æfter symle* ("sleeping after the feast") is a metaphor for "death after life."[7] The "prepared place" or "resting bed", of course, is the grave.[8] What is interesting about this particular instance of the theme is its gnomic—rather than narrative—nature. Nonetheless, this variation of the scene shows the enduring association between sleeping, feasting, and death, in Old English poetic tradition and for the *Beowulf*-poet, in particular.

Instance 5

In the fourth instance of the Sleeping After the Feast type-scene and the final night-attack passage, the Danes are once again caught unawares, this time by Grendel's mother. In this instance, the innovation on the type-scene concerns its emphasis on element 5 ("unawareness of danger"), as the Geats and Danes now believe the danger to be over. Indeed, Beowulf has defeated Grendel. Therefore, mentions of sleep, in this iteration of the scene, are continually paired with indications of the men's lack of awareness of danger. The feast celebrating Grendel's death ends, like the others, with the onset of night (1232b-37a):

(2) Þær was symbla cyst;
druncon win weras. (3) Wyrd ne cuþon,
geosceaft grimme, swa hit agangen wearð
eorla manegum, (1) syþðan æfen cwom
ond him Hroþgar gewat to hofe sinum,
rice to ræste
["(2) The best of feasts was there; the men drank wine. (3) They were unaware of fate, of grim destiny—this has happened to many men—(1) after the evening came, and mighty Hrothgar departed to his dwelling to sleep."]

The poet mentions the Danes' ignorance of fate two more times in this passage. He says that *Beorscealca sum/fus ond fæge fletræste gebeag* (1240b-41, "one of those revelers was fated to die as he sank onto his bed"), and ten lines later, adds, *Sigon þa to slæpe. Sum sare angeald æfenræste* (1250–51a, "Then they went to sleep. One of them paid dearly for that evening's rest"). Then Grendel's mother appears on the scene, making her way toward Heorot, *ðær Hringdene/geond þæt seld swæfun* (1279b-80a). In all, the poet mentions five times that the Danes are asleep, and therefore unaware, when she attacks.

How do we know that the collocation of the key elements—sleeping, feasting, and danger—is not simply chance? After all, it would be natural

144 *Type-Scene Sequences within Single Works*

for the Danes to sleep after drinking. However, three points suggest otherwise. First, the *Beowulf*-poet combines these elements in contexts where this is not "natural" (cf. *swefan æfter symle*,1008a, in the gnomic passage). Second, the fact that the Geats sleep when Grendel attacks is not "natural" either. And third, there are other, more innocuous feast-scenes in the poem, but these *never* mention sleeping. The long feast-description after the hero's return (1977–2199) does not conclude with Hygelac, Beowulf, and the other Geats falling asleep. It is the combination of feasting and sleeping that signals danger. And the *Beowulf*-poet never fails to fire Chekhov's gun. It is one of the chief means for generating tension and irony in the first half of the poem.

Instance 6

A particularly illuminating passage of sleep as the danger-signaling element in the "Sleeping after the Feast" scene is Beowulf's mutilation of Grendel's dead body in the mere-dwelling. In this instance, variation of the scene concerns the poet's emphasis on the hero's righteousness, even as now becomes the aggressor and mimics the monsters' behaviors. Though the scene does not employ the feasting-sleeping pattern, it does shed light on its emotional and psychological dynamics. Having killed Grendel's mother with the giant-sword, Beowulf looks about for Grendel's body and discovers it lying in repose: *he æfter recede wlat*, 1572a ("he looked around the hall"), and then *he on ræste geseah/guðwerigne Grendel licgan*, 1585b-86 ("he saw the battle-weary Grendel lying there, on a resting-place"). Then Beowulf mutilates Grendel's body by cutting off its head. We should note that the description in 1572a and 1585b-86, especially, exactly mirrors Grendel's earlier actions in Heorot: *geseah he in recede rinca manige,/swefan . . .*, 729–30a ("in the hall, he saw many warriors, sleeping . . ."), after which he *nam þa mid handa . . . rinc on ræste* 746–47a ("then, with his hands he grabbed one of the warriors lying on the resting-place"). These similarities are not coincidental. Rather, they express in verbal terms the ritual eye-for-an-eye retribution of blood vengeance. The poet himself draws this connection (1577b-83a): Beowulf

> . . . hraþe wolde
> Grendle forgyldan guðræsa fela
> ðara þe he geworhte to Westdenum
> oftor micle ðonne on ænne sið,
> þonne he Hroðgares heorðgeneatas
> sloh on sweofote, slæpende fræt
> folces Denigea . . .

[(Beowulf) quickly wanted to repay him for the many attacks that he had perpetrated upon the West-Danes—on many more than one foray—when he killed Hrothgar's household troops in their sleep, when he devoured the sleeping Danes.][9]

Then, as Beowulf desecrates the dead body, the poet once again comments on this (using an ironic figure) as an act of retribution: *he him þæs lean forgeald*, 1584b ("he repaid him for his favors"). This passage twice mentions that the Danes were asleep (*on sweofote, slæpende*) when Grendel killed them; in revenge, Beowulf now maims Grendel's body "lying at rest" (*on ræste licgan*), an expression that is used elsewhere of the sleeping Danes killed by Grendel (122b, 1298b) and of Beowulf as the monster reaches for him (747a). Just as Grendel earlier penetrated the Danes' dwelling and killed the defenseless, sleeping warriors, so Beowulf has invaded the home of the Grendel-kin (explicitly described as *reced*, "hall") and now takes vengeance upon the "sleeping" Grendel.

In essence, the plot of *Beowulf*, especially in its first half, consists of a series of Sleeping After the Feast scenes, six in all (with others, off-stage, implied): 1) a feast initially provokes Grendel's first intrusion into Heorot, where he attacks sleeping warriors; 2) Beowulf employs the scene in relating his earlier slaying of sea-monsters, where he plays the attacker; 3) after the feast occasioned by Beowulf's arrival, Grendel attacks once more during the night; 4) Grendel's wounded retreat from Heorot and impending death is rendered metaphorically as "sleeping" (to mean "dying") after the feast; 5) Grendel's mother strikes during the night following the third feast at which the Danes had celebrated Grendel's death; 6) and Beowulf's retaliatory attack on the mere-dwelling of the Grendel-kin echoes the type-scene yet again. Five of these scenes follow the night-attack "Sleeping After the Feast" pattern (115–25, 642–736a, and 1232–82a), while one follows the morning-attack model. In each case, the poet varies the basic formula of the type-scene by emphasizing one of its six elements over the others, so that each individual iteration of the scene "specializes" in one element (e.g. "unawareness of attack," "sleep," "looking"). The three passages involving the Grendel-kin resemble one another remarkably, especially in their almost cinematographic description of the monsters' approach to Heorot as well as in details and wording. The other passages use the feasting-sleeping pattern not in order to flesh out a narrative skeleton, but allusively, and therefore, have less in common with each other (or the other passages); paradoxically, it is nevertheless the allusive uses of the theme which demonstrate its conventional character. Ultimately, the preponderance of this single type-scene in *Beowulf* attests not only to its emotional and spiritual resonance for the early English audience but also to the opportunity it afforded the Old English poet to display infinite creative possibilities through finite means.

Notes

1 See especially Hugh Magennis, *Images of Community in Old English Poetry*, CSASE 18 (Cambridge, 1996).
2 Jeff Opland, "*Beowulf* on the Poet," *Mediaeval Studies* 38 (1976): 442–67, at 447–48.
3 *Beowulf* 679a, 567a, *Genesis A* 2533a, *Andreas* 72a, *The Battle of Brunanburh* 30a, *The Fates of the Apostles* 69a, *Juliana* 603a, *Judith* 321a.
4 This chapter derives from published and unpublished work on this type-scene by Paul Battles. See "Dying for a Drink: 'Sleeping after the Feast' Scenes in *Beowulf*, *Andreas*, and the Old English Poetic Tradition," *Modern Philology* 112 (2015): 435–57.
5 Like "to serve," *þegnian* can mean both "to obey, to wait upon" or "to serve food or drink" (see Bosworth-Toller, s.v. *þegnian* I and II). Though, grammatically, it fits better with the clause that follows (*þæt hie me þegon*), *ðære fylle* also puns on *Ic him þenode / deoran sweorde*, creating an ironic contrast between the "feast" they are expecting (Beowulf's body) and what they actually receive (his blade). Compare the translation by Howell D. Chickering, Jr.: "I served them well / with my noble blade, as was only fitting. / Small pleasure they had in such a sword-feast, / dark things in the sea that meant to eat me" (560–63).
6 As noted by Marilynn Desmond, "*Beowulf*: The Monsters and the Tradition," *Oral Tradition* 7 (1992): 258–83, 269.
7 See Magennis, "*Swefeþ Æfter Symle*," and Harry E. Kavros, "*Swefan Æfter Symble*: The Feast-Sleep theme in *Beowulf*," *Neophilologus* 65 (1981): 120–28, 122.
8 *Legerbedd* usually means "grave," and its use is not confined to poetry, so one may question whether an audience would have been aware of the literal meaning, "rest-bed." But the poet seems to be activating that literal meaning by punning on the etymological sense. I would see the compound as a not-quite-dead metaphor. Compare the foregoing discussion concerning the "bed" as "grave."
9 Translation by Paul Battles.

Part III

One Type-Scene in Three Different Works

Medieval Cultural Profiling
The Wise Woman Type-Scene in Middle English Romance

The Middle English poems *Floris and Blancheflour*, *Sir Degrevant*, and *Athelston*, among others, all feature a rare and refreshing instance of a prominent wife dispensing sound political advice to her ruler-husband in the midst of a crisis of his own making.[1] While sometimes rejected in the moment, her advice proves ultimately successful as her husband's plans implode, and he finds no alternative but to follow her earlier lead. This domestic scene between husband and wife becomes a recurring scene containing stock elements intended to evoke certain narrative and moral expectations in the reader. Mary Housum Ellzey first called attention to scenes of this pattern nearly thirty years ago, as part of her examination of female counsel in several Middle English poems, including *Athelston*.[2] Exploring these scenes for their unusual depiction of woman's political insight and agency, however limited, Ellzey focused primarily on the wives themselves, as they question their husbands' political decisions and propose reasonable alternatives.

The present study approaches these and other instances of female counsel in two new ways: first, it identifies and names the recurring scene of the Wise Woman *as* a type-scene, comparable to type-scenes like the Arming of the Hero, with preconceived rules and aims that dictate interpretation. Second, it focuses, instead, on the husbands standing corrected, exploring how the Wise Woman type-scene signals his cultural difference from the English audience of the poem. While the ruler's foreignness may be obvious in some cases, as with the Muslim parents of *Floris and Blancheflour* (and comparable poems such as *The King of Tars*), in other instances, the cultural difference of the family depicted has gone largely unnoticed until recently.[3] The scene consistently profiles these men as cultural Other, playing on negative cultural stereotypes, and using the wives as a mouthpiece for the poems' larger, English agendas in the region, whether ideological, political, territorial, or religious, singly or in combination. Although the Wise Woman type-scene prominently features a woman assuming a man's role, the scene is not so much intended to honor the woman as to dishonor

DOI: 10.4324/9781003369592-7

her ruler-husband by casting him as a cultural outsider deserving of censure. More than that, the Wise Woman type-scene signals a distinct story-type of cultural assimilation, using the domestic apparatus to transform the political landscape. It therefore becomes a diagnostic tool, alerting the reader to questions of foreign policy in the poem and enabling us to identify commonalities between seemingly unrelated poems on the basis of this type-scene.[4]

On the whole, the scenes of female counsel discussed in this chapter have highlighted the strength and fortitude of the wife standing up to her tyrant-husband, focusing attention primarily on questions of gender.[5] While meaningful for their insights into some of the most distinctive features of these scenes and texts, these studies have tended to obscure or overlook questions of cultural difference, mainly because, with the exception of *Floris*, the foreign settings and cultures of these texts have largely eluded scholars up to now. Yet, matters of cultural difference not only dictate the framework of the scenes in which these women offer counsel but also change the terms of how we judge these women, as they themselves are generally foreigners. Moreover, these studies approach the wise wife as primarily a *challenger* who critiques public policy and exposes the consequences of tyrannical leadership, of which her husband is a prime example. Yet, in each instance, in challenging her husband, the woman becomes a *collaborator* with English interests in the region. Finally, on the whole, these studies have focused on English *domestic* policy, and have sometimes correlated the tyrannical ruler with an *English* king—notably, Richard II. However, these scenes invariably occur within a foreign culture, whether it be Muslim Spain, Scotland, or the lost world of pre-Conquest English kingship. These women are not aberrations from the English norm. With a single exception, they are not English at all. Above all, approaching the scenes of female counsel through the lens of cultural difference rather than gender alone shifts attention away from the woman and onto her wider culture and its leader, her impossible husband. In so doing, we see, in most cases, the politically astute wife not as an *internal* challenger of English *domestic* policy in the hands of an *English* king, but as a *foreign* agent, and a *proponent* of English *foreign* policy, within enemy territory, under the rule of a *foreign* (and unfit) leader. Above all, given the pattern of foreign settings in which the Wise Woman type-scene occurs, the scene can serve as a diagnostic tool, prompting the reader to look for signs of cultural difference that may not be immediately evident.

Before discussing specific iterations of the Wise Woman scene, it is necessary to establish its parameters as a type-scene. The scene dramatizes a particular emotional distribution between man and woman, used primarily to discredit a male-ruler—specifically, one of foreign descent. The components of the scene are as follows: 1) a non-English setting, either in another country entirely or along the border of the realm, and a noble household within that country/region, 2) a ruler who serves as the poem's antagonist, and who belongs to a culture and/or religious tradition other than that of the English/Christian audience of the poem, 3) the antagonist's wife, who critiques her husband's political and/or religious choices, and in some cases, offers an alternative plan of action. Her plan accords with the "enemy" political/religious agenda at play in the poem, and she unwittingly becomes an agent of political and/or religious subversion, and 4) in many cases, the only child of the antagonist, who is endangered by his/her father's actions, and later, knowingly joins the wife/mother as an agent subverting his/her father's plans.[6] These four core elements occur in each of the instances of the Wise Woman type-scene discussed below, and the subtle variations introduced by each individual poet become so many keys for unlocking the poem's larger concerns, precisely by locating the work within a particular territory where the English crown had political and/or religious claims at stake.

The scene follows a prescribed choreography. We have a domestic setting involving an emotionally volatile ruler pursuing a destructive course of action that encroaches on the rights of others, and often endangers his child. Thus, the scene profiles him doubly as both a political leader and a parent. Encountering a setback in his plan, the ruler retreats to his home and stews in frustration. Where the ruler himself is emotionally fraught, his wife maintains a cool detachment, both from her husband and from the crisis at hand. She enters the hall where he sits alone, patiently questions his motives, and suggests an alternative course of action, revealing her superior grasp of the conflict at hand. In some instances, her advice initially fails to divert him from his foolish path, but, in the end, she prevails and her husband relinquishes his control of the crisis. It becomes a stock scene clearly intended to highlight the shortcomings in the husband as a leader, as in each case, his inability to control his emotions of anger and jealousy overwhelms his capacity to make effective decisions, and his wife sounds more like a patient mother than a spouse.[7] Above all, however, this scene occurs in instances where the ruler in question belongs to a different racial/cultural background than the audience of the poem.

The emotional map of the Wise Woman scene, in effect, undercuts the masculine authority of a foreign ruler by feminizing him. The ruler falls victim to his own powerful emotions of frustration, anger, and confusion, which impedes his ability to reason, let alone govern, thereby taking on the role normally reserved for a female character. In turn, his wife exhibits the emotional profile normally expected of a male ruler; she maintains professional distance from the crisis at hand and displays greater objectivity and maturity in her understanding of the matter, even as it puts her own side in the wrong. Her superior emotional poise renders the ruler himself more feminine than a woman, therefore disqualifying him from rule. As we shall see, this character profile originates in western stereotypes of the Middle East, and indeed, it appears first in Middle English in *Floris and Blancheflour*— one of the earliest ME romances, set in Muslim Spain. As it happens, however, the type-scene proved remarkably versatile for subsequent medieval English poets, who adapted the Wise Woman scene to a variety of cultural and territorial frontiers where the English crown had designs.

The Wise Woman scene forms a brief domestic interlude with a direct bearing on the poem's larger public and political drama by exposing internal weakness in the region. The personal and intimate workings of the scene, therefore, prove every bit as germane to the story's political agenda as any of the scenes of combat and diplomacy.[8] As a rule, these poems systematically discredit a ruler of foreign descent, and, if anything, the Wise Woman scene forms the most damning of all the scenes intended to incriminate the ruler, as it exposes his failings, even within his own household and private life. We see the ruler taken to task by his own wife, and in some cases, undermined by his own child. Despite his earlier bravado in the face of his enemy, we see him weak, frustrated, and confused within his inner family circle; hardly a leader to anyone. Here is a ruler who cannot even keep his own house in order, and his wife has more common sense than he does. His resistance to and detachment from his own wife becomes a metaphor for his political detachment.[9] In the same vein, his often-hostile attitude toward his own child, whose life is endangered by his actions, becomes a further and final metaphor for the unsustainability of his entire cultural and political picture. His way of life has no future, as symbolized by his struggling child. Thus, far from being a break from the main action of the poem, the domestic scene of the Wise Woman offers the deepest insight into the ruler's misguidedness at home and abroad.

Adding insult to injury, the wife and, in some cases, child of the poem function as infiltrators working in tandem to undermine the ruler in question. First, the wife enters into the hall to confront her husband and voices precisely the political objections that would most appeal to an English, Christian audience, becoming a mouthpiece for the opposing side of the conflict, right there in the ruler's own home. Husband and wife then reverse roles; he, the emotive one occupying a domestic space, listens as she assumes the part of political advisor pointing out the shortcomings of his strategy or recommending diplomacy, in the end suggesting a plan that later works against her husband. In this way, she becomes an unwitting ally of the poem's English (or English-allied) hero, working for him behind the scenes, unawares. It is worth noting that she herself, as the wife of the foreign ruler, is culturally Other, allowing for a greater range of permissible behavior, as the rules of conduct for English wives do not apply entirely.[10] Her role, in general, stays at the level of verbal advice, since, as a woman of some stature, she cannot take direct action in the public arena, and since her advice often fails to alter her husband's actions.

However, if the wife's subversion works on the level of thought, the child's subversion works on the level of action. The banner of resistance passes to her child (in those tales featuring a child), who later knowingly works to cross-purposes to his/her father, notably by fraternizing with the "enemy," be that the hero or a sympathetic Christian, becoming yet another counteragent working behind enemy lines. In fact, the actions and fate of the child pronounce the larger political policy at stake in the poem, whether it be religious conversion, territorial expansion, or dynastic viability, all of which bear the banner of "progress." Taken as a pair, the wife and child of these poems transcend limitations of gender and/or age by bringing to an end the destructive policies of the flawed ruler in ways that serve the hero's purposes and affirm the rightness of his cause. Thus, the Wise Woman scene lays the foundation, to a great extent, for later scenes in which the child, charting a new direction that happens to align with the political message of the poem, out-performs his or her father as both a political agent and a spouse, newly wedded outside of the faith/culture of origin.

Floris and Blancheflour

The Wise Woman type-scene occurs in one of the earliest Middle English romances, *Floris and Blancheflour*, dating to c.1250, whose plot revolves around the interfaith and cross-cultural love affair between a Muslim prince and the daughter of a Christian slave.[11] Surviving in four manuscripts of varying incompleteness, the English version of the story belongs to the "aristocratic," as opposed to the "popular," version of the story, a division traced to thirteenth-century French manuscript witnesses, which idealizes the innocent, if forbidden, love of the youthful pair,[12] steering the story out of its roots in the *chanson de geste*, and matters of empire, and toward matters of the heart, both emotional and spiritual.[13] In this regard, concerns of religious conversion continually attend the experience of youthful love.[14] The poem takes us into the household of Floris' Muslim parents living (by earlier French accounts) in Almeria, in southern Spain, and remains almost exclusively in Muslim lands for the duration of the plot, creating a sustained cultural portrait of the Muslim world and "the rare example of a Saracen setting for a story designed for a Christian audience."[15] In this household, we see Floris' father as an eastern ruler, husband, and father, and all three roles come together at the beginning of the tale, where the Wise Woman type-scene forms the first major scene of the poem, followed closely by two further iterations of the same scene, to similar purposes, thereby structuring the entire initial third of the poem (ll. 41–308). The scene, moreover, is prefaced by matters of cultural difference, with references to "Þe Cristen woman" (Blanchefloure's mother, l. 3) and Floris' obligation to marry according to Islamic law ("wyfe after þe lawe," l. 40), which precipitates the central crisis of the poem.[16] While the English adaptation of the legend of Floris undoubtedly prioritizes matters of love over empire, I would suggest that the English poet merely proposes alternate tactics to carry out the story's original mission of religious conversion, using women and children to do the political work formerly and typically assigned to armies—a plan unveiled in the Wise Woman type-scene.[17]

The prominence of the Wise Woman scene in the ME *Floris and Blancheflour*, and its political preoccupations, in fact, distinguishes it from its French antecedents. In her study of the tale, Geraldine Barnes details the English poet's "conscious selectivity" in shaping the narrative specifically around scenes of counsel and strategy.[18] To this end, the poet abridges descriptive passages of objects such as the tomb and the cup, omits formal portraits of the hero and heroine, along with most of the floral imagery, and excises most of the declarations of love, joy, grief, and fidelity.[19] Instead, the English poet emphasizes scenes of dialogue involving advice, planning, and deceit, whereby the Wise Woman type-scene, in its multiple iterations and lengths, comes to predominate. The result is a narrative concerned more "in the manipulative than in the sentimental side of the story" and driven "by a cast of intriguers."[20] As with all of the versions of the story that "expand the conversion material," the English Floris' efforts to rescue and wed Blanchefloure amount to a story whereby Floris and his country "are led on the inexorably path to Christianity, despite all the efforts of his parents to save their country by thwarting the union of their son and the Christian maiden."[21] *Amour*, in all its private ideals, comes to serve concrete, public strategy on the ground which, given the story's eastern setting, revolves around religious conversion of the region. The Wise Woman type-scene(s) in the story participates in this strategy by offering scenes of counsel that expose the eastern leader's shortcomings, while unfolding a plan that will simultaneously lead to his demise and to the rise of an agent (Floris) more in line with European Christian values.

The Wise Woman type-scene pivots on the negative portrayal and discrediting of a foreign leader, in this case, Floris' father, a Muslim King. One of the most pervasive western stereotypes of the Muslim man assumes a violent, irascible, impulsive, and irrational temperament given to extremes of emotion and rooted, to some extent, in the hot climate of Middle

Eastern lands.[22] We see this profile in Floris' father, a Spanish Muslim king, who appears in the narrative almost exclusively within the domestic sphere, as a father and husband, amidst his most intimate relationships.[23] The poem, therefore, gives us a behind-the-scenes glimpse into the private affairs of this foreign ruler. At first, the king acts as any other responsible, loving father, seeing to his young son's education, "on þe book letters to know" (l. 11), and tenderly consenting to Floris' wish that Blancheflour attend lessons with him, saying "'she shal lerne for þy loue'" (l. 24). However, the king grows increasingly concerned when he "vnderstod þe grete amoure/Bytwene his son and Blanchefloure" (ll. 35–6), a situation bound to interfere with Floris' obligation to "wyfe after þe lawe" (l. 40), at which point, the king's tenderness swings toward the opposite extreme. Over several iterations of the Wise Woman type-scene, we watch the king become increasingly overwhelmed by his own emotions, at first by simple "þouȝt," "care," and "woo" (ll. 42–3) in the first scene, then escalating to "wreth" (ll. 137 and 139) in the second, and ending in silent defeat in the third scene, as "Þe kinges hert was al in care" (l. 253) in witnessing his son's own emotional distress at the rumor of Blancheflour's death.

The king's emotional extremes translate into extreme measures in dealing with the crisis, which begins with the nuclear option in the first Wise Woman scene "þat Blaunchefloure be do to deed," "yslawe" (ll. 46–7), a notion that intensifies in the second scene as he specifies the method of execution with "'Fro þe body þe heued shal goo.'" (l. 141). Such extremity bespeaks his struggle to think rationally and subtly or to anticipate future consequences. The king's child-like inability to understand and manage his own emotions short-circuits his judgment, driving him to his wife, on whom he increasingly relies, and who consistently does the thinking for him, exposing him as emotionally and mentally weak and dependent. As the king's ideation regarding Floris' private life invariably affect Floris' future in the political sphere as the next ruler of the kingdom, this series of Wise Woman scenes have political resonance in discrediting the Muslim king's viability as a leader in public affairs by revealing his deficiencies as a leader in his own private affairs.

True to the pattern of the Wise Woman type-scene, the king's wife in *Floris and Blancheflour* not only reinforces the negative cultural stereotypes surrounding her eastern husband-ruler but also becomes an internal agent of western influence within the foreign household, often by means of her own cultural otherness. The crisis concerns the destabilizing Christian element (Blancheflour) in their midst, and its hold on their son's heart, a private danger with broad social and political ramifications. The queen's relationship with the king solidifies the portrait of him as weak, indeed feminine, as she routinely assumes the masculine role of royal advisor, usually at his request, patiently weighing competing options and anticipating future repercussions, thereby playing on western stereotypes of the politically inept eastern ruler. However, in so doing, she also plays into western stereotypes of the "disquieting [Muslim] female" as assertive, unfeminine, and even belligerent in advancing the plot.[24] The total absence in the poem of any male royal advisors to the king only heightens her unusual function.

The queen's role manifests in the first two iterations of the Wise Woman scene, as the king approaches and/or summons her to consult about his plans, at first confessing to her "of his woo,/Of his þouȝt and of his care" (ll. 42–3), awash in emotions and asking her explicitly "'Dame, rede vs what is to do'" (l. 64), while later he "cleped þe queene/And tolde hur all his teene" (ll. 137–8), this time in an emotional rage. Each time, he reveals his dependence on her in matters of state, and each time, he concedes to her plan over his. In the final scene, her authority over the king sheds all pretense when, having just saved Floris from suicide, she rushes to the king in tears and commands "'For Goddes loue, sir, mercy!'" (l. 316) and reminds him that, of their twelve children, only Floris survives, once again overriding the king with her better sense. Their relationship reveals a kingdom governed by weak schemes and even weaker kings, reliant on female counsel and devoid of male competence, confirming western negative stereotypes of the East.

More than that, in her efforts to alleviate her son's anguish, the queen inadvertently becomes an internal advocate for the Christian presence in their lives, ironically by means of her own Muslim identity. As a non-Christian, the queen is not bound by European Christian customs that would limit her agency in matters of state, thereby affording her a broader range of behavior and increased influence.[25] Where her husband consistently plots Blanchefour's death, the queen repeatedly counter-plots the girl's salvation, albeit on other pretexts, always getting her way, and in this sense, working toward western interests in ensuring the future spread of Christianity in Muslim lands.[26] She becomes an agent of future assimilation of her people into the Christian fold—a recurrent role of the Muslim woman in medieval European texts.[27] Perhaps for this reason, the poet ascribes laudable motives to the queen, in part expressed in her private, ulterior motive to "Saue þe mayde fro þe deed" (l.54), in part through her successful counterplots that save Blanchefour, and in part through her repeated insistence to the king "'For Goddes loue, sire, mercy!'" (ll. 144 and 316).

At the same time, however, the queen displays the hallmark trait of trickery often associated with eastern peoples, as she skillfully manipulates her husband to spare Blanchefour by appealing to his wish that Floris "'lese not his honour'" (ll. 57) as a result of the girl's execution, while also deceiving her own son by feigning Blanchefleur's death and burial.[28] Indeed, her scheme to sell Blanchefleur into slavery behind her son's back is comparable to outright execution in its lack of ethics. Each of her thoughts and actions emerge not from love of the Christian Blanchefleur, *per se*, or from any larger moral code, so much as from concern for her son alone. In this sense, preserving the Christian presence becomes a mere byproduct of her narrow ethics as a Muslim woman, brought about by shady means, all of which fail.[29] Thus, the queen's Muslim identity affords her a wider range of agency and influence than comparable Christian queens bound by a stricter ethical code found elsewhere in Middle English literature, traits that conveniently serve western rather than eastern interests, a banner taken up by Floris himself.

From the start, Floris emerges as an agent of religious and political change in the poem, an internal agent of values external to his people. Given his youth, innocence, and undying devotion to his childhood sweetheart, scholars have tended to view him primarily through the lens of *amor courtoise*, an embodiment of a largely ahistorical emotional ideal.[30] Similarly, and in keeping with the courtly ideal, Floris' earthly love for the mortal Blanchefleur transmutes into spiritual love, resulting in his own conversion in the end, again focusing on Floris' inner, private life.[31] However, Floris' emotional preoccupation with Blanchefleur leads him to do concrete political work, at his parents' own expense, no less, rendering him as much a political actor as a literary and spiritual ideal.[32] His function as an internal agent of religious conversion expresses itself immediately in the opening lines of the Middle English version, as the poet specifies, twice, how Blanchefleur's mother "Þe Cristen woman fedde hem thoo" (l. 3) and "she fedde hem in feere" (l. 5) until the age of "seuen ȝere" (l. 6). Christianity is "in the water," so to speak, as Floris is literally nourished by a Christian nurse throughout his infancy.[33] At Floris' own insistence, he and Blanchefleur then attend school together and "myȝt neuer parte atwoo" (l. 30), suggesting that these two children come to share the same mind through a shared education. Likewise, color imagery involving the "white flower" (Blanchefleur) and "red" (Floris), evoking the Christian symbolism of purity and divine love permeates the entire poem.[34] Similarly, Floris' journey to rescue Blanchefleur in Babylon becomes a pilgrimage of sorts, "a literal road to his eventual spiritual salvation," while, by some interpretations, the butterfly imagery during Floris' infiltration into Babylon alludes to similar imagery surrounding the resurrection and rebirth.[35] Thus, Floris' attachment to Blanchefleur inadvertently doubles as adherence to Christian influence. In this way, in body, mind, and heart, Floris orients to Christianity early in life, despite his Muslim identity.

At the same time, true to the pattern surrounding the Wise Woman type-scene, Floris becomes a double agent of sorts, as his portraiture hinges on key negative stereotypes of the eastern character, yet cast in somewhat more acceptable form, and as he works against his own people. For example, the very qualities of youth and innocence that render him so sympathetic as an ideal of *amor courtoise* also render him effeminate and militarily impractical, fulfilling western stereotypes of eastern men as unmanly, and setting him apart from the more typical, mature, and physically formidable heroes of Middle English romance, so many of whom are lovers as well.[36] Indeed, he exerts authority in the narrative not through any martial feats, as would a western hero, but largely through his extravagant wealth, playing on stereotypes of the riches of the East.[37] A. B. Taylor suggests that Floris, as a hero, is somewhat "too fragile and delicate for English tastes," perhaps compromising the extent to which we should take his emotional pathos seriously.[38] That same emotional intensity, which overrides all other aspects of his young life, fuels western stereotypes of the irrational and sensuous eastern male temperament.[39] Floris' youthful nature, therefore, while garnering sympathy for him, simultaneously perpetuates negative stereotyping of the East.

Floris' eastern disposition enables him to effectively both navigate and undermine the eastern landscape he inhabits. His mission to rescue his Christian beloved requires him to engage in trickery and bribery, another negative stereotype of eastern conduct roundly discouraged by the knightly ideal. For instance, he gains entry into Babylon, disguised, through a series of premeditated chess matches and by bribing the gatekeeper with the valuable cup—a task he embraces readily and effectively. Moreover, as Edmund Reiss notes, the game of chess in the narrative comes laden with associations of eastern culture (where it originated), including demonic bargains for the soul, and magic, thus shrouding Floris' otherwise pristine character in western cultural suspicions of the East.[40] To be sure, English heroes, too, sometimes adopt a disguise as a lower-ranking man in order to infiltrate a stronghold (e.g. Horn, Havelok, Orfeo). However, in *Floris and Blancheflour*, the poet he amplifies Floris' skill at trickery and bribery in the infiltration scene, in a departure both from comparable Middle English romances as well as from the source text for this particular scene (discussed later), thereby framing Floris within a more permissive ethical system than that of the English audience.[41] In these aspects, Floris stands apart from the more mature, martially competent, and morally unambiguous heroes of Middle English literature, gaining, for sure, in his range of acceptable behavior, yet losing somewhat in his social and moral stature. Thus, he does important political work benefitting western interests, ironically by means of his eastern traits, while never becoming a serious threat to western ideals—political or otherwise.

Floris' political function in the story crystallizes in his mission to retrieve Blancheflour from Babylon, where he usurps the role of leader formerly occupied by his father. First, he transforms from the role of son, about whom decisions are made, to the role of leader making his own decisions, proclaiming "'Hur to seken y woll wend'" (l. 345). Second, when his father tries to dissuade him from going, he overrides his father's authority, shaming him for "synne" (l. 350) in even asking such a thing, effectively denouncing his father's decision-making. Third, he travels to Babylon not as a lone knight-lover but with a caravan, disguised as wealthy merchants. In preparation for the journey, he demotes his father from one who gives orders to one who takes them, saying "'Leue fader . . . y telle þee/Al þat þow shalt fynde me'" (ll. 355–6), and his list of essentials includes horses laden "'wiþ seluer and wyþ golde,'" "'clothes ryche/Þe best of al þe kyngryche,'" and an entourage including seven horses and seven men, merchants to conduct them, and "'þyn own chamburlayn'" (ll. 360–67).[42] Rather than traveling lightly, swiftly and discretely, as other love-struck heroes of romance would, Floris creates a traveling spectacle of authority in what amounts to his political coming-of-age.[43] Thus, even though Floris' youth and emotional state would lend itself to privacy in this endeavor, the poet, instead, has Floris assume, indeed demand, the public spotlight as he moves through his kingdom into Babylon, commanding his father's wealth, suggesting a latent, timely political function within this timeless tale of love. Even as he, as a young Muslim, ascends politically, the western audience of the poem roots for him as his success smooths the way for Christian, not Muslim, expansion.

While readers tend to focus on the pairing of Floris and Blancheflour, in fact, the poet prioritizes Floris' relationship with his mother as a co-conspirator against his foreign father. The primacy of the mother-son pair is signaled through another type-scene, involving a magic protective ring. As Floris is about to set forth on his journey in search of Blancheflour, his mother removes a ring from her finger and gives it to Floris, promising him that "'While þou hit hast, doute þe no þing,/Ne fir þe brenne, ne drenchen in se,/Ne iren ne stel schal derie þee'" (ll. 392–4). We find similar protective rings elsewhere in medieval literature granted to heroes such as Yvain by his beloved Laudine in Chrétien's *Yvain*, and Horn by Rymenhild in *King Horn*, where the ring signals the centrality of the female love interest in the hero's trajectory of progress.[44] In *Floris and Blancheflour*, however, the hero receives the protective ring not from his lover, but instead, from his mother, locating the hero's source of power not in Blancheflour but in the queen.[45] While one could argue that such a ring would remain out of Blancheflour's purview, given her diminished social status compared to the granters of similar rings, nonetheless, the queen's bestowal of this powerful protective ring to her son binds the hero more to her narrative function as a political counteragent within her (Muslim) kingdom than with Blancheflour's function as the love interest for the hero. Moreover, Floris later uses this ring as he infiltrates the defenses of a fellow Muslim leader, the Emir, and grants it to Blancheflour (l. 1149)—while mentioning his mother—as protection against impending execution by the same leader, thereby undermining the Emir's power. Again, the hero's amorous goals serve political aims, however indirectly, of challenging Muslim religious and political authority.

In fact, Floris follows in the footsteps of crusading armies infiltrating a Middle Eastern city. The second half of the poem involves Floris' search for Blancheflour, which takes him to the city of Babylon (Cairo), where she is held captive in a harem. With the guidance of a bridge warden of Babylon, a man named Daire, Floris secures insider cooperation and infiltrates the city through a fortified tower. He and Blancheflour are reunited and hide within the city, only to be discovered two weeks later by the Emir. The couple is placed on trial and sentenced to death, but manages to escape sentencing by impressing on the Emir the intensity of their love and mutual devotion, even in the face of death. Here, we have a young, Muslim prince infiltrating the stronghold of a fellow Muslim ruler in an eastern setting, rescuing a Christian subject, and redirecting public, legal policy through an emotional appeal centered in love, all of which capture the aims, tactics, and religious underpinnings of the crusader mentality. While early scholars find meaningful parallels between this segment of the story and similar plots of various eastern tales, the English poet overlays the plot of a particularly pivotal episode of western accounts of the First Crusade in rendering Floris' efforts at this point.[46]

In an earlier study, I trace the source of the scene for Floris' entry into the city of Babylon to rescue Blancheflour to a similar scene involving the siege of Thebes in the OF *Roman de Thèbes*, itself rooted in chronicle accounts of the Siege of Antioch (1097–8) during the First Crusade.[47] The *Thèbes*—the first vernacular re-telling of the classical legend of the Theban War—recasts the story of the civil war between the sons of Oedipus found in Statius' *Thebaid* (90 A.D.) as a crusade, reframing the forces of Pollinicés as western crusaders overcoming the forces of Ethïoclés of Thebes, a city allied with various eastern peoples, including Turks, Persians, and Slavs.[48] To enhance the eastern flavor of the narrative, the French poet introduces into the story several scenes modeled on chronicle accounts of the First Crusade. One such scene is the story of Daire le Roux, which, itself, draws on the famous Pious Traitor episode from chronicle accounts of the Siege of Antioch, whereby Pirus, a citizen of Antioch, covertly aids the forces of Bohemund in infiltrating the city by means of a fortified tower.[49] The Babylon episode in the story of *Floris* and the story of Daire le Roux in the

Roman de Thèbes share a series of interconnected plot elements, including the setting of a fortified city of eastern aspect, the strategic importance of a fortified tower within that city, secretive conversation with an eye toward subversion between the hero and an insider of the city named "Daire," treacherous infiltration, an arrest and trial, and the reversal of a death sentence on the basis of amorous appeal. Like the crusaders, Floris proves triumphant in not only protecting a Christian subject, Blancheflour, but more importantly, in making meaningful inroads in "converting" the heart of an eastern ruler, the Emir; witnessing the self-sacrificing love of the young pair, "Weping he turned his heued awai,/And his swerd hit fil to grounde" (ll. 1228–9). Floris, a lone, unarmed, and militarily unproven young Muslim, disarms a Muslim foe by modeling the core Christian concept of love, doing the work normally carried out by a crusading army.

The dual religious and political nature of Floris' mission is perhaps best distilled in the magnificent cup he carries with him on his journey, a cup intimately connected to Blancheflour. The cup, "good and ryche" (l. 163), forms part of the steep price the merchants of Babylon pay for Blancheflour, along with "Twenty mark of reed golde" (l. 162). As the price received by Floris' parents on the sale of Blancheflour to merchants, the cup unquestionably emblematizes Blancheflour's commodification as a slave.[50] However, the story engraved on the cup, and the provenance of the vessel provided by the poet, raise its significance above the level of the mercantile through a series of images evoking empire. Portrayed on the cup, we see the story of "How Paryse ledde awey þe queene" (ll. 168–9), that is, Paris' abduction of Helen. While the story of Paris and Helen undoubtedly evokes passionate love, it equally evokes notions of empire, as the love affair that initiates the destruction of Troy and subsequent founding of Rome.[51] The poet then provides a political lineage for the cup that traces the founding of the West: "Enneas, þe king, þat nobel man,/At Troye in batayle he it wan/And brouȝt it into Lumbardy/And gaf it to Lauine, his amy" (ll. 177–80). The cup accompanies Aeneas from the siege of Troy to Italy, where he founds the kingdom that will become Rome. It then ends up in the "tresour hous" of "Cesar" (l. 181–2), from whom it is stolen by a thief, who then uses it as currency for Blancheflour (l. 183–4). In effect, Blancheflour, the Christian slave-girl, stands in a long line of distinguished empire-builders reaching back to the origins of western power. Moreover, the cup distills the same blend of the amorous (Paris and Helen; Aeneas and Lavinia) and the imperial (Troy and Rome) that permeates the entire poem of *Floris*. Above all, the cup's function in the story does not end with the sale of Blancheflour, but rather, transforms into a tool of state, becoming Floris' "key" into a Muslim stronghold to rescue a captive Christian subject.[52]

Floris' triumph at the end of the poem proves as much, if not more, political as personal and establishes what will become a hallmark of poems featuring the Wise Woman type-scene, whereby the child of the foreign ruler outdoes his/her father in statecraft while steering the country in a new direction in line with the poem's English, Christian audience. Floris and Blancheflour manage to avoid the Emir's punishment on the strength of their love. They marry and soon return to Spain, becoming king and queen of the kingdom. However, religious conversion of the Muslim occurs at both ends of this finale. The Emir, witnessing the selfless love of the pair, "Boþe him chaungede mod and chere" (1224), putting that change of heart into action by having Floris and Blancheflour led "To one chirche" (l. 1273), where they marry as Christians. In the same church, the Emir, "þourgh conseil of Blauncheflour" (l. 1277), marries Clarice as "quene" (l.1279), presumably on Christian terms, and further offers Floris his own kingdom. The potency of this religious transformation in the city of Babylon accords with medieval notions of Babylon as both a symbol of "religious deviance and perversion" as well as a seat of enormous wealth and imperial power, magnifying Floris' achievement all the more.[53] The poet finalizes the conversion as the young pair "bitauʒt þe Amerail oure Driʒt" (l. 1299). Finally, at least one manuscript witness of the poem extends the momentum of conversion further, by having Floris return to Spain to receive his kingdom, where he now, as king, "vnderfeng Cristendom of prestes honde" (l. 1303), ushering his kingdom into the Christian fold.[54]

In effect, any character development in the poem occurs not in the young lovers, who remain steadfast in love throughout, but rather in the political leadership of the poem, where changes of heart create changes of regime that, in turn, precipitate large-scale religious conversion. Conversion is not a simply an added bonus of Floris' quest to rescue Blancheflour, but rather, his main achievement, with love of Blancheflour providing the occasion by which he accomplishes this. Ultimately, *Floris and Blancheflour* brings about the same ends of conversion of the infidel through internal rather than external means. Rather than a Christian force infiltrating and overcoming a Muslim stronghold, the English poet creates the ironic scenario of a Muslim prince, Floris, infiltrating and "vanquishing" not one but two Muslim kingdoms, bloodlessly and at his own expense, no less. Disguised in the end as an engineer ("ginour," l. 748), he breeches Muslim defenses in Babylon better than any engineers of siege warfare. In Floris' father and the Emir of Babylon, we have two Muslim leaders subdued by a boy of their own kind, who instills in these lands values and beliefs that flatter the poem's English audience.

The Wise Woman type-scene in *Floris and Blancheflour* forms a prototype of what later becomes a narrative tool for signaling cultural difference and transformation, even as the settings and political agendas shift. In this instance, the matter of cultural difference is hardly subtle, given the Middle Eastern settings, and how the profiling of both Muslim rulers—Floris' father and the Emir—draws upon medieval western stereotypes of eastern men as effeminate, emotive, and irrational. Nonetheless, this same cultural profile will come to apply to non-Muslim leaders in later poems, where poets coopt these negative stereotypes of eastern peoples to signal Otherness in general, often in fellow Christians, in instances where cultural difference may be less pronounced.

Sir Degrevant

The Wise Woman type-scene occurs in a later Middle English poem, the fourteenth-century/early fifteenth-century *Sir Degrevant*, where cultural difference manifests closer to home.[55] Surviving in two manuscripts, the poem takes place in the war-torn landscape of modern-day Lothian, along the Anglo-Scottish border, a region devastated by border raids involving small units of fighting men that ravage livestock, farmland, and people alike.[56] While less exotic than Muslim Spain or Egypt, the culturally distinct world of the poem nevertheless exhibits itself in terms of the nature and styles of combat, terms of land-tenure, domestic architecture, international relations, and tastes in imported luxury goods.[57] As with *Floris and Blancheflour*, the main cast of characters belong to a culture other than the English audience of the poem, in this case, Scotland, accounting for the peculiar situation whereby the hero himself commits atrocities that typically violate the chivalric code so prized by English poets.[58] Degrevant, a latter-day Agravain, one of King Arthur's Scottish knights of the Round Table (another being Gawain, Agravain's older brother), models the career familiar to the *scoti anglicati*, or "English Scots," Scottish men recruited by the English crown to further its interests in the region.[59] The poem announces the world of the border in the seemingly pointless and unprovoked vandalism of Degrevant's lands by the Earl of the poem, and in Degrevant's identical retaliatory raid on this neighbor that culminates in a military stalemate. The failure of traditional masculine strategies in settling the dispute sets the stage for the Wise Woman type-scene and its subtler methods.

The type-scene follows the same choreography established in *Floris*. Finding himself temporarily bested by Degrevant, the Earl retreats to his castle—a late-medieval tower-house characteristic of the border region—and stews over this latest humiliation. His wife, the countess, enters and initiates the narrative pattern of the Wise Woman type-scene. Here, the scene does not introduce the central dilemma of the poem, as it does in *Floris and Blancheflour*, so much as redirect it, therefore falling somewhat later in the narrative. Nevertheless, as with *Floris and Blancheflour*, the poem concerns itself with influencing affairs in a foreign land, and, as in *Floris*, the Wise Woman type-scene in *Sir Degrevant* introduces an alternate, less violent solution to affecting political change, again using women and children to do the work normally assigned to armies, with far greater success.

Sir Degrevant dramatizes, with striking realism, the array of tactics employed by the English crown to exert its influence in Scotland. Beginning in 1296 with Edward I's invasion of Scotland with an eye to dominion and escalating over subsequent centuries, the English crown used a range of tools for securing and maintaining a political foothold among the Scottish population in the critical areas along the Border, including Lothian—Agravain's home. Territorial dominance formed the key to this political endeavor, a game that the Scottish border lords had long mastered while vying amongst themselves. One of the chief mechanisms both the English and Scottish leaders employed to punish or reward their "officer ranks" involved confiscating the estates of the disloyal and redistributing them to the loyal. The frequency with which the Scottish barons, in particular, shifted allegiance for and against the English, and for and against one another, using land as currency, resulted in a kaleidoscopic pattern of shifting lordly estates all along the Scottish Border, not to mention endless animosity over property rights and unrelenting armed disputes. Such is the picture arising in *Sir Degrevant*, where Degrevant, a Scottish knight holding the English military title of "banneret," lives on estates that were bestowed on him ("sesyd in hys hand," l. 65), rather than inherited, and about whose boundaries he takes special care—terms of ownership the Earl refuses to acknowledge, accounting for his attacks.[60]

Degrevant's attempts to safeguard his estate and his right to be there take the reader through the range of options available to newly installed landholders (Scots or English) loyal to the crown. We first see Degrevant try to "werke be lawe" (l. 151) in dispatching a letter to the Earl, identified as a writ *praecipe*, a standard tool of English justice issued by the crown in cases involving unlawful use of, or seizure of, land.[61] When English law fails, Degrevant then resorts to English military might, notably, ranks of archers, or longbowman, a tool first discovered during the reign of Edward III in the Scottish campaigns and that "dominated in English hands," in France as well as Scotland.[62] Degrevant then tries to meet the Earl on his own terms, arriving at his home wielding an axe, a non-knightly weapon, but the distinctive weapon of the medieval Scot, a challenge also refused by the Earl.[63] Finally, the hero launches a retaliatory raid on the Earl's lands, duplicating the pattern of vandalism visited earlier upon his own estates, in which he finds no satisfaction ("hym lykys no pley,/To honte ne to revey," ll. 521–2). However, into this last campaign, the poet introduces another strategy, tamer and far less expensive, involving the hero's love for his enemy's daughter (ll. 523–44), that hearkens to yet another royal tactic for securing loyalty and territorial gain: marriages "sponsored by the crown . . . designed to bind Scots more firmly into the English king's allegiance."[64] Thus, as the men continue the fight, the countess and her daughter, Melidor, pursue a parallel strategy, unveiled in the Wise Woman type-scene and carried out in secret, that expands landholdings rather than laying them waste.

To illustrate the need for an alternate, non-violent approach for advancing English dominion in Scotland, the poet shows both the hero and his foe, alike, employing and failing at the same armed strategies. In the first half of the poem, we see Degrevant and the Earl mimic one another in mood, motivation, and aggressive conduct, launching nearly identical raids on one another's lands, with nearly identical casualties. Despite his earlier characterization of Degrevant as a "comelych knyght," "dowghty," and a "fayre man and free" (ll. 20, 25, and 33), the poet shows Degrevant as not unlike the villain of the story. For example, when more civilized tactics of diplomacy fail in his conflict with the Earl, Degrevant readily turns to armed retaliation driven by revenge. Just as the Earl boasts verbally of his planned attack on Degrevant's lands, Degrevant, too, despite his supposed "'gentriese'" (l. 497), boasts to the Earl's wife that "'Tyll his [the Earl's] freth wyl Y fare,/Y woll no wyld best spare/For soth all this day'" (ll. 502–4). Like the Earl, who conducts unauthorized hunting on Degrevant's lands, Degrevant "hontede [the Earl's] for[e]ste" (l. 515) without permission. Just as the Earl slays Degrevant's deer, "sexty on a day" (l. 111), Degrevant "breng þe dere to þe grond" (l. 507) in the same number of sixty (l. 511). Just as the Earl dredges Degrevant's rivers and compromises the fish supply (l. 113), Degrevant similarly drags the Earl's ditches with nets for their supply of pike ("Grete luces y-nowe", l. 519).[65] Like the Earl, who delights in frustrating and angering his neighbor, Degrevant vandalizes the Earl's land, we are told, for the sake of "Ten[e]de þe Eorl on þe beste," or angering the Earl as best he can (l. 514). Not surprisingly, many scholars have struggled to make sense of Degrevant's arrogant and destructive behavior, some seeking ways of justifying it given its deviation from the knightly norm.[66]

However, this unusual hero portrait speaks to the central political conflict in two ways, first, in establishing the hero's own foreign (Scottish) identity, despite his English loyalties. Second, the duplication of behavior in Degrevant and the Earl calls into question current English tactics in dealing with Scottish resistance, as both men end up weary of the whole situation and devoid of better ideas. Subsequent skirmishes produce more casualties but no lasting victories. Thus, the Earl's wife proves "wyese" ("wise," l. 449L), indeed, when she articulates the futility of the standard armed approach to the political scene, where good guys and bad guys start to look more or less the same.

The Earl of the poem shares with the Muslim king of *Floris and Blancheflour* the same emotive and volatile portrait, traits that overlap remarkably well with English negative stereotypes of a Scottish lord. L.F. Casson, the poem's early editor, rightly characterizes the Earl as "a man of violent and predatory nature."[67] Indeed, the poet tells us he "wax w[ro]th/And swor many a gret owth" (ll. 209–10) when publicly challenged for his actions, and later, "wax wode/And swor be bonus and blode" ("ll. 1753–4) when he learns of Melidor's secret dealings with Degrevant. Thus, as with the king in *Floris*, his own child becomes the target of his aggression. The Earl's impulsivity, in all events, assumes broader range, however, as it gets compounded with excessive pride, leading to provocative trespasses onto Degrevant's lands "Wyth his brag and his bost" (247) and vengeance toward Degrevant, for whom "He hade a grete spyt" (l. 101). The emotional portrait of the Earl of the poem essentially distills medieval English stereotypes of the Scots, as detailed, for instance, in Bartholomeus Anglicus' encyclopedia *De proprietatibus rerum* (c.1235–1240), which characterizes the Scottish people as desiring "to be praised and valued above all other people," "envious of their neighbors," "not ashamed to lie," xenophobic, and taking "pride in their misdeeds and dislik[ing] peace."[68] Thus, violent emotion becomes, once again, a hallmark of the foreign ruler.

This portrait of the Earl also corresponds to what we know of the leadership style of the Scottish border lords, who vied mercilessly with one another for regional dominance, engaging in frequent destructive raids on neighboring lands, using bands of loyal men in combat-ready units, such as we see in the poem. In this regard, the Earl's emotional volatility spans more lordly spheres than in *Floris and Blancheflour*. Floris' father appears in the poem almost exclusively in the domestic sphere, as a husband and father; we never see him out among his people, presiding over a banquet or adjudicating in state business. In *Sir Degrevant*, however, the Earl's primary conflict focuses not so much on his child's actions (as in *Floris*) as on his neighbor, Degrevant's, actions as a rival lord, and therefore, he expresses emotional impulsivity in the form of bravado, anger, aggression, and revenge—on the battlefield as well as in the home. Nonetheless, the Earl's emotive style of leadership marks him as a foreigner and an inferior, a leader whose days are numbered.

The bearer of the hard truth regarding the Earl's unsustainable course of action comes from his wife, the countess, in the first instance of the Wise Woman type-scene in the poem. The same pattern witnessed in *Floris and*

Blanchefleur obtains here in *Sir Degrevant*, whereby the foreign leader, at an impasse with his own approach to the crisis, finds himself at home, nursing his wounds; in this case, emotional as well as physical ones. If he exhibited brag and boast out on the battlefield, here, in the home with his wife, he reverts to the opposite extreme. The Wise Woman type-scene opens after he has just fled from battle with Degrevant (l.347), who chased him home "Mor þen enleue m[y]le" (l. 358), so that ". . . whan þe Eorl com ham/He was wonded to scham" (ll. 373–4). The countess enters the room, finds him wounded, and cries out "'Alas!/Haue ye nat parkus and chas?/What schuld ye do at is place/Swych costus to kythe?'" (ll. 377–80). While the poet frames this question within a swoon (she "swouned full swyth" l. 376), her question implies exasperation rather than desperation, as she assumes the tone of an impatient mother questioning the whole point of his incursions on Degrevant's estate when he has estates of his own.[69] Also, unlike in *Floris and Blanchefleur*, the countess's advice to her husband is unsolicited, tipping the power dynamic between husband and wife even further. Her question essentially incriminates him—a conclusion borne out by his sheepish, child-like apology, "'Dame . . . Y was thare,/ And me rews now full sar/Y take m[y] leve] for eueremare/Swych wronges to wrythe'" (ll. 381–4). He admits to his mistake and promises not to do it again, his private submissiveness here contrasting with his earlier public arrogance. Toward the end of the poem, when the Earl's control over his own household reaches its lowest point, the countess again questions his incursions on Degrevant's lands, justifying the hero's retaliation and insisting "'ʒe haue ben to long foas'" ("'you've been enemies too long,'" l. 1762), again speaking the voice of wisdom, this time getting her way. As with Floris' father, the Earl reveals his own ineptitude as a leader when he cowers before, and defers to his wife's greater wisdom, exposing internal weakness behind enemy lines, and making the wife the key agent of this exposé.

Indeed, the Earl's home becomes the primary arena of his undoing, the site of a series of scenes of "diplomacy" between the wife, the daughter, and the enemy (Degrevant), adhering to the pattern of narratives featuring the Wise Woman scene, where the wife and child serve external political interests. For instance, the poet duplicates the Wise Woman scene almost immediately with a similar scene, in the same home (in "þe hall," l. 417), where the countess and her daughter meet privately with Degrevant, who has just arrived to challenge the Earl to a duel. The Earl dispatches the porter to refuse the challenge ostensibly due, we are told, to his secret "drede" of Degrevant (l. 416). In a seeming act of betrayal, the countess seizes the opportunity to speak separately with Degrevant, questioning him along similar lines as she did her husband earlier and assuming the same masculine stance of political advisor; she asks that he stop his attacks on their property, and even after he justifies his actions to her, she insists "'Ye haue well good men y-slayn,/Y rede ye be at an/Or ther dey any moo'" (ll. 450–2), presuming to tell him what to do. As with her husband, she assumes the tone of the patient adult in the room. Her plan, in both scenes, involves reconciliation of the warring sides, which she herself models by praising Degrevant as a "man marvelus," whom "Gode hath lent . . . grace" (ll. 423–5), laying a foundation of good will between the rival households.

Interestingly, this second variant of the Wise Woman scene (involving Degrevant) in the poem affirms the narrative function of this type-scene as a marker of cultural difference in a man in a leadership role. To be sure, as a knight in English employ, Degrevant represents emerging English presence in the region. Nonetheless, he, too, is a Scot, and he, too, pursues an ineffectual path early in the poem; thus, the choreography of this second iteration of the Wise Woman scene replicates the earlier scene involving the Earl—again, tipping the gender roles. The countess assumes a superior social position as the one hosting the meeting as well as a superior political position as the one dictating terms and strategies to a foreign male leader, terms he clearly feels obligated to respond to as he tries to justify his non-compliance. She also fulfills the same narrative purpose of furthering English political interests in negotiating with him at all, and the poet announces his approval of her plan by referring to her in this scene as "wyese in wane" ("wise in this life," l. 449L). True to the Wise Woman scene, where the woman herself is a cultural Other, the countess' Scottish identity affords her the poetic license to assume a public, political role as a woman working within the domestic sphere, affecting the most subtle infiltration into a foreign household. Above all, the quiet presence of the daughter, Melidor, in this scene lays the groundwork for the non-violent solution to the conflict via intermarriage ushered in later in the poem.

True to the pattern of poems containing the Wise Woman type-scene, the child of the foreign leader—in this case, his daughter, Melidor, a girl approaching marriageable age—imagines a future at odds with her father's way of life and becomes a counter-agent working against him in ways that alter the trajectory of the entire region. As in *Floris and Blancheflour*, the contest between foreign and domestic cultural systems takes the form of a generational divide, with the father embodying the foreign (and endangered) way of doing things and the child embracing and integrating a new way of being in line with English political interests. The divide becomes apparent after the child's exposure to influences unacceptable to the parent.

Melidor, like Floris, initiates political change, first, through personal, romantic connections. Just as Floris develops a lifelong attachment to

Blancheflour that ultimately foments conflict with his father, Melidor conducts a love affair with her father's enemy, Degrevant, provoking the Earl's public death-threat to his daughter. Not long after Degrevant's secret meeting with the countess where he first spies Melidor, who "lokyd on that aunterous" (l. 421), he confesses to his squire, "'My loue is leliche y-lyeght/On a worthly wyeght'" (ll. 529–30), and the two soon sneak into the Earl's barmkin (a tower-house enclosure) to see Melidor, whom they encounter on her way to the chapel.[70] The tension of this early encounter gives way to regular amorous rendezvous between the pair in a lavishly described "chaumbur of loue" (l. 1439), with equally lavish delicacies (ll. 1409–32), under her father's own roof, meetings which continue, no less, a "ȝere,/ Pre [qua]terus, and mare" (ll. 1567–8). As in the case of *Floris*, the infiltration of external influence into the foreign leader's household happens under his very nose, under his own roof, with his own child, though, in this case, without his express knowledge or approval. While Melidor's love affair with Degrevant fulfills the generic amorous element we expect of late medieval romance, it does specific political work in exposing the foreign leader's lack of control over his people, starting with his own family. It also illustrates the pattern of the Wise Woman type-scene, where the mother introduces the idea of change (reconciliation) that the child then enacts.

In fact, at every turn, Melidor's actions speak to and shape all of the international competing powers at play in the region, including Scotland, England, France, and even Germany.[71] As a Scottish woman and the love interest for a Scottish hero in service to England, Melidor distills key aspects of the Anglo-Scottish conflict. For example, her first appearance in the poem comes in the midst of negotiations between her mother and Degrevant, capturing the divisive landscape of the border, with some Scots, such as Degrevant, siding with the English, and other Scots, such as Melidor's family, resisting English encroachments into their lands—a situation that fueled the border raids between rival lords. Undoubtedly, the poet frames her in traditional amorous terms in this scene, as a young woman "jentell and small/And louesom to seyght" (ll. 419–20). Nevertheless, Degrevant's subsequent disclosure to his squire of his budding fancy for Melidor foregrounds her political situation and function, as the squire reminds Degrevant that "'ȝe er enemys'" (l. 578), thus fusing the love with the war. In turn, Degrevant identifies her as "'þe Eorlus owun eyer'" (l.570), dangling the prospect of territorial expansion, the object of English policy in the region.

The political implications of her affair with Degrevant are by no means lost on Melidor. Her first conversation with Degrevant only sharpens the political tenor of their relationship, as she frames him not as a lover but as an outlaw among their people. She accuses him of trespassing into their barmkin "'armid on werre'" (l. 709), and then, upon hearing his name, twice accuses him of political high crime. She shouts, "'Tratur, lat be þe!/. . . . My lord hym-self shal þe see/Hanged on hyȝth'" (ll. 733–6; 753 and 758), naming the crime as well as the appropriate punishment for cases of treason, a crime perpetrated by an insider for the benefit of outsiders.[72] Just like her mother, she assumes command over Degrevant in this scene, echoing her mother in reminding him of "'our folk þat þou hast slayn'" (l. 757) while closing ranks with her people, calling him out for misconduct and dictating his likely future—hardly the manner of a lady love—thus, positioning herself as a leader in the relationship, with all its ramifications, from here on in. Melidor's first tryste with Degrevant, too, reveals yet another corner of the Scottish tapestry; perceiving her maid's ruse to arrange the lovers' first meeting, she says to her maid, "'Damesele, so haue I rest,/þou hast geton þe a gest/Off wylde men of þe west . . .'" (ll. 1365–1367), referring here to the *Scoti sylvestres*, or "Wild Scots," men of the Highlands and Western Isles of Scotland, whose language and cultural practices distinguished them from the Lowland Scots such as Melidor's family, and whose presence posed as much a threat to them as the English.[73] Thus, Melidor expresses a full awareness of the complexities of border life both among the Scottish people themselves and between the Scots and the English—political knowledge she will use for political purposes.

In accordance with the Wise Woman type-scene, Melidor displays greater acumen than her father in steering the political crisis endemic to the region to fruitful ends. Again, matters of the heart dovetail with matters of state in Melidor's dealings with the hero. For example, whereas her father amplified armed conflict with Degrevant, suffering humiliating setbacks in his plans, Melidor indirectly disarms the enemy, as Degrevant, issuing a raid on the Earl's property, suddenly recalls Melidor and finds "Now hym lykys no pley,/To honte ne to revey" (ll. 521–2). Love weakens his resolve to retaliate. When, later, he sneaks into her barmkin "Y-armede" (l. 632), he leaves the castle peacefully, despite her harsh tone with him. While standing her ground, she manages to tame his fury. Once disarmed, Degrevant becomes her guest, and here too, Melidor applies her skills of diplomacy.

True to poems containing the Wise Woman scene, the domestic sphere, mastered here by Melidor, serves English political ends. At first glance, it would appear that Melidor's nightly trysts with Degrevant, conducted over the course of a year, occur despite the political currents enveloping them. After all, they meet after hours, in private, undetected by official oversight. However, the poet uses the love affair to hypothesize a parallel, alternate, and ultimately more effective line of statecraft, rendering the lovers' first meeting with a degree of pageantry and ceremony more befitting a public occasion of state than a private rendezvous. As Degrevant is shown into the Melidor's chamber, she greets him as one would greet a dignitary, as she "Knelyd doun in þe floure,/And fel hym to feet" (ll. 1379–80), a formal gesture of respect appropriate to heads of state, which I discuss more later. Furthermore, despite the intimacy of this meeting of two, the poet describes a lavish banquet, spanning thirty-five lines, of delicacies and beverages, specifying wines from Italy, Greece, France, and the Low Countries, served with fine linens. The opulence of the table is matched by the opulence of the chamber itself, a vaulted room decorated from ceiling to floor in murals—a passage running one hundred fifty-one lines (1339–1488)—not including furnishings.[74] In other words, their first private meeting in this "chaumbur of loue" (l. 1439) comes clothed in language the audience would expect of a great state occasion, where Melidor showcases her own social stature while also acknowledging his, suggesting political implications of this private meeting. As the evening progresses and Degrevant presumes to ask the privilege of a bridegroom (ll. 1523–28), Melidor insists he will have no such thing "'Or þou wed me with a ryng'" (l. 1535), dictating the terms of their relationship while introducing the notion of marriage, laying the groundwork for reconciliation between the feuding parties. Above all, consistent with the Wise Woman type-scene, her skillful diplomatic efforts inadvertently serve English interests, as marriage with Degrevant, a knight serving the crown, would bring her lands and people into the English fold. Thus, Melidor redirects the Anglo-Scottish conflict besetting her region within the confines of her own room in ways that would please English readers.

Melidor's love affair with Degrevant serves English interests, as well, for its implications in Franco-English relations. Early in the relationship, Degrevant learns from Melidor's maid that the Earl has arranged for her to marry a certain Duke of Gerle, a French nobleman and ally of her father, who arrives from "ouer þe see" (l. 1009) with "a ful grete meyne" (l. 1010). The Earl receives Melidor's French suitor with the same level of pomp and formality as Melidor will soon receive her English-allied suitor, Degrevant, forming visual parallels between the official and unofficial, public and private, with both courtships taking place at the Earl's home. The Duke, however, represents more than a rival lover to Degrevant, as his character captures the spirit of the Franco-Scottish alliance forged during this period between England's two primary enemies. While France and Scotland had a long relationship of reciprocity, the two countries formalized their mutual political interests in 1295 in what became known as the "Aulde Alliance," when John Balliol of Scotland forged an alliance with Philip IV of France against Edward I of England, who planned to exploit the occasion of the crisis of succession in Scotland to bring that country under English rule.[75] As was typical for Scottish border lords, who often brokered their own overseas political alliances irrespective of royal authority, Melidor's father seems to have acted independently in arranging her marriage to a French nobleman, with nine other French peers mentioned in the poem as his allies (l. 1870), a fictional incarnation of the Franco-Scottish alliance. Indeed, interests of mutual defense accompany the wedding preparations as the Earl confides to the Duke of his ongoing "vylany" (l. 1035) with Degrevant, referring to him here using the English military title "Baneret" (l. 1033). In reply, the Duke promises his support to the Earl, swearing "'Here my trouþ I þe plyȝth,/Whedur he wol tornay or fyȝth,/He shal haue inow'" (ll. 1038–40), an historically appropriate exchange. Nor is the political significance of this lost on Degrevant, who prepares to fight the Duke at the tournament with the intent "'I wol se þe countenauns/Of þe chyualrye of Frauns,/As euer mote I go'" (ll. 1182–84), specifically framing his upcoming contest within national terms.

It stands to reason, therefore, that, as Melidor happens to serve English interests on the border by secretly courting Degrevant, she simultaneously undermines the Franco-Scottish alliance as represent in her father's choice of French suitor. Moreover, she publicly reveals her loyalty for Degrevant for the first time on the field of battle itself, as she strides across the tournament field to supply him with a fresh horse, where "she spekys a word of pride:/'On þis stede wol I ryde/By my lemmanus syde,/I[n] lond whare I go'" (ll. 1317–20). In essence, by choosing this stage to disclose her personal inclinations, she invariably invokes their public ramifications, placing herself in the arena of the political tensions at play in the region as she proclaims a new allegiance that will nullify them all, working one person at a time, all the while upstaging her father.

As in *Floris and Blancheflour*, where the English poet exploits stereotypically Muslim qualities of trickery in particular to serve Christian ends, in *Sir Degrevant*, the poet, at times, vivifies Melidor's Scottish qualities by way of equipping her for the active role she must take, despite her gender and young age. While Melidor serves English interests in the poem, she does so by means of her Scottish qualities, accounting for her mixed reception among scholars who have assumed her English origin.[76] Two gestures, in particular, mark her as a Scottish woman. As noted previously, Melidor transgresses against the behavior deemed acceptable for medieval heroines in her bold appearance on the tournament field, leading a horse to Degrevant. This bold gesture, where Melidor publicly proclaims her love for and loyalty to her father's enemy and the rival to the Duke of Gerle for her hand in marriage, on the battlefield, amidst ranks of fighting men accords, in fact, with Scottish practice of the time, as recorded in chronicle accounts of the time. For example, fourteenth-century chronicle *Scalacronica* by Thomas Gray—a soldier and local administrator in the Anglo-Scottish and French wars of the time—records a similar scene occurring outside the walls of Norham castle, which had recently been seized by the Scots (1355). Sir Thomas de Gray, the author's father and constable, brings his own army out to meet the Scots, and battle ensues. During a lull in the fighting, "the women of the castle [then] brought out horses to their men, who mounted and gave chase, slaying those whom they could overtake."[77] Thus, Melidor proclaims her defection to the English side through a distinctly Scottish custom for women.

Likewise, Melidor's unusual reception of Degrevant into her chamber, where she falls on her knees before him only to be swooped up in his arms and kissed, carries similar cultural resonance. A comparable scene occurs in *The Wallace* by Blind Hary (c. 1477), where William Wallace accepts an invitation to meet with the English queen to negotiate peace. As he enters the room, the queen falls to her knees before him, presumably observing Scottish custom, only for him to scoop her up and kiss her.[78] While *The Wallace* postdates *Sir Degrevant* by about seventy years, nevertheless, these parallel scenes of etiquette, just the like parallel scenes on the tournament field, share the same distinctive choreography and motivation against a backdrop of the Scottish Wars of Independence.

Such precise cultural practice helps to account for some of Melidor's other, more provocative behavior in general, which also expresses her Scottishness while doing English political work. For example, like all the children featured in the Wise Woman scene, Melidor finds her life threatened by her own father when, after her public display on the battlefield, the Earl rightly accuses her collaborating with the enemy and causing "'slauȝthtur of my mene'" through "'ȝowr false treyn'" (ll. 1739–40). He grows enraged and swears "Þis day shall þou de[de] be'" (l. 1742), vowing "'Mete ne drynk shall do me gode/Ar I se þe dye!'" (ll. 1753 and 1755–6). Like Floris, Melidor has resorted (one might say, stooped) to trickery (*treyn*) to achieve her ends. Just as Floris' mother must remind the king that Floris is their only surviving child, the countess reminds the Earl that "'We hade neuer chyl but hyr on'" (l. 1759), urging him to accept their daughter's choice of Degrevant as mate. However, Melidor hardly needs defending, as she retorts "'He is my loue and my lorde,/Myn hele and my counforde,'" matching her father's threat to "'neuer ete mete'" (ll. 1781–2 and 1786). Far from being obedient toward her father, as a medieval heroine would, Melidor matches his stubbornness, pride, and aggression, becoming his political equal as she guides her family's allegiance away from the French Duke and toward the knight serving an English king. Perhaps her most shocking behavior, however, involves entertaining

Degrevant regularly, alone in her chamber, for more than a year, violating all polite social norms. As with Floris, sensuousness and trickery, otherwise taboo qualities, combine to enable Melidor to affect the reconciliation between feuding sides that her mother could only wish for. Above all, all of these daring and deviant gestures empower Melidor not only to motivate Degrevant into action, but to become an active agent herself on the political stage in ways that happen to facilitate plans for English territorial expansion along the border.

Interestingly, Melidor, like Degrevant earlier, mirrors her father's behavior, but to more auspicious ends. Where Degrevant matches the Earl on the field of battle, Melidor matches him in the negotiation chamber, as she courts a "foreign" suitor in the family home with the same gracious formality and diplomatic command as her father does with the Duke, and to the same interpersonal ends of establishing a foundation of mutual trust and cooperation. Also, like Degrevant, she stands up to her father, inciting his wrath and endangering herself, but unlike Degrevant, who escalates the conflict, she brings about her father's capitulation. Thus, where Degrevant mimics the Earl in ways that fail, Melidor does so in ways that prevail, aligning her with powerful men on both sides of the conflict, her father and her lover, both of whom she surpasses politically.

At the end of the poem, the poet specifically links the marriage to territorial gain, at the Scottish Earl's expense, advances brought about entirely by insiders, again replicating the pattern we see in poems featuring the Wise Woman type-scene. In getting her choice of bridegroom, Melidor effectively puts an end to her father's feud with Degrevant, disarming both sides with regard to one another, while giving Degrevant an English foothold into yet another Scottish family on the border. Melidor's actions find backup in her mother's words, as she continues to incriminate her husband while defending Degrevant, castigating him for his final ambush of Degrevant on his way out of the barmkin, insisting "'[He] was not to blame'" (l. 1768), and dredging up his earliest crimes against Degrevant's lands while the knight "'werred in Spayn'" (l. 1770). Mother and daughter, maintaining their narrative function in the Wise Woman scene, thus grow more brazen in opposing their own husband, father, and leader, justifying English efforts to quash such border lords in their tracks, making these women agents of progress in English eyes. This progress takes concrete form, for, in marrying Melidor, "Syr Degriuaunt by-lefte þer eyr/With brod londus and fair" (ll. 1901–2). Degrevant's marriage to Melidor marks a shift in political allegiance for her family as well as a territorial gain for Degrevant—an outcome that accords with border conflict, in general, in which "the aim of warfare was to make men switch allegiance," something Melidor and her mother achieve without ever going to war.[79]

Typical of narratives featuring the Wise Woman scene, the poem celebrates shifting political alliances in the end. The international guest list at the wedding, drawn from the very highest ranks of France, Germany, Portugal, and the Church, becomes a testament to the international reach of their otherwise modest efforts. While Degrevant, our hero, reaps the rewards of land and influence, the credit for such progress goes to the diplomatic efforts of Melidor and her mother, the countess, both Scottish insiders, who give voice to the English agenda in the region and make it happen at their own expense. They are the ones who get to the Earl to concede to Degrevant in saying "'Welcome to þis place,/We haue ben to longe fase'" (ll. 1814–15). Thus, *Sir Degrevant* exposes the standard handling of the border conflict, rendered so vividly at the start of the poem, as destructive, expensive, and ultimately ineffectual, while proffering intermarriage as an alternative, sustainable, and far more cost-effective strategy for subduing the Scots. Once again, women and children succeed where armies failed.

Athelston

The presence and particular trajectory of the Wise Woman type-scene in the late fourteenth-century *Athelston* points to a still subtler exploration of cultural difference in Middle English romance.[80] Many scholars have rightly identified the poem's preoccupation with the dangers of absolutist royal power and its prescription of an ecclesiastical corrective—a general theme that has generated a meaningful corpus of historical interpretations referencing analogues spanning the twelfth to the fourteenth centuries.[81] However, the question remains as to why the poet casts him as an outsider in his own country, a status announced by the Wise Woman type-scene, and a status that sets him apart from other, more favorably portrayed, pre-Conquest monarchs found elsewhere in the corpus of Middle English romance, including *King Horn* and *Havelok the Dane*.[82] Indeed, who would think to consider an Anglo-Saxon, Christian monarch ruling from his royal seat in London as a foreigner? Yet, the presence of the Wise Woman type-scene, used elsewhere in Middle English romance to delineate cultural difference, prompts us to consider Athelston not simply as a tyrant but as a foreigner within England. *Athelston*, I argue, splices cultural difference more finely than either of the previous poems discussed in that it differentiates between types of Englishness; notably, the social divide between Anglo-Saxon and Anglo-Norman (and later Angevin) ushered in by the Conquest of 1066. Specifically, the poem denigrates the king's pre-Conquest, Anglo-Saxon identity and its associated world view in preference for post-Conquest, Anglo-Norman ways of doing things that defined late fourteenth-century society, a world captured vividly, and insistently, in the poem's contemporary, late fourteenth-century setting.[83] Moreover, the scene's outcome, both for the queen and their unborn child, amounts to a harsh verdict of Athelston's cultural identity and its future within the realm. In essence, the Wise Woman scene in *Athelston* reveals post-Conquest cultural prejudice against early English identity.

Though *Athelston* falls within a group of Middle English tales, commonly referred to as the "Matter of England" romances, that explore pre-Conquest English history, it stands apart from these and other Middle English romance for its raw mean-spiritedness.[84] By far the meanest scene in the entire poem just so happens to be its rendition of the Wise Woman type-scene. The scene occurs after King Athelston, having assumed the throne and awarded his three "weddyd breþeryn" (l. 10) prominent political seats, succumbs to a rumor that one of these "breþeryn," Egelond, "'wolde þat þou were slayne'" so that "'He wole be kyng off þy lande'" (ll. 162 and 164). As Athelston arranges for the immediate arrest and execution of Egelond, his wife, and their children, the queen enters into the hall where Athelston sits, pondering his decision. Deferring to him as "Sere kyng" (l. 259) as well the father of their unborn child (l. 260), she appeals to him to pause and investigate the matter through the established procedure of "playne parlement" (. 266), a request he rejects outright, saying "'þy bone schal nouȝt igrauntyd be'" (l. 268). When she falls to her knees in tears to pray for all of them, the king grows angrier and more defiant, accusing her of disobedience. His verbal rejection extends into physical rejection when "Wiþ hys foot. . . . He slowȝ þe chyld ryȝt in here wombe" (ll. 282–3), resulting in the miscarriage of their male baby, his future heir. The queen's bid for parliamentary procedure involving "comoun sent" (ll. 265 and 447) gains further credence from Alryke, the archbishop whom she summons. Meeting with similar rebuttal from the king, Alryke recommends the alternative of a trial by fire involving nine hot ploughshares (ll. 570–2), a judicial practice commonly attributed to Anglo-Saxon legal tradition.[85] What ensues is a contest between the sensible and rejected "playne parlement," an innovation of post-Conquest legal practice, and the trial by fire, associated with Anglo-Saxon legal custom, brutally applied in the poem to an innocent, pregnant woman and her children, creating a clear legal winner.[86] Scholars have explored the well-known scene of "the kick" in *Athelston* for its unusual depiction of woman's superior political wisdom, discussions that focus primarily on the queen herself.[87] However, as an instance of the Wise Woman type-scene, this scene is equally, if not more, distinctive for what it tells us about the king, Athelston, not only as a monarch but as a foreigner in his own land.

In many ways, the Wise Woman scene in *Athelston* constitutes the most innovative application of this stock scene so far, starting with its domestic, rather than foreign, setting. Unlike *Floris* and *Sir Degrevant*, the poem takes place entirely in England and features an exclusively English cast of characters. One of *Athelston*'s most distinctive features includes its geography, which specifies neighborhoods and landmarks of late-medieval London and a particular area of northern Kent that includes the villages of Stone (l. 43ff.), Sittingbourne (*Steppyngbourne*, l. 342), Osprynge (l. 346), and Gravesend (l. 751).[88] Within the city of London, the poem specifies landmarks, such as Fleet Street and Charing Cross that only appear in the post-Conquest period, underscoring the poem's contemporary, fourteenth-century setting.[89] The poem, therefore, takes place in an everyday, English setting familiar to the audience. Furthermore, the character names overwhelming derive from the Anglo-Saxon, rather than French, compounding the decidedly English setting with a solidly—indeed, self-consciously—English cast of characters.[90] Englishness saturates the poem. Moreover, the poet portrays these characters, especially Athelston and Alryke, as devout Christians; amidst the political and personal turmoil enveloping Athelston, he retreats to the chapel "To praye God for þe ryȝt . . . And on hys knees he felle" (ll. 416 and 419). Spying Alryke in the choir, he greets him as "'erchebysschop,/ Oure gostly fadyr vndyr God'" (ll. 435–6), who then expresses his own desire for guidance in Christian terms (ll. 441–52). We see English characters working within Christian institutions to which they feel devoted.

However, the presence of the Wise Woman scene in the poem, consistently used elsewhere to denote cultural difference, prompts us to look for signs of foreignness and inferiority within the English/Christian household of King Athelston. I argue that the poem draws lines of difference through time rather than space; rather than locating the Other in another country beyond the boundaries of England, the poet engages in what we might call "racial profiling" within the realm itself by casting a pre-Conquest king (Athelston) on the stage of post-Conquest, fourteenth-century England, where he does not belong.[91]

The Wise Woman type-scene in *Athelston* denigrates Athelston as an Anglo-Saxon in several ways, first, by casting him in the role of the antagonist despite there being a clear villain in the poem. By all accounts, the scene should take place in the household of Wymond of Dover, labeled "traytour" no fewer than twelve times in the poem (ll. 128, 139, 148, 175, 181, 294, 700, 760, 784, 790, 801, 811)—ten of them evenly clustered within just two scenes (91–179; 754–812). Emotionally envious like the Earl of *Degrevant*, Wymond launches an unprovoked attack that precipitates the crisis of the poem, only to receive his just deserts at the end, qualifying him as the antagonist of the poem, the figure typically profiled in the Wise Woman scene. Athelston, whose struggles against the treachery of Wymond form the main action of the poem, would appear to assume the role of hero. However, while, in comparable poems, the hero and antagonist work to cross purposes, Athelston and Wymond initially share a close bond, placing these men on the same side, blurring the lines between hero and villain. We also get no heroic challenger comparable to Sir Degrevant. In this sense, none of the other poems discussed abandon the English readers so completely to the danger represented by the foreign figurehead than *Athelston*, whose unpredictable king reigns in their very midst.

The poet's choice of Athelston as the ruler in the Wise Woman scene compounds the long-standing ambiguity as to who the hero of this poem actually is. The absence of a title announcing the hero in the single manuscript witness of the poem (the only poem within the manuscript a title), compounds the confusion. Additionally, the introduction of four men, rather than one, in the narrative's opening lines, not to mention their often-questionable behavior, has led scholars to either discount any hero for the work or to propose new candidates entirely.[92] I would argue, however, that the confusion is deliberate. Athelston's virtual interchangeability with his other "breþeryn," each of whom (with the exception of Egelond) eventually grows menacing, can be seen as a form of type-casting, where a character's role is predetermined by the traits of his/her social or ethnic group.[93] In the poem, we see Athelston, first and foremost, with his cultural group, all of whom bear Anglo-Saxon names, and the casting of Athelston in the Wise Woman type-scene, which hinges on negative racial/cultural stereotypes, invites us to lump these men together as both problematic and ineducable.

The group dynamic of Athelston and his "breþeryn" functions similarly to account for Athelston's imperviousness to the queen's influence in the Wise Woman scene, further incriminating him as an Anglo-Saxon. While all the wives in the Wise Woman scene meet with resistance from their incalcitrant husbands, the queen's rejection in *Athelston* is unparalleled in ways that highlight not so much an issue (i.e., territorial expansion) as a mind-set. *Athelston* stands apart from most other Middle English romances in having female characters but no romance. As students of the poem so often note, the queen appears in the story as if out of thin air. The poem provides no background for her character, no courtship between her and Athelston, no lovesickness on his part (or hers), and no verbal declarations of affection between them—anywhere. We see her for the first and last time in the Wise Woman scene and immediately following, where she sustains verbal and physical abuse from him and promptly summons help from another man. Interestingly, Athelston's marriage in the poem is a fictional expansion on the life of the historical King Athelstan, a bachelor king, and yet, the queen does not fulfill the predictable role of love interest for Athelston.[94] His later, similar abuse of his sister Edith, also in advanced pregnancy, reinforces the portrait we have of Athelston's studied insensitivity to women, even at their most vulnerable.

Athelston's emotional excesses, a hallmark of the Wise Woman scene, also conform to pre-Conquest patterns. Perhaps the most salient feature of Anglo-Saxon literature that distinguishes it from post-Conquest chivalric romance concerns its emphasis on the bonds among men, as opposed to the bonds between men and women. This ethos characterizes Athelston, who orients himself completely to his male companions, Wymond, Alryke, and Egelond. The poem documents their opening pact of sworn brotherhood and their subsequent mutual admiration (ll. 100, 104), jealousies ("gret envye," l. 79), rumored rivalries ("'He wole be kyng off þy lande,'" l. 164), threats (ll. 170–4, 453–7), and reconciliation with one another (ll. 549–60). Any emotional sickness Athelston experiences in the poem concerns one of his male "breþeryn," mimicking the powerful bonds among men that underlie Anglo-Saxon heroic tradition—only here, seen in forms that trivialize them. Athelston and his male companions come across as somehow emotionally unevolved. Even in the final scene involving the trial by fire, Athelston offers recompense for the suffering he caused not to Edith, his own sister who survived the fire, but to her newborn male baby, Edmund (l. 656–61). To be sure, other historicizing English romances feature (and in some cases invent) prominent and sustaining male friendships for the hero, but the hero's affinity for these men does not contrast with hostility to women, as it does in *Athelston*.[95] Instead, the marriage showcases his cultural primitivism toward women. Ironically, while Athelston's volatile and immature emotional life, in the Wise Woman scene and beyond, discredits him by infantilizing and therefore feminizing him, as we saw earlier with comparable rulers, nevertheless, his exclusively masculine emotional orientation over-masculinizes him, exposing his Anglo-Saxon identity as a major impediment to his ability to rule.

The Wise Woman type-scene in *Athelston*, in fact, constitutes one of several type-scenes structuring this short poem that profile and incriminate Athelston as an Anglo-Saxon within England. As discussion in Part II of this volume, the poem opens with a scene derived from the English Outlaw Tradition, and ends with a type-scene from hagiographic tradition, both of which cast him as a problematic outsider in his own country.[96] In the opening lines, the four men, as yet nameless, "By a forest gan þey mete/Wiþ a cros, stood in a strete/Be leff vndyr a lynde . . . (ll. 16–18), and enter into a pact of sworn brotherhood. The phrase "under the leafy" forms a verbal formula distinctive to the English Outlaw Tradition, as found in *The Tale of Gamelyn* and the later Robin Hood tales.[97] By several accounts, the English Outlaw Tradition has its roots in Anglo-Saxon resistance to the Norman Conquest, where dispossessed Anglo-Saxon noblemen, stripped of their titles and estates, took refuge in the forests where they waged a guerilla war against the Normans, becoming known the *silvatici* ("forest-dwellers," or "wild men").[98] In using the Outlaw Tradition to introduce these four men, who have entered into a pact of mutual cooperation of undisclosed design, the *Athelston*-poet plays upon post-Conquest negative stereotypes about Anglo-Saxons and outlawry. We know *what* these men are before we know who they are, and the Anglo-Saxon derivation of their names, later disclosed, only confirms our early suspicions.[99] In an additional type-scene, occurring during the trial by fire, Edith assumes the part of the innocent Christian martyr suffering persecution by a heathen despot in a foreign land, only the despot in this instance is neither heathen nor foreign but English and Christian. Viewed alongside these other type-scenes intended to denigrate Athelston politically and spiritually, the Wise Woman scene becomes charged as a tool for negative stereotyping; in this case, one aimed at early English cultural identity. The poem frames King Athelston as an outsider, despite his clear status as an insider in terms of ethnicity, faith, and even territory. In this sense, he becomes an object of scorn among his own people—the very worst kind of rejection.

Yet another subtle and revealing variation the *Athelston*-poet introduces to the Wise Woman type-scene concerns the wife herself, Athelston's queen, by far the highest ranking yet most yielding wife of any of the scenes discussed previously. Scholarly discussions of this and related scenes tend to focus on the powerful threat posed by women's social agency, as embodied in the queen.[100] However, when placed alongside the other wives of the Wise Woman scenes, the queen grows less formidable. First, unlike her counterparts, the queen is not ethnically or culturally Other. Nor is she Anglo-Saxon, like her problematic husband. Rather, her character gestures toward post-Conquest English culture and values, as she is most likely based on Queen Emma of Normandy, successive queen of Aethelred the Redeless (nicknamed the "Unready") (978–1016), and the Danish conqueror, Cnut (1016–1035), and the mother of Edward the Confessor (1042–1066).[101] According to a legend that originated sometime during the thirteenth century, Emma, in 1042, found herself having to clear her name from the unfounded rumor of unchastity by undergoing an ordeal by fire involving nine hot ploughshares. While not an exact blueprint for the story of *Athelston*, the two share many narrative features, including the ordeal by fire undergone by a woman, a villainous royal advisor living in Dover, a gullible king (in this case, Edward the Confessor), and a Bishop named Alwyn (cf. Alryke), all rooting *Athelston* in earlier, pre-Conquest events.[102] In Emma, we see a Norman woman, the daughter of Richard I, Duke of Normandy, who becomes a queen in Anglo-Saxon England, finding herself subjected unfairly to early English judicial practice, framing early England in primitive terms. The context of the Emma legend places Athelston's queen in Anglo-Norman rather than Anglo-Saxon tradition, distancing her from her retrograde husband.

Second, the Wise Woman scene in the poem is less private than in other texts, as Athelston and the queen are not the only people in the room; the poet indicates "Ladyys and maydenys þat þere were" (l. 285), another important departure from the narrative norm for this scene that compromises the queen's ability to speak and act independently.[103] Hers is a public performance. Her conduct, therefore, is altogether more formal than in early Wise Woman scenes. She enters the hall and addresses Athelston formally: "'Sere kyng, I am before þe come'" (l. 259), mentioning their unborn child to gently further her case. She then makes a formal appeal, rather than a demand, asking he "'Graunte me my bone'" (l. 261), expressing none of the easy familiarity between husband and wife we find in comparable scenes.[104] In other words, the queen approaches Athelston less like a spouse than like any other royal subject appealing to the crown.

Third, unlike comparable wives in the Wise Woman scene, the queen of *Athelston* does not openly admonish her husband, either through leading questions or damning conclusions. Rather, the queen remains deferential and courteous throughout. She avoids criticizing her husband's recent action of imprisoning Egelond, Edith, and their children and merely asks if she might "borwe" Egelond and Edith "'Out off here paynys stronge,'" "'Tyl þe nexte day at morwe'" (ll. 262–3), to release them just for a day, carefully evading any suggestion of wrongdoing on Athelston's part. Even her suggestion to convene a "playne parlement" treads lightly as a mere tool for gathering more information "'þat we mowe wete þe comoun sent'" (l. 265), and when he refuses, she submits to him still further through shedding "teeres" (l. 275), and "On here bare knees doun sche felle" (l. 277). We get no criticisms, veiled or otherwise, of Athelston's conduct, and her tone and body language remain non-confrontational. In fact, when the queen eventually furthers her cause shortly thereafter, she works through other men entirely—Archbishop Alryke and the royal messenger who delivers her emergency summons—avoiding further direct confrontation. In short, unlike her counterparts in other instances of the Wise Woman scene, the queen is the soul of decorum.

Finally, while each of the wives in other instances of the Wise Woman scene merely suffer some verbal rebuff, the queen of *Athelston* endures sharp physical harm and humiliation, shocking in its severity, when Athelston kicks her in the womb, causing her to collapse and miscarry the baby.[105] Whereas, in other instances of the Wise Woman scene, the wife, if anything, overpowers her husband verbally and/or strategically, in *Athelston*, the wife's weaker status as a (pregnant) woman weakens still further as Athelston overrules her verbally ("'Þy bone schal nouȝt igrauntyd be,'" l. 268) and incapacitates her physically so that "Sche swownyd amonges hem alle" (l. 284). That the queen's recommendation of a "playne parlement" never gets any traction only confirms the pattern of powerlessness surrounding this queen, certainly in comparison with the other wives. Thus, at every turn, the poet seems to diminish the wife's force as an internal challenger to the ruler's dangerous actions.

However, in *Athelston* as elsewhere, the wife in the Wise Woman typescene highlights the cultural difference and perceived inferiority of the ruler to whom she is married, and the queen in *Athelston* proves no exception, as the variations in her characterization reveal. One way *Athelston* incriminates Anglo-Saxon culture, as measured by post-Conquest, Anglo-Norman values, concerns the relative positioning of women within the literary project. To be sure, English romance deviates from French romance from which it derives in tying the hero's project equally, and in some cases, more, to masculine concerns and alliances while aligning the woman he loves to the hero's concurrent martial and political goals. Such is the pattern in *King Horn*, *Havelok the Dane*, *Sir Orfeo*, and the *Erl of Tolouse*, to name a few.[106] Nonetheless, the hero of each of these poems follows the model of French romance in how he comes to the aide of the woman he loves, and most of them exhibit the profound emotional attachment for the woman so characteristic of the romance hero, and so absent in the Anglo-Saxon hero.

The Middle English *Athelston* features a treatment of women that could not violate the chivalric code more, and Athelston's violence toward the queen in the Wise Woman scene caricatures the late-medieval perceived cultural primitivism of the Anglo-Saxon. He is not simply emotionally indifferent toward her—he is abusive. In her study of Chaucer's depiction of the pagan Other with regard to marital relations, Lynn Shutters identifies a pattern of abusive men and their willing spouses, suggesting images of culturally sanctioned abuse of women as a marker of difference.[107] Elizabeth Ashman Rowe argues relatedly for the politicization of the queen in *Athelston* as a symbol for the vulnerable political subject at the mercy of absolutist rule.[108] The Wise Woman scene in *Athelston* combines these two gestures of cultural denigration for political aims, using the queen as the test case. Her power in this scene derives not from her *in*subordination, but rather, from her flawless *sub*ordination to the king, through unwavering social decorum, even in the face of life-threatening odds, unlike the typical wife of the Wise Woman scene.[109] Moreover, her powerful vulnerability expresses not only her own Christ-like virtue but, through contrast, Athelston's un-Christ-like brutality, from a man who should know better, given where and when he is.[110] The problem, however, is who he is. The queen's violated body becomes forensic evidence not only of the endangered "body politic" but also of the culturally specific threat posed to it by outmoded and hyper-masculinized, early English modes of governance.

Thus, Athelston's apparent and unusual victory over his wife's meddling in the Wise Woman scene, in fact, spells his defeat as a viable ruler in the eyes of the audience, precisely in how it contrasts so painfully with one of the core tenets of post-Conquest chivalric romance regarding the treatment of women, especially high-ranking ones.

One final way the *Athelston*-poet innovates with the Wise Woman typescene involves disempowering and duplicating the child character, while retaining its narrative function of charting progress for the ruler and the kingdom. At first, it would seem that the child figure undergoes a similar diminishment to its mother's. First, while the children of the foreign rulers in other instances of the Wise Woman scene appear in the story as named, young adults possessing growing powers of judgment and agency, the child in *Athelston* is a nameless, powerless, unborn infant. Second, while the young adult children of other tales suffer yet triumph over their fathers' abuse, the child in *Athelston* suffers and dies under direct attack from his father. In this sense, while other fathers fail to quash the futures of their children, Athelston succeeds. Third, the children of the other foreign rulers forge a new and better future for their fathers and kingdoms, whether it be religious conversion or territorial unification. In *Athelston*, the death of the royal heir seems to deny any future to the kingdom. Fourth, the poet displaces the child in favor of another baby, St. Edmund, also born prematurely under duress caused by Athelston, also of Anglo-Saxon descent, also related to Athelston (nephew), and also marked as a future royal child. Thus, Athelston's son, rather than exercising agency as other children of the Wise Woman scene do, is deprived of any agency through death and replaced by a similar baby boy. Why does the *Athelston*-poet make the king's son disposable?

Unlike the earlier children discussed, who align with the colonizer's notions of progress, at odds with their fathers, Athelston's baby aligns with the backward ways of the "colonized." Whereas Floris and Melidor appear as fully developed characters, the nameless infant of *Athelston* bears only three markers of identity: gender and age ("a knaue-chyld," l. 289) and rank ("Hys owne fadyr hym slowȝ," l. 293), each of which mark him first and foremost as Athelston's royal heir—a status underscored by the queen's words "'I am before þe come/Wiþ a chyld, douȝtyr or a sone,'" ll. 259–60). This baby represents the foreign ruler, Athelston, rather than any opponent of his. In part, this relates to the absence of any hero comparable to Floris or Degrevant who actively undermines the ruler's agenda. Nonetheless, this child, like the others, factors into the foreign ruler's demise even more intensely than previously seen; unlike the Emir of *Floris* or the Earl of *Degrevant*, both of whom are defeated by children akin to them, Athelston defeats himself by murdering his own heir, tantamount to death-by-self-destruction—the soundest form of defeat. Equally unwittingly, he then prompts the premature birth of another child, this one, according to the poet, pre-canonized and named as "seynt Edemound" (l. 649), or Edmund the Martyr (855–869), and the hagiographic flavor of Edith's trial by fire, where she follows in the footsteps of the innocent Christian undergoing persecution, marks her baby, as sanctioned by God.[111] Interestingly, in this scene, Athelston plays the role normally assigned to the heathen despot torturing innocent Christians, despite his English/Christian status, becoming yet another way the poem frames him as a force to be overcome.[112]

If the death of the earlier baby marks the end of Athelston's archaic brand of governance, this new baby embodies a progressive and salvific future that will not include the likes of Athelston. St. Edmund, shown here in the usual form of an infant, parallels the earlier infant damned by his own father and effectively takes the future of the kingdom out of Athelston's hands.[113] Just as Athelston undermines himself, without the need for outside intervention, when he kills his own baby, he also voluntarily relinquishes control over the future of the kingdom when he bequeaths to Edmund "'Halff my land . . . Also longe as I may leue,/Wiþ marykys and with pounde,/And al afftyr my dede-/Yngelond to wysse and rede'" (657–61). By this gesture, Edmund becomes the successor to Athelston without being his actual offspring and heir; he marks a break in the royal line, a break brought about by Athelston himself, not by any challenger. As a fellow king and the early patron saint of England, Edmund, in this scene, represents, specifically, the political salvation of England, now wrested from the grip of a tyrant.[114] Athelston and Edmund, as I have argued elsewhere, form competing versions of Anglo-Saxon identity that came to dominate the political landscape of the late fourteenth century, cutting along class lines and finding indelible expression in the Peasant's Revolt of 1381.[115] Whereas Athelston represents the confrontational and dangerous image of Anglo-Saxon kingship championed by the peasant protesters of the time, Edmund represents a conciliatory model of Anglo-Saxon kingship, rooted in a shared faith tradition and sanctioned by the crown, which triumphs at the end of the poem.

In sum, the Wise Woman type-scene in *Athelston*, through its infrastructure of cultural difference, casts a version of the "domestic" (early English identity) as essentially "foreign." In this way, it reverses the usual direction of infiltration into a foreign land found in other poems containing the scene by casting an early English king as the "foreign" ruler who has wrongfully infiltrated the English throne. He holds the throne, and therefore, holds the nation's institutions of governance (namely Parliament) hostage to his own subjective and arcane ideals of community and justice. In doing so, he becomes indistinguishable from the poem's villain, Wymond, in his child-like propensity for jealousy and vengeance. The absence of any hero, such as Degrevant, who fights the good fight against tyranny, effectively removes all defenses shielding both the other characters as well as the English readers of the poem, who watch Athelston and his cronies move through familiar English towns and byways in the poem's contemporary setting. In victimizing innocent women and children, including his wiser wife, and killing his only child, Athelston effectively delegitimizes and excises Anglo-Saxon identity, as exemplified by him, from English political life, rendering it un-English.

Conclusion

The Middle English *Floris and Blancheflour*, *Sir Degrevant* and *Athelston* bring to light a recurring scene sharing a fixed constellation of narrative elements, with a common choreography and trajectory, constituting a type-scene all its own: what I have termed the Wise Woman type-scene. The scene features a culturally foreign land and/or mindset and a family native to that land, including a troubled leader, his clever wife, and their resourceful child, all of whom find their old, native ways of doing things challenged by a newer, non-native value system that outclasses theirs in every way. The English audience peers into the private, domestic life of a non-English family whose wider culture seems to have entered its final phase before obsolescence. The foreign lord, in these texts, features in the roles of husband, father, and leader, and gets none of them right, exposing his own ineptitude and inferiority as a political figure. Progress in the situation falls to his wiser wife and resourceful child, both of whom, knowingly or not, collude with outside forces, whether they be western, English, Christian, or all three. Mother and child act in tandem, with the parent waging resistance through verbal criticism of her husband, and the child forging a practical way forward that brings his/her family and society closer to English values. Cultural difference is obvious in the earliest instance of the Wise Woman type-scene in Middle English, in the thirteenth-century *Floris and Blancheflour*, set exclusively in Muslims lands of southern Spain and North Africa. In the later, fourteenth-century *Sir Degrevant*, however, set along the Anglo-Scottish border and featuring a Scottish border lord, cultural difference proves more subtle, yet equally potent, if not more timely, as English kings of the time were pursuing various means for bringing Scotland into the English fold. In the late fourteenth-century *Athelston*, cultural difference takes its most nuanced form, manifesting across time periods rather than terrain, exploring pre- and post-Conquest chapters of English history and governance. It unfolds a fictional scenario whereby a tenth-century Anglo-Saxon king, Athelston, finds himself on the throne of late-fourteenth-century England and out of step with its citizenry. He may be English and Christian, but the poet casts him as an "outsider" from a by-gone era, who spells his own extinction by killing his only son and heir.

The pattern observed suggests that the Wise Woman type-scene, occurring, as it does, early in the narrative, encodes cultural difference, and therefore, announces a more complex social and political terrain than may otherwise seem apparent. The central conflict in these poems entails a collision of two different codes of conduct, rather than a shared code enacted dissimilarly, with one deemed more primitive, unjust, and immoral, and therefore, nonviable. The wise woman and her child straddle both cultures, participating in one while serving the other, working behind enemy lines, non-violently, to bring about social progress from within, and modeling effective diplomacy in the private sphere that shapes the public sphere. The scene's diverse application across texts and cultures demonstrates its continuing utility for poets seeking to portray and critique cultures other than their own. For the most part, English poets affirm official English policy but question its strategies. The Wise Woman scene explores alternate, less militarily destructive, and more sustainable methods of political progress using women and children as the prime—and secret—agents.

Notes

1 Similar scenes also appear in the ME *King of Tars* (c.1330) between the Christian heroine and her husband, the Muslim king of Damas (Damascus), and the late fourteenth-century ME *Erl of Toulouse* between Dame Beaulybon and her husband, the German emperor.
2 See Mary Housum Ellzey, "The Advice of Wives in Three Middle English Romances: *The King of Tars, Sir Cleges,* and *Athelston,*" *Medieval Perspectives* 7 (1992): 44–52. Her exclusion of comparable scenes in the texts forming the subject of the current chapter, and her inclusion of episodes not sharing the core emotional picture found in the Wise Woman scene, suggests that Ellzey may not have considered the Wise Woman episode to be a type-scene, as such.
3 On cultural and religious difference in *The King of Tars*, see Siobhain Bly Calkin, *Saracens and the Making of English Identity: The Auchinleck Manuscript* (New York and London: Routledge, 2005), 97–128. For cultural difference in *Sir Degrevant*, see Dominique Battles, "The Middle English *Sir Degrevant* and the Scottish Border," *Studies in Philology* 113 (2016): 501–45. For Athelston as a cultural Other, see Battles, "The Middle English *Athelston* and 1381, Part I: the Politics of Anglo-Saxon Identity" *Studies in Philology* 117 (2020): 1–39.
4 These poems include the OF *Roman de Thèbes, Floris and Blancheflour, The King of Tars, Sir Degrevant,* the *Erl of Tolouse,* and *Athelston*. Themes of political reform and/or cultural and religious assimilation govern all these poems.
5 See Ellzey, "The Advice of Wives in Three Middle English Romances." In the case of *Athelston*, Elizabeth Ashman Rowe interprets the queen's role as a mirror of the king, Athelston, but admittedly, does not account for the

Anglo-Saxon elements permeating the poem. See "The Female Body Politic and the Miscarriage of Justice in *Athelston*," *Studies in the Age of Chaucer* 17 (1995): 78–98, 96. Similarly, Nancy Mason Bradbury reads the queen in *Athelston* as an example of a generalized cultural anxiety of female interference in public policy, but not does account for the Anglo-Saxon profile of the king and his sworn brothers. See "Beyond the Kick: Women's Agency in *Athelston*," in Corinne Saunders, ed., *Cultural Encounters in the Romance of Medieval England* (Cambridge: D.S. Brewer, 2005), 149–58, 157.

6 Ellzey identifies the element of political subversion for the Middle English *Athelston*, a concept that applies equally to *Sir Degrevant*, the *Erl of Tolouse*, and *Floris and Blancheflour*. See "The Advice of Wives in Three Middle English Romances," 50–51.

7 See Ellzey, "The Advice of Wives in Three Middle English Romances," 48–51; John Carmi Parsons, "The Pregnant Queen as Counsellor and the Medieval Construction of Motherhood," in John Carmi Parsons and Bonnie Wheeler, eds., *Medieval Mothering* (New York: Garland Publishing, Inc., 1996), 31–61, 44 and 51.

8 Ellzey, "The Advice of Wives in Three Middle English Romances," 45.

9 See Elizabeth Ashman Rowe, "The Female Body Politic and the Miscarriage of Justice in *Athelston*," 85.

10 Ellzey attributes the public voice these wives exercise to the homiletic and "non-chivalric nature" of the romances she examines and does not factor in their cultural picture. See "The Advice of Wives in Three Middle English Romances," 45 and 51.

11 On the dating of the poem, see A.B. Taylor, *Floris and Blancheflour: A Middle English Romance* (Oxford: Clarendon Press, 1927), 7–8. Also Lillian Herlands Hornstein, "Miscellaneous Romances," in J. Burke Severs, gen. ed., *A Manual of the Writings in Middle English 1050–1500*, 11 volumes, vol. 1 (New Haven: The Connecticut Academy of Arts and Sciences, 1967), 144–74, 145–46; also Erik Kooper's edition of *Floris and Blancheflour* in *Sentimental and Humorous Romances* (Kalamazoo: Medieval Institute Publications, 2006), 1–38, 1–3.

12 The French "aristocratic" version of the story dates to 1160, while the "popular" version dates to c.1200. See A.B. Taylor, *Floris and Blancheflour*, 7–8, 15; Hornstein, "Miscellaneous Romances," 146.

13 Hornstein, "Miscellaneous Romances," 145–46; Erik Kooper, *Sentimental and Humorous Romances*, 8; Patricia E. Grieve, *Floire et Blancheflor and the European Romance* (Cambridge: Cambridge University Press, 1997), 18–20. One of the French redactions of *Floris* aligns the story with national epic by making the young lovers the parents of Charlemagne's mother, Bertha. See William Henry Schofield, *English Literature from the Norman Conquest to Chaucer* (New York: Macmillan and Co., 1906), 307; also W.R.J. Barron, *English Medieval Romance* (London and New York: Longman, 1987), 183.

14 See Grieve, *Floire et Blancheflor and the European Romance*, 2–6, 53–57. Conversion permeates the entire tradition of *Floris and Blancheflour*, and expresses itself in the aristocratic versions of France and England, where Grieve notes the emphasis on "conversion material," including the "persecuted heroine" theme involving Blancheflour and her mother, the role of magical objects denoting divine intervention, and Floris' "love-pilgrimage." Siobhain Bly Calkin locates religious difference at the heart of *Floris*, one of several Middle English romances in the Auchinleck MS that uses the Saracen Other to

explore the anxieties Muslim civilization engendered in the European Christian imagination. See *Saracens and the Making of English Identity: The Auchinleck Manuscript*, 3–7.
15 Taylor, *Floris and Blancheflour*, 17.
16 All references to the poem are from Taylor, *Floris and Blancheflour*.
17 W.R.J. Barron voices the consensus opinion of *Floris and Blancheflour* as a purely incidental love story with a "fairy-tale ending . . . whose tenuous relationship with reality must be seen in light of contemporary concepts of love and marriage." See *English Medieval Romance*, 185.
18 See "Cunning and Ingenuity in the Middle English *Floris and Blauncheflur*," *Medium Aevum* 53 (1984): 10–25, 13.
19 Ibid.
20 Ibid., 14.
21 See Grieve, *Floire et Blancheflour and the European Romance*, 55.
22 See Suzanne Conklin Akbari, *Idols in the East: European Representations of Islam and the Orient, 1100–1450* (Ithaca, NY and London: Cornell University Press, 2009), 159–73, 282–83.
23 Taylor, *Floris and Blancheflour*, 17.
24 See Mohja Kahf, *Western Representations of the Muslim Woman: From Termagant to Odalisque* (Austin: University of Texas Press, 1999), 53–54.
25 In her analysis of the Saracen princess Floripas from *Fierabras*, Suzanne Conklin Akbari notes the far-ranging, often paradoxical behavior, blending both feminine and masculine traits, exhibited by the Saracen woman. See *Idols in the East*, 175–85; Mohja Kahf, *Western Representations of the Muslim Woman: from Termagant to Odalisque*, 53–54.
26 In the leadership function she plays in the kingdom, often through subversion, the queen in *Floris and Blancheflour* resembles other medieval fictional Muslim women such as the Sultaness in Chaucer's *Man of Law's Tale*, and Nicolette in *Aucassin et Nicolette*. See Kahf, *Western Representations of the Muslim Woman: from Termagant to Odalisque*, 46–48.
27 Ibid., 54.
28 Ibid., 2.
29 On the "poetic amorality" governing the basic plot of the story in both French and English versions, where good comes about in the absence of moral or religious conscience among the main players, see M. Lot-Borodine, *Le Roman idyllique au moyen Âge* (Paris: A. Picard, 1913; rpt. Geneva: Slatkine Reprints, 1972), 68; Geraldine Barnes, "Cunning and Ingenuity in the Middle English *Floris and Blauncheflur*," 11.
30 See William C. Calin, "Flower Imagery in *Floire and Blancheflour*," *French Studies* 18 (1964): 103–11, 106–8; Kooper, *Sentimental and Humorous Romances*, 8; Taylor, *Floris and Blancheflour*, 16–17.
31 Grieve discusses "the road to conversion" as a guiding theme in several medieval versions of the legend, generally emphasizing Floris' personal spiritual journey and divine intervention pertaining to it. See *Floire et Blancheflour and the European Romance*, 53–57.
32 In her discussion of the OF *Floire et Blancheflour*, Sharon Kinoshita argues that the story advances a more fluid, reciprocal, accommodating model of East-West relations than that found in the tradition of the *chanson de geste*—which it does. However, both the French version, and at least one English versions of the tale (the Auchinleck MS), conclude with conversions away from Islam and towards Christianity, suggesting a consistent political and theological vision

despite evolving methods. See *Medieval Boundaries: Rethinking Difference in Old French Literature* (Philadelphia: University of Pennsylvania Press, 2006), 77–104.
33 This detail resonates with medieval iconographic depictions of the nursing Virgin. See *Floire et Blancheflour and the European Romance*, 97–98. Carol F. Heffernan argues that this arrangement suggests some level of incestuous love between the young lovers, either biological or spiritual. See *The Orient in Chaucer and Medieval Romance* (Cambridge: D.S. Brewer, 2003), 84–99. On the metaphorical image of the nursing Christian mother and European mores, see Anna Czarnowus, *Fantasies of the Other's Body in Middle English Oriental Romance* (Frankfurt am Main: Peter Lang, 2013), 111–12.
34 Edmund Reiss, "Symbolic Detail in Medieval Narrative: *Floris and Blancheflour*," *Papers on Language and Literature* 7 (1971): 339–50, 341–42.
35 Grieve, *Floire et Blancheflour and the European Romance*, 55; Reiss, "Symbolic Detail in Medieval Narrative: *Floris and Blancheflour*," 344–45.
36 On western stereotypes of the feminized Orient, see Suzanne Conklin Akbari, *Idols in the East*, 284.
37 Kathleen Coyne Kelly speaks of Floris' "very bourgeois way towards Babylon," encountering none of the hostile foes that typically plague the medieval knight-errant. See "The Bartering of Blancheflur in the Middle English *Floris and Blancheflur*," *Studies in Philology* 91 (1994): 101–10, 107.
38 *Floris and Blancheflour*, 19.
39 See Akbari, *Idols in the East*, 283.
40 See "Symbolic Detail in Medieval Narrative: *Floris and Blancheflour*," 346–48. Reiss reads the chess game as part of his larger Christian allegorical interpretation of the poem, but he provides copious evidence of the game's moral ambiguity for western audiences.
41 In comparable scenes in Middle English literature, the disguise itself is the trickery. In *Floris*, the poet adds the trickery of the chess game on top of disguise. For the theme of disguise and infiltration in Middle English romance, see Dominique Battles, *Cultural Difference and Material Culture in Middle English Romance* (New York: Routledge, 2013), 112–20, 134–35, 137–39, as well as the entry on "Disguise and Infiltration" in Part I of this volume.
42 See Kooper, *Sentimental and Humorous Romances*, 41.
43 In this sense, Floris' *persona* on this journey, even disguised as a merchant, is somewhat akin to the journey we see in the "popular" version of this tale, where Floris scorns the use of disguise and insists on proclaiming his knightly status. See Taylor, *Floris and Blancheflour*, 12–13.
44 See Joseph Hall, ed., *King Horn: A Middle English Romance* (Oxford: Clarendon Press, 1901). I refer to the Cambridge manuscript of *Horn* (l. 563ff.) For a discussion of magical protective rings, including those of *King Horn* and *Floris and Blancheflour*, see Corinne Saunders, *Magic and the Supernatural in Middle English Romance* (Woodbridge, Suffolk: D.S. Brewer, 2010), 125–30, 160, 165. Also, the "Magic Ring type-scene in Part I of this volume.
45 N.H.G.E. Veldhoen reads the ring as adding a "feminine aspect to [Floris'] male personality, thus making him whole," but does not identify the variant of this particular topos, whereby feminine influence extends not from the love object, Blancheflour, but from a feminine figure exerting political resistance, the queen. See "Floris and Blancheflour: To Indulge the Fancy and to Hear the Love," in N.H.G.E. Veldhoen and H. Aertsen, eds., *Companion to Early Middle English Literature* (Amsterdam: VU University Press, 1995), 51–65, 60.

46 Gédéon Huet, for example, aligns the Babylon episode in the Old French *Floire et Blancheflaur* with two Arabic tales involving a man's infiltration into a harem. One is titled "The Steward's Tale: the Young Man from Baghdad and the Lady Zubaida," by Ibn-al-Djouzi, based on the fourteenth-century Syrian manuscript of *Alf Layla wa-Layla*, and the other, "The History of the Moneylender of Baghdad." See Huet, "Sur l'Origine de *Floire et Blancheflaur*," *Romania* 28 (1899): 348–59. Carol F. Heffernan traces the Babylon episode in the Middle English *Floris and Blancheflour* to an Arabic tale entitled "The Story of Nur-al-Din ibn-Bakkar and the Slave-Girl Shams al-Nahar." See *The Orient in Chaucer and Medieval Romance*, 103–4. While all of these tales involve disguise, infiltration into a harem, and romantic love, they all have the love affair emerge only after the man has entered the harem, in contrast to *Floris and Blancheflour*, where the young couple are already in love prior to the infiltration. Floris rescues a woman he already loves. See also S. Singer, "Arabische und europäische Poesi im Mittelalter," in *Abhandlungen der preussischen Akademie der Wissenschaften, philos-hist. Klasse* (Berlin, 1918), 4–6; Dorothee Metlitzki, *The Matter of Araby in Medieval England* (New Haven, CT and London: Yale University Press, 1977), 243–44.

47 See "The City of Babylon in the Middle English *Floris and Blancheflour*," *Anglia* 128 (2010): 1–7. The *Roman de Thèbes* (1155–60) is contemporary with the French antecedent of the ME poem, *Floris et Blancheflaur*. On the influence of the *Roman de Thèbes* on various Old French works, including *Floris et Blancheflaur*, see Leopold Constans, *Le Roman de Thèbes*, 2 vols. (Paris: Librairie de Firmin Didot, 1890), vol. 2, cxlv–cliii.

48 See Dominique Battles, *The Medieval Tradition of Thebes: History and Narrative in the* OF Roman de Thèbes, *Boccaccio, Chaucer, and Lydgate* (New York: Routledge: 2004), 19–59.

49 The story survives in multiple chronicle accounts of the First Crusade, but the fullest account of the Pious Traitor episode occurs in William of Tyre, *Deeds Done Beyond the Sea*, trans. Emily Atwater Babcock and A.C. Krey, 2 vols. (New York: Columbia University Press, 1943), 1: 242. Composed between 1167 and 1184, William's account, in fact, postdates the *Roman de Thèbes* by a few years. For a comparison of the different versions of this episode in the chronicle accounts, see Robert Levine, "The Pious Traitor: Rhetorical Reinventions of the Fall of Antioch," *Mittellateinisches Jahrbuch* 33 (1998): 59–80.

50 Kathleen Coyne Kelly reads the cup, Blancheflour, and Helen (depicted on the cup) as "articles of trade." See "The Bartering of Blancheflur in the Middle English *Floris and Blancheflur*," 106. Also, Czarnowus, *Fantasies of the Other's Body in Middle English Oriental Romance*, 113–15.

51 On the cup as a "an emblem of physical passion," see Karl P. Wentersdorf, "Iconographic Elements in *Floris and Blancheflour*," *Annuale mediaevale* 20 (1981): 76–96, 78–83.

52 Grieve suggests a similar reading of the cup in relation to Boccaccio's *Il Filocolo*. See *Floire et Blancheflour and the European Romance*, 64.

53 See Akbari, *Idols in the East*, 286.

54 The Auchinleck MS (Edinburgh, National Library of Scotland, Advocates 19.2.1) contains the most complete ending of the four extant manuscripts of the poem. See Calkin, *Saracens and the Making of English Identity: The Auchinleck Manuscript*, 129–31. On the various endings to the story, see Marijane Osborn, *Nine Medieval Romances of Magic* (Peterborough, ON: Broadview Press, 2010), 219.

55 On the dating of *Sir Degrevant*, see L.F. Casson, ed., *The Romance of Sir Degrevant* EETS OS 221 (London: Oxford University Press for the Early English Text Society, 1949), lxxii–lxxiii; Hornstein, "Miscellaneous Romances," in J. Burke Severs, gen. ed., *A Manual of the Writings in Middle English 1050–1500*, 11 volumes, vol. 1 (New Haven: The Connecticut Academy of Arts and Sciences, 1967), 144–74, 147–48.

56 *Sir Degrevant* survives in two well-known manuscript anthologies: the Findern Anthology (Cambridge University Library, MS Ff.1.6), dating to the late fifteenth and early sixteenth centuries, and the Lincoln Thornton MS (Lincoln, Dean and Chapter Library, MS 91), dating to the mid-fifteenth century. For facsimile editions of each, see Richard Beadle and A.E.B. Owen, *The Findern Manuscript: Cambridge University Library MS Ff.1.6* (London: Scolar Press, 1977); D.S. Brewer and A.E. B. Owen, *The Thornton Manuscript: Lincoln Cathedral MS 91* (London: Scolar Press, 1975; rev. ed. 1977). For a discussion of these manuscripts, see Casson, ed., *The Romance of Sir Degrevant*, ix-xv.

57 See Battles, "The Middle English *Sir Degrevant* and the Scottish Border," *Studies in Philology* 113 (2016): 501–45; also "The Middle English *Sir Degrevant* and the Architecture of the Border," *English Studies* 96 (2015): 853–72; also "Behind Enemy Lines: The German Connection in the Middle English *Sir Degrevant*," *Neophilologus* 100 (2016): 489–501; also "Melidor and the 'wylde men of þe west' in the Middle English *Sir Degrevant*," *American Notes and Queries* 33 (2020): 15–18.

58 Hornstein notes the "unusual interest derive[d] from the realistic treatment of the feudal situation" (148), while Dieter Mehl characterizes the hero as "impulsive," "down-to-earth," and thereby "individualized," commending the poem for the "refreshing absence of meaningless clichés." See his *The Middle English Romances of the Thirteenth and Fourteenth Centuries* (London: Routledge and Kegan Paul, Ltd., 1968; reprt. 2011), 68–71. Other scholars justify Degrevant's violent, vengeful actions. Arlyn Diamond, for instance, claims that "he is a chivalric hero, who is aggressive in his own defense." See his "*Sir Degrevant*: What Lovers Want," in Nicola McDonald, ed., *Pulp Fictions of Medieval England: Essays in Popular Romance* (Manchester: Manchester University Press, 2004), 82–101, 93; also A.S.G. Edwards, "Gender, Order and Reconciliation in *Sir Degrevant*," in Carol M. Meale, ed., *Readings in Medieval English Romance* (Woodbridge, Suffolk: D.S. Brewer, 1994), 53–64, 55.

59 See J.O. Halliwell-Phillips, *The Thornton Romances: The Early English Metrical Romances of Perceval, Isumbras, Eglamour, and Degrevant* (London: Camden Society, 1844), 288–89; Casson, ed., *The Romance of Sir Degrevant*, 116. Other variant spellings of Agravain include "Aggravain," "Agrafrayn," "Agravan," "Agreveins," "Engrevains," "Egrefayn," and "Engrevain." See Christopher Bruce, *The Arthurian Name Dictionary* (New York: Garland, 1999), now available full-text online; G.D. West, *An Index to Proper Names in French Arthurian Verse Romances 1150–1300*, University of Toronto Romance Series, vol. 15 (Toronto: University of Toronto Press, 1969); Edith Rickert, *Early English Romances in Verse: Done into Modern English: Romances of Love* (New York: Cooper Square Publishers, 1966), xlviii–xlix. On Degrevant as an example of the *Scoti Anglicati*, see Battles, "The Middle English *Sir Degrevant* and the Scottish Border," 505–14.

60 All citations are from Casson, ed., *The Romance of Sir Degrevant*. Casson provides a facing-page edition of the Thornton and Findern manuscripts of the poem; I quote the Findern manuscript. References to the Lincoln Thornton

MS contain an "L." Under Edward III, the banneret became one of an entire class of "new nobility," many of them men of lesser means, who owed their position, and therefore their allegiance, directly to the crown. These "new men" became indispensable to King Edward, a vital and loyal cohort of servants he could draw upon in his ongoing wars with France and Scotland. See James Bothwell, "Edward III and the 'New Nobility': Largesse and Limitation in Fourteenth-Century England," *English Historical Review* 112 (1997): 1111–40. Bothwell argues that Edward III created these new men not necessarily as permanent hereditary nobility, but rather, as a shorter-term arrangement for "somewhat more limited aims" dictated by the wars with France and Scotland (1132).

61 See Sheryl L. Forste-Grupp, "'For-thi a letter has he dyght': Paradigms for Fifteenth-Century Literacy in *Sir Degrevant*," *Studies in Philology* 101 (2004): 113–35, 121–22.

62 See Matthew Bennett, Jim Bradbury, Kelly DeVries, Iain Dickie, and Phyllis Jestice, eds., *Fighting Techniques of the Medieval World* (New York: St. Martin's Press, 2006), 31; Matthew Bennett, ed., *The Medieval World at War* (London: Thames and Hudson, 2009), 166, 170, and 174.

63 Robert Bruce, for instance, fought with a battle-axe at Bannockburn in 1314. For this and a full description of the Battle of Bannockburn, see Bennett, Bradbury, DeVries, Dickie, and Jestice, eds., *Fighting Techniques of the Medieval World*, 36–43.

64 Michael H. Brown, "*Scoti Anglicati*: Scots in Plantagenet Allegiance during the Fourteenth Century," in Andy King and Michael A. Penman, eds., *England and Scotland in the Fourteenth Century: New Perspectives* (Woodbridge, Suffolk: Boydell Press, 2007), 94–115, 110, also 107–9.

65 Craigmillar Castle, an early fifteenth-century tower-house located in Midlothian, includes a fine example of a fishpond, both functional and ornamental (this one in the shape of a "P" for the Preston family), connected to a tower-house. See Richard Fawcett, *Scottish Architecture From the Accession of the Stewarts to the Reformation 1371–1560* (Edinburgh: Edinburgh University Press, 1994), 274.

66 W.A. Davenport sees the hero as a model of "powerful and virtuous lordship." See "*Sir Degrevant* and Composite Romance," in Judith Weiss, Jennifer Fellows, and Morgan Dickson, eds., *Medieval Insular Romance: Translation and Innovation* (Cambridge: D.S. Brewer, 2001), 111–34, 120. Arlyn Diamond sees Degrevant as a "chivalric knight" who happens to be aggressive in defending his own rights. See "*Sir Degrevant*: what lovers want," 93. A.S.G. Edwards argues the extreme violence of the poem serves primarily to highlight the necessity of the "harmonizing female role" in conflict-resolution. See "Gender, Order and Reconciliation in *Sir Degrevant*," 64. Dieter Mehl reframes the hero's vengeful side as an example of "his reckless daring and his undaunted spirit." See *The Middle English Romances of the Thirteenth and Fourteenth Centuries*, 96.

67 See *The Romance of Sir Degrevant*, 121 n. 184.

68 Cited in Philippe Contamine, "Froissart and Scotland," in Grant G. Simpson, ed., *Scotland and the Low Countries* (East Linton: Tuckwell, Press, 1996), 43–58, 45. Contamine cites from MS Bibliothèque Nationale, fr. 22531, fol. 253r.

69 With his extensive lands, including arable land yielding rents ("demaynus," l. 69), enclosed deer parks ("parkes," and "haynus," meaning boundary markers, l. 70), domesticated animals ("tame store," l. 72), not to mention his many castles and stables ("stallus," l. 75) full of horses ("Lyard and soore" (l. 76)

meaning "dappled grey" and "sorrel"), Degrevant possesses landholdings befitting his station. The pattern of late medieval emparkment often included arable lands as well as settlements of the people working the land, which appears to be the case in *Sir Degrevant*. On the history of emparkment in England, and its associated communities, see Oliver Creighton, *Designs Upon the Land: Elite Landscapes of the Middle Ages* (Woodbridge, Suffolk: Boydell and Brewer, 2009), 122–66.

70 The word in the poem indicating barmkin architecture is "barnekynch" (l. 391). Variant spelling includes "barnekynnys," found in the Middle Scots *The Wallace* (VIII.782 and 1046). See Dominique Battles, "The Middle English *Sir Degrevant* and the Architecture of the Border," 855–57. Also, Jackson W. Armstrong, *England's Northern Frontier: Conflict and Local Society in the Fifteenth-Century Scottish Marches* (Cambridge: Cambridge University Press, 2020), 75–93.

71 See Dominique Battles, "Behind Enemy Lines: The German Connection in the Middle English *Sir Degrevant*," 1–13.

72 Melidor's second accusation of treason specifies hanging, drawing, and quartering (l. 758), the method of punishment reserved for cases of crimes against the state. See J.G. Bellamy, *The Law of Treason in England in the Later Middle Ages* (Cambridge: Cambridge University Press, 1970), 13; W.R. J. Barrow, "The Penalties for Treason in Medieval Life and Literature," *Journal of Medieval History* 7 (1981): 187–202; also the chapter titled "The Matter of Britain: Defining English Identity in Opposition to Torture," in Larissa Tracy, ed., *Torture and Brutality in Medieval Literature: Negotiations of National Identity* (Cambridge: D.S. Brewer, 2012).

73 See Battles, "Melidor and the 'wylde men of þe west' in the Middle English *Sir Degrevant.*"

74 Melidor's chamber resembles a similar painted, vaulted chamber in Longthorpe Tower near Peterborough, a towerhouse of the same period as the poem. For the first study done of the murals at Longthorpe, see E. Clive Rouse and Audrey Baker, "The Wall-Paintings at Longthorpe Tower Near Peterborough, Northants," *Archaeologia* 96 (1955): 1–57. L.F. Casson mentions the murals of Longthorpe, a recent find at the time, in his edition of *Sir Degrevant* (p. lxviii); W.A. Davenport, "*Sir Degrevant* and Composite Romance," 125–27; also N.J.G. Pounds, *The Medieval Castle in England and Wales: A Social and Political History* (Cambridge: Cambridge University Press, 1993), 284–85.

75 See Elizabeth Bonner, "Scotland's 'Auld Alliance' with France, 1295–1560," *History* 84 (1999): 5–30.

76 Arlyn Diamond frames her behavior in the positive when he observes how Melidor lives in the "declarative mode," as does Forste-Grupp, who sees her as "a new ideal of woman." See Arlyn Diamond, "*Sir Degrevant*: What Lovers Want," 87; Forste-Grupp, "'For-thi a lettre has he dyght': Paradigms for Fifteenth-Century Literacy in *Sir Degrevant*," 129. Casson, however, judges her more harshly in saying "Melidor ceases to be the conventional romantic heroine of rather shrewish temper." See Casson, ed., *The Romance of Sir Degrevant*, lxxv.

77 The passage reads "Lez femmes du chastelle enamenerent lez cheueaux a lours homs, qi mounterent, [et] firent la chase . . ." ["The women of the castle brought horses to their men, who mounted and gave chase . . ."]. See Andy King, ed. and trans., Sir Thomas Gray, *Scalacronica 1272–1363* (Woodbridge, Suffolk: The Boydell Press, 2005), 80–81.

78 See Matthew P. McDiarmid, ed., *Hary's Wallace*, 2 vols. (Edinburgh: William Blackwood and Sons Ltd., 1968), VIII.1235.
79 Michael H. Brown, *The Wars of Scotland 1214–1371* (Edinburgh: Edinburgh University Press, 2004), 194.
80 *Athelston* survives in the unique fifteenth-century manuscript Cambridge, Gonville and Caius 175, fols. 120v–131v. The dating of the poem has been set at around 1400. See A.M. Trounce, ed., *Athelston: A Middle English Romance*, EETS 224 (London: Oxford University Press, 1951), 1–2, 60–61; Elaine Treharne, "Romanticizing the Past in the Middle English *Athelston*," *The Review of English Studies*, n.s. 50 (1999): 1–21, 9–11. On the poem's origins based upon dialect, see Trounce, ed., *Athelston*, 49–52.
81 See Gordon Gerould, "Social and Historical Reminiscences in the Middle English *Athelston*," *Englische Studien* 36 (1906): 193–208; Geraldine Barnes, *Counsel and Strategy in Middle English Romance* (Cambridge: D.S. Brewer, 1993), 55–57; Ellzey, "The Advice of Wives in Three Middle English Romances," 49–50. Also, Susan Crane, *Insular Romance: Politics, Faith, and Culture in Anglo-Norman and Middle English Literature* (Berkeley: University of California Press, 1986), 69–73; Elaine M. Treharne, "Romanticizing the Past in the Middle English *Athelston*," 18–21; Rowe, "The Female Body Politic and the Miscarriage of Justice in *Athelston*," 79–98; Nancy Mason Bradbury, "Beyond the Kick: Women's Agency in *Athelston*"; Daniel F. Pigg, "The Implications of Realist Poetics in the Middle English *Athelston*," *English Language Notes* 32 (1994): 1–8; Rosalind Field, "*Athelston* or the Middle English *Nativity of St. Edmund*," in Rosalind Field, Phillipa Hardman, and Michelle Sweeney, eds., *Christianity and Romance in Medieval England* (Woodbridge, Suffolk: D.S. Brewer, 2010), 139–49. Elaine Treharne and Laura Hibbard detail the Anglo-Saxon portraiture of this particular absolutist ruler. See Treharne, "Romanticizing the Past in the Middle English *Athelston*," 12–18; Laura A. Hibbard, *Mediaeval Romance in England* (New York: Burt Franklin, 1969), 143–44.
82 King Murry of *King Horn* is "þe gode king" (l. 30), and King Orfeo of *Sir Orfeo* is characterized as is "an heiȝe lording,/A stalworþ man & hardi bo" (ll. 40–1), while King Athelwold of *Havelok the Dane* is called "Engelondes blome" (l. 63). See W.W. Skeat, ed., and rev. by K. Sisam, *The Lay of Havelok the Dane* (Oxford: Clarendon Press, 1939); Hall, ed., *King Horn: A Middle English Romance*; A.J. Bliss, ed., *Sir Orfeo*, 2nd ed. (Oxford: Clarendon Press, 1966). On the portrayal of these kings as Anglo-Saxons, see Dominique Battles, *Cultural Difference and Material Culture in Middle English Romance: Normans and Saxons* (New York: Routledge, 2013), 20–22, 27, 30–34, 125–26; also "*Sir Orfeo* and English Identity," *Studies in Philology* 107 (2010): 179–211.
83 See Treharne, "Romanticizing the Past in the Middle English *Athelston*," 2. A.M. Trounce notes the poem's highly specific geography as "quite peculiar" within the corpus of Middle English romance. See *Athelston*, 38. More recently, Christine Chism explores the geographic mapping of the poem in "The Romance of the Road in *Athelston* and Two Late Medieval Robin Hood Tales," in Valerie Allen and Ruth Evans, eds., *Roadworks: Medieval Britain, Medieval Roads* (Manchester: Manchester University Press, 2016), 220–48, 225–37. On parallels between the poem's geography and the major sites of the Peasant's Revolt of 1381, see Dominique Battles, "The Middle English *Athelston* and 1381, Part II: The Road to Rebellion," *Studies in Philology* 117 (2020): 469–87.

84 *Athelston* is commonly classified under "The Matter of England" romances, despite the fact that it has no known source. Charles W. Dunn categorizes it under "Romances Derived from English Legends," in J. Burke Severs, ed., *A Manual of Writings in Middle English* (New Haven: Connecticut Academy of Arts and Sciences, 1967), 2–37, 33–34; also Rosalind Field, "Romance as History, History as Romance," in Maldwyn Mills, Jennifer Fellows, and Carol M. Meale, eds., *Romance in England* (Woodbridge, Suffolk: D. S. Brewer, 1991), 163–73; the poems most recent editors have adopted the same classification, grouping it with *King Horn*, *Havelok the Dane*, and *Bevis and Hampton*, all poems concerning legendary English history. See Ronald B. Herzman, Graham Drake, and Eve Salisbury, eds., *Four Romances of England* (Kalamazoo: Western Michigan University Press, 1999), 341–84. Within the general heading of "Matter of England" romances, W.R.J. Barron includes *Athelston*, tentatively, under the sub-heading "Romances of Greenwood," as a precursor, of sorts, to the later Robin Hood tales. See *English Medieval Romance* (London: Longman, 1987), 63–88, 81. Nancy Mason Bradbury characterizes *Athelston* as a "strange and angry narrative." See "The Erosion of Oath-Based Relationships: A Cultural Context for *Athelston*," *Medium Aevum* 73 (2004):189–204, 189.

85 See Treharne, "Romanticizing the Past in the Middle English *Athelston*," 15; Helen Young, "*Athelston* and English Law: Plantagenet Practice and Anglo-Saxon Precedent," 116; Robert Allen Rouse, *The Idea of Anglo-Saxon England in Middle English Romance* (Cambridge: D.S. Brewer, 2005), 129–32; also Robert Bartlett, *Trial by Fire and Water: The Medieval Judicial Ordeal* (Oxford: Clarendon Press, 1986), 62–69. Bartlett notes that while such ordeals were banned by the Fourth Lateran Counsel in 1219, they continued in judicial practice into the post-Conquest period (p. 64).

86 The great innovation of post-Conquest English law is the jury system, whereby legal cases were determined by a jury of peers who have examined the evidence of the case. On the development of the jury system in medieval England, see Doris M. Stenton, *English Justice Between the Norman Conquest and the Great Charter 1066–1215* (Philadelphia: The American Philosophical Society, 1964), 13–17; Alan Harding, *The Law Courts of Medieval England* (London: George Allen & Unwin, Ltd., 1973), 32–63.

87 See Bradbury, "Beyond the Kick: Women's Agency in *Athelston*," 150–51; Ellzey, "The Advice of Wives in Three Middle English Romances, 50; Rowe, "The Female Body Politic and the Miscarriage of Justice in *Athelston*," 82–83; Parsons, "The Pregnant Queen as Counsellor and the Medieval Construction of Motherhood," 43–51.

88 On the poem's detailed, contemporary geography, see "Romanticizing the Past in the Middle English *Athelston*," 2. A.M. Trounce notes the poem's highly specific geography as "quite peculiar" within the corpus of Middle English romance. See *Athelston*, 38. Also, Christine Chism, "The Romance of the Road in *Athelston* and Two Late Medieval Robin Hood Ballads," 220–48. Also, Battles, "The Middle English *Athelston* and 1381, Part II: The Road to Rebellion."

89 The name "Fleet Street" is first recorded in 1280; see J.E.B. Gover, *Place Names of Middlesex* (London: Longmans, Green, and Co., 1922), 29–30. Charing Cross, is one of the twelve Eleanor crosses, dates to the reign of Edward I (1272–1307) in commemoration of his queen Eleanor of Castile (c.1244–90).

90 For a discussion of the names in the poem, see A.M. Trounce, ed., *Athelston*, 25–28; Laura A. Hibbard, "*Athelston*, a Westminster Legend," *Publications of the Modern Language Association* 36 (1921): 223–44, 224–25; also, Edith

Rickert, ed. and trans., *Early English Romances of Friendship* (New York: Cooper Square Publishers, Inc., 1967), 175.

91 Robert Allen Rouse argues that *Athelston* "is clearly set in Anglo-Saxon England" but in such a way that blurs the boundaries of past and fourteenth-century present, a reading that does not fully account for the poem's copious, at times excessive, handling of contemporary authenticating markers of setting. See *The Idea of Anglo-Saxon England in Middle English Romance*, 132.

92 Nancy Mason Bradbury speaks of the poem's "absent hero," and the lack of "straightforward goodness" in the poem's four "brethryn" compared to other Middle English heroes. See "The Erosion of Oath-Based Relationships," 91–92 and 94; also Susan Crane, *Insular Romance*, 69. Rosalind Field argues for Edmund, born at the end, as the poem's intended focus. See "*Athelston* or the Middle English *Nativity of St. Edmund*," 141, 149.

93 In addition to Wymond's rumor mongering, the poet portrays Alryke as equally capable of disrupting the realm when, challenged by Athelston, he threatens to raise a contingent of men to destroy the churches and reduce the countryside to famine and ruin (ll. 477–81 and 486–94).

94 Sarah Foot, *Aethelstan: The First King of England* (New Haven, CT: Yale University Press, 2011), 69.

95 Some examples include *King Horn* with Horn's lifelong friendship with Athulf, whose trajectory mirrors Horn's relationship with Rymenhild; *Havelok the Dane* and Havelok's bonds with his adoptive brothers, William Wenduth, Huwe Raven, and Roberd the Rede, all sons of Grim, who accompany him to Denmark to reclaim his throne, a detail not found in French antecedents of the story; and Gamelyn's bonds with his merry men of the forest in *The Tale of Gamelyn*. See Battles, *Cultural Difference and Material Culture in Middle English Romance*, 25–27, 35–36, 139–40.

96 See Battles, "The Middle English *Athelston* and 1381, Part I: The Politics of Anglo-Saxon Identity," 10–13, 34.

97 Hibbard, "*Athelston*, a Westminster Legend," 231–32; also, Nancy Mason Bradbury, "The *Tale of Gamelyn* as a Greenwood Outlaw Talking," *Southern Folklore* 53 (1996): 207–23, 216. For similar language and imagery of meeting under greenery, sometimes involving oaths, in the Robin Hood tradition, see *Adam Bell, Clim of the Clough, and William of Cloudesley* (ll. 1–4, 189–90, 380–81,405), and *A Gest of Robyn Hode* (ll. 316, 704, 844, 948, 1096, 1136, 1189–92ff.). Both are collected in Stephen Knight and Thomas Ohlgren, eds., *Robin Hood and Other Outlaw Tales* (Kalamazoo, MI: Medieval Institute Publications, 2000), 235–67 and 80–168. See also Nancy Mason Bradbury, "The *Tale of Gamelyn* as a Greenwood Outlaw Talking," 221, n.17.

98 See Maurice Keen, *The Outlaws of Medieval Legend*, 2nd ed. (London: Routledge, 2000), 11 and 23. Keen devotes two chapters to the legend of Hereward, 9–38. Concurring with Keen's assertion that this tradition emerged out of the political conflicts of the Norman Conquest, Thomas Ohlgren identifies the story of Earl Godwin, whose conflicts with a French advisor of Edward the Confessor are preserved in the anonymous *Vita Ædwardi Regis* (c.1065–1067), as the "earliest extended account of outlawry in English literature." See Thomas H. Ohlgren, ed., *Medieval Outlaws: Ten Tales in Modern English* (Stroud and Gloucester: Sutton Publishing, 1998), "General Introduction," xvii, and Timothy S. Jones' introduction to the *Vita*, 1–4.

99 For a discussion of the names in the poem, see A.M. Trounce, ed., *Athelston*, 25–28; Hibbard, "*Athelston*, a Westminster Legend," 224–25.

100 Ellzey, "The Advice of Wives in Three Middle English Romances," 49–51; Rowe, "The Female Body Politic and the Miscarriage of Justice in *Athelston*," 82–83. Nancy Mason Bradbury calls the queen "an agent national politics rather than . . . a pawn." See "Beyond the Kick: Women's Agency in *Athelston*," 155.
101 See Laura A. Hibbard, "*Athelston*: A Westminster Legend," 223–44.
102 Ibid., 227–29.
103 Bradbury distinguishes between public (masculine/political) and private (feminine/domestic) space in *Athelston*, noting how the queen, and later Edith, both "abandon their chambers and assert themselves in the public spheres." See "Beyond the Kick: Women's Agency in *Athelston*," 151. The presence of other royal subjects in the scene emphasizes this movement.
104 Ellzey, "The Advice of Wives in Three Middle English Romances," 49.
105 Ellzey attributes the severity of the queen's abuse to the fact that Athelston, as a monarch, occupies the highest social rank, and to the political rather than personal or domestic nature of the advice she offers, as opposed any negative cultural stereotypes that Athelston's behavior plays upon. See "The Advice of Wives in Three Middle English Romances," 50.
106 Sheila Fisher, "Women and Men in Late Medieval English Romance," in Roberta L. Krueger, ed., *Cambridge Companion to Medieval Romance* (Cambridge: Cambridge University Press, 2000), 150–64, 161–62; Battles, *Cultural Difference and Material Culture in Middle English Romance*, 149–50.
107 Shutters discusses primarily the "Clerk's Tale" and the *Legend of Good Women*, where "feminine suffering *requires* cruel men." See "Griselda's Pagan Virtue," *The Chaucer Review* 44 (2009): 61–83, 71.
108 Rowe reads the poem in light of Lancastrian propaganda against Richard II and does not tie Athelston's conduct toward the queen—and later, Edith—to his Anglo-Saxon portraiture. Similarly, she reads the violence against women in the poem as emblematic of medieval misogyny in general, rather than as targeted commentary on native English values. See "The Female Body Politic and the Miscarriage of Justice in *Athelston*," 80, 85–87, 96.
109 Elizabeth Ashman Rowe suggests that the queen "increases the threat to royal power posed by Parliament by associating it with the threat to male power posed by insubordinate women." See "The Female Body Politic and the Miscarriage of Justice in *Athelston*," 83. However, when we place the queen in *Athelston* within the literary context of the Wise Woman type-scene, she appears remarkably conciliatory, compared with the typical wife of this scene, and her power derives from her submissiveness.
110 Ellzey, "The Advice of Wives in Three Middle English Romances," 50.
111 The hagiographic key of the final scene of the poem has led Dieter Mehl to classify *Athelston* as a "homiletic romance." See *The Middle English Romances of the Thirteenth and Fourteenth Centuries*, 146–52. See Rosalind Field has developed this angle of *Athelston* most fully. See "*Athelston* or the Middle English *Nativity of St. Edmund*," 145–49.
112 See Battles, "The Middle English *Athelston* and 1381, Part I: The Politics of Anglo-Saxon Identity," 34.
113 In her recent study of imagery of St. Edmund, Rebecca Pinner notes that sixty percent of the images of St. Edmund depict him as adult and glorified. Other popular images of Edmund depict him as an individual, adult figure flanked by Danish archers, in keeping with stories of his martyrdom, being bound and shot full of arrows. Two-thirds of these images, moreover, date to around

1400, forming an important context for what we see in *Athelston*. See *The Cult of St. Edmund in Medieval East Anglia* (Woodbridge, Suffolk: Boydell Press, 2015), 195–96, 198, 208. For parallelism between the two infants of the poem, see Rowe, "The Female Body Politic and the Miscarriage of Justice in *Athelston*," 88; Bradbury, "Beyond the Kick: Women's Agency in *Athelston*," 157. Rosalind Field reads the poem against the Gospel of Luke, where we also see two pregnant women "whose unborn children contain the transformed future" (145). See "*Athelston* or the Middle English *Nativity of St. Edmund*," 145–49.

114 Edmund was the patron saint of England until he was supplanted in the fourteenth century, when Edward III associated St. George with the Order of the Garter. See Christopher Daniell, *From Norman Conquest to Magna Carta, 1066–1215* (London and New York: Routledge, 2003), 78.

115 "The Middle English *Athelston* and 1381, Part I: The Politics of Anglo-Saxon Identity," 35–38; and "The Middle English *Athelston* and 1381, Part II: The Road to Rebellion."

Bibliography

Primary Sources

Alighieri, Dante. "De vulgare eloquentia." In *Opere minori*. Edited by P.V. Mengaldo. 2 vols. Milan and Naples: Ricciardi, 1979.

Battles, Paul, ed. *Sir Gawain and the Green Knight*. Peterborough, ON: Broadview Press, 2012.

Beadle, Richard, and A.E.B. Owen. *The Findern Manuscript: Cambridge University Library MS Ff.1.6*. London: Scolar Press, 1977.

Bede, "The Venerable." In *The Life of St. Cuthbert*. Edited by Edward Consitt. London: Burnes and Oats, 1904.

———. *Ecclesiastical History of the English People*. Translated by Leo Sherley-Price. Harmondsworth: Penguin Books, 1990.

Benson, Larry D., ed. *The Riverside Chaucer*. New York: Houghton Mifflin, 1987.

Bliss, A.J., ed. *Sir Orfeo*. Oxford: Clarendon Press, 1966.

Boccaccio, Giovanni. "Teseida delle Nozze di Emilia." In *Vol. 2 of Tutte Opere di Giovanni Boccaccio*. Edited by Alberto Limentani and Vittore Branca. 10 vols. Verona: Arnoldo Mondadori, 1964.

———. *The Filostrato: A Translation with Parallel Text*. Translated by Nathaniel Edward Griffin and Arthur Beckwith Myrick. New York: Biblo and Tannen, 1967.

———. *The Book of Theseus*. Translated by Bernadette Marie McCoy. New York: Medieval Text Association, 1974.

Brewer, D.S., and A.E. B. Owen. *The Thornton Manuscript: Lincoln Cathedral MS 91*. Rev. ed. 1977. London: Scolar Press, 1975.

Burgess, Glyn S., and Keith Busby, ed. and trans. *The Lais of Marie de France*, 73–81. Harmondsworth: Penguin Books, 1986.

Casson, L.F. *The Romance of Sir Degrevant*. EETS, o.s. 221. London: Oxford University Press for the Early English Text Society, 1949.

Chandler, John H., ed. *The King of Tars*. Teams Middle English Texts. Kalamazoo: Medieval Institute Publications, 2015.

Chaucer, Geoffrey. *The Riverside Chaucer*. Edited by Larry D. Benson. Boston, MA: Houghton Mifflin, 1987.

Colonne, Guido delle. *Historia Destructionis Troiae*. Edited by Nathaniel Edward Griffin. Cambridge: Medieval Academy of America, 1936.

———. *Historia Destructionis Troiae*. Translated by Mary Elizabeth Meek. Bloomington and London: Indiana University Press, 1974.
Constans, Léopold, ed. *Le Roman de Thèbes*. 2 vols. Paris: Librairie de Firmin Didot, 1890.
Crossley-Holland, Kevin, trans. *Beowulf*. Oxford: Oxford University Press, 1999.
de Lorris, Guillaume, and Jean de Meun. *The Romance of the Rose*. Translated by Charles Dahlberg. Hanover and London: University Press of New England, 1983.
Donovan, Leslie A., ed. and trans. *Women Saint's Lives in Old English Prose*. Cambridge: D.S Brewer, 1999.
Fitzgerald, Robert, trans. *The Aeneid of Virgil*. New York: Random House, 1983; reprint Vintage, 2013.
French, Walter Hoyt, and Charles B. Hale, eds. *Middle English Metrical Romances*. New York: Russell and Russell, 1964.
Geoffrey of Vinsauf. "Poetria Nova." In *Medieval Literary Criticism: Translations and Intepretations*. Edited by O.B. Hardison, Jr., et al., 123–44. New York: Frederick Ungar Publishing Co., 1974.
Gower, John. *Confessio Amantis*. Edited by Russell A. Peck. Toronto: University of Toronto Press, 1980.
Gray, Sir Thomas. *Scalacronica 1272–1363*. Edited and translated by Andy King. Woodbridge, Suffolk: The Boydell Press, 2005.
Hahn, Thomas. *Sir Gawain: Eleven Romances and Tales*. Kalamazoo, MI: Western Medieval Institute Publications, 1995.
Hall, Joseph, ed. *King Horn: A Middle English Romance*. Oxford: Clarendon Press, 1901.
Halliwell-Phillips, J.O., ed. *The Thornton Romances: The Early English Metrical Romances of Perceval, Isumbras, Eglamour, and Degrevant*. London: Camden Society, 1844.
Herzman, Ronald B., Graham Drake, and Eve Salisbury, eds. *Four Romances of England*. Kalamazoo, MI: Western Michigan University Press, 1999.
Homer. *The Odyssey*. Translated by Robert Fagles. New York: Penguin Books, 1996.
Kibler, William W., ed. and trans. *Chrétien de Troyes: Arthurian Romances*. New York: Penguin Books, 1991.
Knight, Stephen, and Thomas Ohlgren, eds. *Robin Hood and the Other Outlaw Tales*. Teams Middle English Texts. Kalamazoo: Western Michigan University Press, 2000.
Kooper, Erik, ed. *Sentimental and Humorous Romances*. Kalamazoo, MI: Medieval Institute Publications, 2006.
Krapp, George Philip, and Elliott van Kirk Dobbie, eds. *The Anglo-Saxon Poetic Records*. 6 vols. New York: Columbia University Press, 1931–42.
Krohn, Rüdiger, ed. Gottfried von Strassburg. *Tristan*. 3 vols. Stuttgart: Philipp Reclam, 1980; reprint 2006.
Laskaya, Anne, and Eve Salisbury, eds. *The Middle English Breton Lays*. Teams Middle English Texts. Kalamazoo: Medieval Institute Publications, Western Michigan University, 2001.

Macray, W.D., ed. *Chronicon Abbatiae de Evesham, ad annum 1418*. London: Longman, Green, Longman, Roberts and Green, 1863.
Matthew of Vendôme. *The Art of Versification*. Translated by Aubrey E. Galyon. Ames: Iowa State University Press, 1980.
_____. *Ars Versificatoria (The Art of the Versemaker)*. Translated by Roger P. Parr. Milwaukee: Marquette University, 1981.
McDiarmid, Matthew P., ed. *Hary's Wallace*. 2 vols. Edinburgh: William Blackwood and Sons Ltd., 1968.
Melville, A.D., trans. *The Thebaid of Statius*. Oxford: Oxford University Press, 1995.
Mora-Lebrun, Francine, ed. and trans. *Le Roman de Thèbes*. Édition du manuscrit S (Londres. Brit. Libr. Add. 34114). Paris: Librairie Générale Française, 1995.
Mynors, R.A.B. *P. Vergili Maronis Opera*. Oxford: Clarendon Press, 1969.
Ohlgren, Thomas H., ed. *Medieval Outlaws: Ten Tales in Modern English*. Stroud and Gloucester: Sutton Publishing, 1998.
Ovid (Publius Ovidius Naso), and Peter Green. *The Erotic Poems*. Translated by Peter Green. London: Penguin Books, 1982.
Phrygius, Dares, and Dictys Cretensis. *The Trojan War: The Chronicles of Dictys and Crete and Dares the Phrygian*. Translated by R.M. Frazer, Jr. Bloomington and London: Indiana University Press, 1966.
Rickert, Edith. *Early English Romances in Verse: Done into Modern English: Romances of Love*. New York: Cooper Square Publishers, 1966.
Shakespeare, William. *Romeo and Juliet*. Edited by Jill L. Levenson. Oxford: Oxford University Press, 200.
Sisam, K. *The Lay of Havelok the Dane*. Oxford: Clarendon Press, 1939.
Skeat, W.W., ed. *The Tale of Gamelyn*. Oxford: Clarendon Press, 1893.
_____, and K. Sisam, eds. *The Lay of Havelok the Dane*. Oxford: Clarendon Press, 1915/1939.
Taylor, A.B., ed. *'Floris and Blancheflour': A Middle English Romance*. Edited from the Trentham and Auchinleck MSS. Oxford: Clarendon Press, 1927.
Trounce, A.M.I. *Athelston: A Middle English Romance*. Oxford: Oxford University Press, 1951.
von Strassburg, Gottfied. *Tristan*. Translated by A.T. Hatto. Harmondsworth: Penguin Books, 1982.
William of Tyre. *Deeds Done Beyond the Sea*. Translated by Emily Atwater Babcock and A.C. Krey. 2 vols. New York: Columbia University Press, 1943.
Yunck, John A., trans. *Enéas: A Twelfth-Century French Romance*. New York: Columbia University Press, 1974.

Secondary Sources

Aguirre, Manuel. "'The Voice of Thunder': The Formulaic Nature of the Gothic Type-Scene." *Gothic Studies* 25 (2023): 93–111.
Akbari, Suzanne Conklin. *Idols in the East: European Representations of Islam and the Orient, 1100–1450*. Ithaca, NY and London: Cornell University Press, 2009.

Albrecht, W.P. *The Loathly Lady in "Thomas of Erceldoune."* Albuquerque: University of New Mexico Press, 1954.

Allega, Rob. "Words, Combat, and Genre: A Comparative Analysis of Medieval Flyting." Hanover College: Senior Thesis, 2009.

Anderson, David. *Before the Knight's Tale: Imitation of Classical Epic in Boccaccio's Teseida.* Philadelphia: University of Pennsylvania Press, 1988.

Arend, Walter. *Die typischen scenen bei Homer.* Berlin: Weidmann, 1933.

Armstrong, J. "The Arming Motif in the *Iliad*." *American Journal of Philology* 79 (1969): 337–54.

Armstrong, Jackson W. *England's Northern Frontier: Conflict and Local Society in the Fifteenth-Century Scottish Marches.* Cambridge: Cambridge University Press, 2020.

Atkinson, Stephen C.B. "Malory's 'Healing of Sir Urry': Lancelot, the Earthly Fellowship, and the World of the Grail." *Studies in Philology* 78 (1981): 341–52.

Bailey, M. "Homeric Guest-Reception and Ritual Handwashing." *American Philological Association Abstracts* 126 (1987).

Barnes, Geraldine. *Council and Strategy in Middle English Romance.* Cambridge: D.S. Brewer, 1993.

———. "Cunning and Ingenuity in the Middle English *Floris and Blauncheflur*." *Medium Aevum* 53 (1984): 10–25.

Barnett, Rod. "Serpent of Pleasure: Emergence and Difference in the Medieval Garden of Love." *Landscape Journal* 28 (2009): 137–50.

Barron, W.R.J. *English Medieval Romance.* London: Longman, 1987.

Barrow, W.R.J. "The Penalties for Treason in Medieval Life and Literature." *Journal of Medieval History* 7 (1981): 187–202.

Bartlett, Robert. *Trial by Fire and Water: The Medieval Judicial Ordeal.* Oxford: Clarendon Press, 1986.

———. *England under the Norman and Angevin Kings, 1075–1225.* Oxford: Clarendon Press, 2000.

Battles, Dominique. "Boccaccio's *Teseida* and the Destruction of Troy." *Medievalia et Humanistica, New Series* 28 (2001): 73–99.

———. *The Medieval Tradition of Thebes: History and Narrative in the OF Roman de Thèbes, Boccaccio, Chaucer, and Lydgate.* New York: Routledge, 2004.

———. "The Heroic Voice in Gottfried von Strassburg's *Tristan*." *Tristania* 25 (2009): 1–24.

———. "*Sir Orfeo* and English Identity." *Studies in Philology* 107 (2010a): 179–211.

———. "The City of Babylon in the Middle English *Floris and Blancheflour*." *Anglia* 128 (2010b): 1–7.

———. *Cultural Difference and Material Culture in Middle English Romance: Normans and Saxons.* New York: Routledge, 2013.

———. "The Middle English *Sir Degrevant* and the Architecture of the Border." *English Studies* 96 (2015): 853–72.

———. "The Middle English *Sir Degrevant* and the Scottish Border." *Studies in Philology* 113 (2016): 501–45.

———. "Behind Enemy Lines: The German Connection in the Middle English *Sir Degrevant*." *Neophilologus* 100 (2016): 489–501.

_____. "Melidor and the 'Wylde Men of þe West' in the Middle English *Sir Degrevant.*" *American Notes and Queries* 33 (2020a): 15–18.

_____. "The Middle English *Athelston* and 1381, Part I: The Politics of Anglo-Saxon Identity." *Studies in Philology* 117 (2020b): 1–39.

_____. "Investigating English Sanctity in the Middle English *St. Erkenwald.*" *Studies in Philology* 120 (2023): 603–57.

Battles, Paul. "Chaucer and the Tradition of Dawn-Song." *The Chaucer Review* 31 (1997): 317–38.

_____. "'Contending Throng' Scenes and the *Comitatus* Ideal in Old English Poetry, with Special Attention to *The Battle of Maldon* 122a." *Studia Neophilologica* 83 (2011): 41–53.

_____. "Dying for a Drink: 'Sleeping After the Feast' Scenes in *Beowulf, Andreas,* and the Old English Poetic Tradition." *Modern Philology* 112(3) (2015): 435–57.

_____. "Old Saxon-Old English Intertextuality and the 'Traveler Recognizes His Goal' Theme in the *Heliand.*" In *Old English and Continental Germanic Literature in Comparative Perspectives.* Edited by Larry J. Swain, 5–37. New York: Peter Lang, 2019.

_____. "Christian Traditional Themes and the Cynewulfian Sociolect in Old English Verse." *Studies in Philology* 119 (2022): 555–78.

_____, and Charles D. Wright, "*Eall-feala Ealde Saege*: Poetic Performance and 'The *Scop*'s Repertoire' in Old English Verse." *Oral Tradition* 32(1) (2018): 3–26.

Baumgartner, Emmanuèle. "Romance." In *Medieval France: An Encyclopedia.* Edited by William Kibler and Grover A. Zinn, 811–13. New York: Garland Publishing, Inc., 1995.

Beinfield, Harriet, and Efrem Korngold. *Between Heaven and Earth: A Guide to Chinese Medicine.* New York: Ballantine Books, 1991.

Bellamy, J.G. *The Law of Treason in England in the Later Middle Ages.* Cambridge: Cambridge University Press, 1970.

Bennett, Matthew, Jim Bradbury, Kelly DeVries, Iain Dickie, and Phyllis Jestice, eds. *Fighting Techniques of the Medieval World.* New York: St. Martin's Press, 2006.

_____. *The Medieval World at War.* London: Thames and Hudson, 2009.

Besserman, Lawrence. "A Note on the Sources of Chaucer's *Troilus* V, 540–613." *The Chaucer Review* 24 (1990): 306–8.

Beye, C.R. "Homeric Battle Narrative and Catalogues." *Harvard Studies in Classical Philology* 68 (1964): 345–73.

Bloomfield, Morton W. "Troilus' Paraclausithyron and Its Setting." *Neuphilologische Mitteilungen* 73 (1972): 15–24.

Boatright, Mody C. "The Beginnings of Cowboy Fiction." *Southwest Review* 51 (1966): 11–28.

Boitani, Piero. "Style, Iconography and Narrative: The Lesson of the *Teseida.*" In *Chaucer and the Italian Trecento,* 185–99. Cambridge: Cambridge University Press, 1983.

Bonner, Elizabeth. "Scotland's 'Auld Alliance' with France, 1295–1560." *History* 84 (1999): 5–30.

Bothwell, James. "Edward III and the 'New Nobility': Largesse and Limitation in Fourteenth-Century England." *English Historical Review* 112 (1997): 1111–40.

Bradbury, Nancy Mason. "*The Tale of Gamelyn* as a Greenwood Outlaw Talking." *Southern Folklore* 53 (1996): 207–23.

———. "The Erosion of Oath-Based Relationships: A Cultural Context for *Athelston*." *Medium Aevum* 73 (2004):189–204.

———. "Beyond the Kick: Women's Agency in *Athelston*." In *Cultural Encounters in the Romance of Medieval England*. Edited by Corinne Saunders, 149–58. Cambridge: D.S. Brewer, 2005.

Branca, Vittore. *Boccaccio: The Man and His Works*. Translated by Richard Monges. New York: New York University Press, 1976.

Brewer, Derek. "The Arming of the Warrior in European Literature and Chaucer." In *Chaucerian Problems and Perspectives: Essays Presented to Paul S. Beichner, C.S.C.* Edited by Edward Vasta, Zacharias P. Thundy, and Theodore M. Hesburgh, 221–43. Notre Dame: University of Notre Dame Press, 1979.

Brown, Michael H. *The Wars of Scotland 1214–1371*. Edinburgh: Edinburgh University Press, 2004.

———. "*Scoti Anglicati*: Scots in Plantagenet Allegiance During the Fourteenth Century." In *England and Scotland in the Fourteenth Century: New Perspectives*. Edited by Andy King and Michael A. Penman, 94–115. Woodbridge: Boydell Press, 2007.

Bruce, Christopher. *The Arthurian Name Dictionary*. New York: Garland, 1999.

Byrne, Aisling. *Otherworlds: Fantasy and History in Medieval Literature*. Oxford: Oxford University Press, 2016.

Calin, William C. "Flower Imagery in *Floire and Blancheflour*." *French Studies* 18 (1964): 103–11.

Calkin, Siobhain Bly. *Saracens and the Making of English Identity: The Auchinleck Manuscript*. New York and London: Routledge, 2005.

Cam, Helen. *Law-Finders and Law-Makers in Medieval England*. London: Merlin Press, 1962.

Canter, H.V. "The Paraclausithyron as a Literary Theme." *The American Journal of Philology* 41 (1920): 355–68.

Carmargo, Martin. "Chaucer and the Oxford Renaissance of Anglo-Latin Rhetoric." *Studies in the Age of Chaucer* 34 (2012): 173–207.

Chism, Christine. "The Romance of the Road in *Athelston* and Two Late Medieval Robin Hood Tales." In *Roadworks: Medieval Britain, Medieval Roads*. Edited by Valerie Allen and Ruth Evans, 220–48. Manchester: Manchester University Press, 2016.

Clark, George. "The Traveler Recognizes His Goal: A Theme in Anglo-Saxon Poetry." *Journal of English and Germanic Philology* 64 (1965): 645–59.

Clark, Matthew. "Formulas, Metre and Type-Scenes." In *The Cambridge Companion to Homer*. Edited by Robert Fowler, 117–38. Cambridge: Cambridge University Press, 2004.

Claxton, Guy. *Intelligence in the Flesh*. New Haven, CT, and London: Yale University Press, 2015.

Clover, Carol J. "The Germanic Context of the Unferþ Episode." *Speculum* 55 (1980): 444–68.

Colby, Alice M. *The Portrait in Twelfth-Century French Literature: An Example of the Stylistic Originality of Chrétien de Troyes*. Geneva: Vittorio Klostermann, 1965.

Contamine, Philippe. "Froissart and Scotland." In *Scotland and the Low Countries*. Edited by Grant G. Simpson, 43–58. East Linton: Tuckwell, Press, 1996.
Coomaraswamy, Ananda K. "On the Loathly Bride." *Speculum* 20 (1945): 391–404.
Crane, Susan. *Insular Romance: Politics, Faith, and Culture in Anglo-Norman and Middle English Literature*. Berkeley: University of California Press, 1986.
Creighton, Oliver. *Designs Upon the Land: Elite Landscapes of the Middle Ages*. Woodbridge, Suffolk: Boydell and Brewer, 2009.
Crowne, David K. "The Hero on the Beach: An Example of Composition by Theme in Anglo-Saxon Poetry." *Neuphilologische Mitteilungen* 61 (1960): 362–72.
Curry, Walter Clyde. *The Middle English Ideal of Personal Beauty; as Found in the Metrical Romances, Chronicles, and Legends of the XIII, XIV, and XV Centuries*. Baltimore, MD: J.H. Furst Company, 1916.
Curtius, Ernst Robert. *European Literature and the Latin Middle Ages*. Translated by Willard R. Trask. Princeton, NJ: Princeton University Press, 1953.
Czarnowus, Anna. *Fantasies of the Other's Body in Middle English Oriental Romance*. Frankfurt am Main: Peter Lang, 2013.
Daimond, Arlyn. "*Sir Degrevant*: What Lovers Want." In *Pulp Fictions of Medieval England: Essays in Popular Romance*. Edited by Nicola McDonald, 82–101. Manchester: Manchester University Press, 2004.
Daniell, Christopher. *From Norman Conquest to Magna Carta, 1066–1215*. London and New York: Routledge, 2003.
Davenport, W.A. "*Sir Degrevant* and Composite Romance." In *Medieval Insular Romance: Translation and Innovation*. Edited by Judith Weiss, Jennifer Fellows, and Morgan Dickson, 111–34. Cambridge: D.S. Brewer, 2001.
Deloria, Philip J., and Alexander I. Olson. *American Studies: A User's Guide*. Berkeley: University of California Press, 2017.
Desmond, Marilynn. "*Beowulf*: The Monsters and the Tradition." *Oral Tradition* 7 (1992): 258–83.
Dickson, Morgan. "The Image of the Knightly Harper: Symbolism and Resonance." In *Medieval Romance and Material Culture*. Edited by Nicholas Perkins, 199–214. Cambridge: D.S. Brewer, 2015.
Donovan, Leslie A., ed. and trans. *Women Saints' Lives in Old English Prose*. Cambridge: D.S. Brewer, 1999.
Dunn, Charles W. "Romances Derived from English Legends." In *A Manual of Writings in Middle English*. Edited by J. Burke Severs, 2–37. New Haven, CT: Connecticut Academy of Arts and Sciences, 1967.
Edwards, A.S.G. "Gender, Order and Reconciliation in *Sir Degrevant*." In *Readings in Medieval English Romance*. Edited by Carol M. Meale, 53–64. Woodbridge, Suffolk: D.S. Brewer, 1994.
Edwards, Mark W. "Type-scenes and Homeric Hospitality." *Transactions of the American Philological Association* 105 (1975): 51–72.
———. "Convention and Individuality in *Iliad* 1." *Harvard Studies in Classical Philology* 84 (1980a): 1–28.
———. "The Structure of Homeric Catalogues." *Transactions of the American Philological Association* 110 (1980b): 81–105.

———. "The Conventions of a Homeric Funeral." In *Studies in Honor of T.B.L. Webster*. Edited by J.H. Betts, J. T. Hooker, and J.R. Green, 84–92. Bristol: Bristol Classical Press, 1986.

———. "*Topos* and Transformation in Homer." In *Homer Beyond Oral Poetry*. Edited by J.M. Bremer, I.J.F. de Jong, and J. Kalff, 47–60. Amsterdam: Grüner, 1987a.

———. *Homer: Poet of the Iliad*. Baltimore, MD: Johns Hopkins University Press, 1987.

———. "Homer and Oral Tradition: The Type-Scene." *Oral Tradition* 7(2) (1992): 284–330.

Elizabeth Passmore and Susan Carter. *The English 'Loathly Lady' Tales: Boundaries, Traditions, and Motifs*. Kalamazoo, MI: Medieval Institute Publications, 2007, 100–45.

Ellzey, Mary Housum. "The Advice of Wives in Three Middle English Romances: *The King of Tars, Sir Cleges*, and *Athelston*." *Medieval Perspectives* 7 (1992): 44–52.

Enright, Michael J. *Lady with a Mead Cup: Ritual, Prophecy and Lordship in the European Warband from La Tène to the Viking Age*. Dublin: Four Courts Press, 1996.

Fawcett, Richard. *Scottish Architecture from the Accession of the Stewarts to the Reformation 1371–1560*. Edinburgh: Edinburgh University Press, 1994.

Fell, Christine. "Perceptions of Transience." In *Cambridge Companion to Old English Poetry*. Edited by Malcolm Godden and Michael Lapidge, 172–89. Cambridge: Cambridge University Press, 1991.

Fenik, Bernard. *Studies in the Odyssey*. Wiesbaden: Steiner, 1974.

Field, Rosalind. "Romance as History, History as Romance." In *Romance in England*. Edited by Maldwyn Mills, Jennifer Fellows, and Carol M. Meale, 163–73. Woodbridge, Suffolk: D.S. Brewer, 1991.

———. "*Athelston* or the Middle English *Nativity of St. Edmund*." In *Christianity and Romance in Medieval England*. Edited by Rosalind Field, Phillipa Hardman, and Michelle Sweeney, 139–49. Woodbridge, Suffolk: Boydell and Brewer, 2010.

Fisher, Sheila. "Women and Men in Late Medieval English Romance." In *Cambridge Companion to Medieval Romance*. Edited by Roberta L. Krueger, 150–64. Cambridge: Cambridge University Press, 2000.

Foley, John Miles. "Literary Art and Oral Tradition in Old English and Serbian Poetry." *Anglo-Saxon England* 12 (1983): 183–214.

Folsom, James K. *The American Western Novel*. New Haven, CT: College and University Press, 1966.

Foot, Sarah. *Aethelstan: The First King of England*. New Haven, CT: Yale University Press, 2011.

Forste-Grupp, Sheryl L. "'For-thi a letter has he dyght': Paradigms for Fifteenth-Century Literacy in *Sir Degrevant*." *Studies in Philology* 101 (2004): 113–35.

Freccero, Carla. "From Amazon to Court Lady: Generic Hybridization in Boccaccio's *Teseida*." *Comparative Literature Studies* 32 (1995): 226–43.

Friedman, John Block. *Orpheus in the Middle Ages*. Cambridge, MA: Harvard University Press, 1970.

Gambera, Disa. "Disarming Women: Gender and Poetic Authority from the *Thebaid* to the *Knight's Tale*." Diss., Cornell University, 1995.

Gerould, Gordon. "Social and Historical Reminiscences in the Middle English *Athelston*." *Englische Studien* 36 (1906): 193–208.
Gershon, Michael. *The Second Brain*. New York: Harper Perennial, 1999.
Gollancz, Sir Israel, ed. *Sir Gawain and the Green Knight*. EETS OS 210. Edited by Mabel Day and Mary S. Serjeantson. Oxford: Oxford University Press, 1940.
Green, Richard Firth. *A Crisis of Truth: Literature and Law in Ricardian England*. Philadelphia: University of Pennsylvania Press, 2002.
Greene, Thomas M. *The Descent from Heaven: A Study in Epic Continuity*. New Haven, CT: Yale University Press, 1963.
Grieve, Patricia E. *Floire et Blancheflour and the European Romance*. Cambridge: Cambridge University Press, 1997.
Guidry, Marc S. "The Parliaments of Gods and Men in the *Knight's Tale*." *Chaucer Review* 43 (2008): 140–70.
Haidu, Peter. "The Episode as Semiotic Module in Twelfth-Century Romance." *Poetics Today* 4 (1983): 655–81.
Harding, Alan. *The Law Courts of Medieval England*. London: George Allen & Unwin, Ltd., 1973.
Hardison, O.B., Alex Preminger, Kevin Kerrane, and Leon Golden, eds. *Medieval Literary Criticism*. New York: Frederick Unger Publishing, Inc., 1974.
Hatto, A.T. *Eos: An Enquiry into the Theme of Lovers' Meetings and Partings at Dawn*. London: Mouton, 1965.
Hayward, Paul Antony. "Translation-Narratives in Post-Conquest Hagiography and English Resistance to the Norman Conquest." *Anglo-Norman Studies* 21 (1999): 67–93.
Heffernan, Carol F. *The Orient in Chaucer and Medieval Romance*. Cambridge: D.S. Brewer, 2003.
Herrick, Samantha Kahn, ed. *Hagiography and the History of Latin Christendom, 500–1500*. Leiden: Brill, 2020.
Hibbard, Laura A. "*Athelston*, a Westminster Legend." *Publications of the Modern Language Association* 36 (1921): 223–44.
_____. *Mediaeval Romance in England*. New York: Burt Franklin, 1969.
Hollander, Robert. *Boccaccio's Two Venuses*. New York: Columbia University Press, 1977.
Hollis, Stephanie J. "The Pentangle Knight: 'Sir Gawain and the Green Knight.'" *The Chaucer Review* 15 (1981): 267–81.
Honegger, Thomas. "Form and Function: The Beasts of Battle Revisited." *English Studies* 79 (1999): 289–98.
Hopkins, Stephen C.E. "Snared by the Beasts of Battle: Fear as Hermeneutic Guide in the Old English *Exodus*." *Philological Quarterly* 97 (2018): 1–25.
Hornstein, Lillian Herlands. "The Historical Background of the *King of Tars*." *Speculum* 16 (1941): 404–14.
Howes, Laura. *Chaucer's Gardens and the Language of Convention*. Gainesville: University Press of Florida, 1997.
Huet, Gédéon. "Sur l'Origine de *Floire et Blanchefleur*." *Romania* 28 (1899): 348–59.
Jones, Timothy S. *Outlawry in Medieval Literature*. New York: Palgrave Macmillan, 2010.

Kaeuper, Richard A. "An Historian's Reading of 'The Tale of Gamelyn'." *Medium Aevum* 52 (1983): 51–62.

Kahf, Mohja. *Western Representations of the Muslim Woman: From Termagant to Odalisque*. Austin: University of Texas Press, 1999.

Kaske, R.E. "An Aube in the *Reeve's Tale*," *English Literary History* 26 (1959): 295–310.

———. "January's Aube," *Modern Language Notes* 75 (1960): 1–4.

———. "The Aube in Chaucer's *Troilus*." In *Troilus and Criseyde and the Minor Poems* vol. 2 of *Chaucer Criticism*. Edited by Richard J. Schoeck and Jerome Taylor, 167–79. Notre Dame: University of Notre Dame Press, 1961.

Kavros, Harry E. "*Swefan Æfter Symble*: The Feast-Sleep theme in *Beowulf*." *Neophilologus* 65 (1981): 120–28.

Keene, Maurice. *The Outlaws of Medieval Legend*. 2nd ed. London: Routledge, 2000.

Kelly, Kathleen Coyne. "The Bartering of Blancheflur in the Middle English *Floris and Blancheflur*." *Studies in Philology* 91 (1994): 101–10.

Ker, W.P. *Epic and Romance: Essays on Medieval Literature*. New York: Dover Publications, 1957.

Kinoshita, Sharon. *Medieval Boundaries: Rethinking Difference in Old French Literature*. Philadelphia: University of Pennsylvania Press, 2006.

Kirkham, Victoria. *The Sign of Reason in Boccaccio's Fiction*. Florence: Leo S. Olschki Editore, 1993.

Kolias, H.D. "The Return Home: A Study of Recognition in the *Odyssey*." *Dissertation Abstracts* 44(8) (1984): 2464A.

Krueger, Roberta L. "Questions of Gender in Old French Courtly Romance." In *The Cambridge Companion to Medieval Romance*. Edited by Roberta L. Krueger, 132–49. Cambridge: Cambridge University Press, 2000.

Lacy Norris J., and Joan Tasker Grimbert, eds. *A Companion to Chrétien de Troyes*. Woodbridge, Suffolk: D.S. Brewer, 2008.

Levine, Robert. "The Pious Traitor: Rhetorical Reinventions of the Fall of Antioch." *Mittellateinisches Jahrbuch* 33 (1998): 59–80.

Lewis, C.S. "Dante's Statius." In *Studies in Medieval and Renaissance Literature* Cambridge: Cambridge University Press, 1966, 94–102.

Librandi, Rita. "Corte e cavalleria della Napoli Angioina nel *Teseida* del Boccaccio." *Medioevo romanzo* 4 (1977): 53–72.

Lord, Albert B. "Homer and Huso II: Narrative Inconsistencies in Greek and Southslavic Heroic Song." *Transactions of the American Philological Association* 69 (1938): 439–45.

———. *The Singer of Tales*. Cambridge: Harvard University Press, 1960.

Lot-Borodine, M. *Le Roman idyllique au moyen Âge*. Paris: A. Picard, 1913; reprinted Geneva: Slatkine Reprints, 1972.

Magennis, Hugh. *Images of Community in Old English Poetry*. Cambridge: Cambridge University Press, 1996.

Magoun, Francis P., Jr. "The Theme of the Beasts of Battle in Anglo-Saxon Poetry." *Neuphilologische Mitteilungen* 56 (1955): 81–90.

Mayer, Emeran. *The Mind-Gut Connection*. New York: Harper Wave, 2018.

McGregor, James H. *The Image of Antiquity in Boccaccio's Filocolo, Filostrato and Teseida*. New York: Peter Lang, 1991a.

———. *The Shades of Aeneas: The Imitation of Vergil and the History of Paganism in Boccaccio's Filostrato, Filocolo, and Teseida*. Athens and London: University of Georgia Press, 1991b.

Mehl, Dieter. *The Middle English Romances of the Thirteenth and Fourteenth Centuries*. London: Routledge and Kegan Paul, 1968; reprinted 2011.

Metlitzki, Dorothee. *The Matter of Araby in Medieval England*. New Haven, CT, and London: Yale University Press, 1977.

Minnis, Alistair J. *Chaucer and Pagan Antiquity*. Cambridge: Cambridge University Press, 1982.

Moretti, Franco. *Signs Taken for Wonders: On the Sociology of Literary Forms*. London: Verso, 1983.

Mursell, Gordon. *English Spirituality from Earliest Times to 1700*. Louisville: Westminster John Knox Press, 2001.

Muscatine, Charles. *Chaucer and the French Tradition*. Berkeley: University of California Press, 1957.

Nickel, Helmut. "Arthurian Armings for War and Love." *Arthuriana* 5 (1995): 3–21.

O'Briain, Helen Conrad. "Listen to the Woman: Reading Wealhtheow as Stateswoman." In *New Readings on Women and Early Medieval Literature and Culture: Cross-Disciplinary Studies in Honour of Helen Damico*. Edited by Helene Scheck and Christine E. Kozikowski, 191–208. Amsterdam: Arc Amsterdam University Press, 2019.

Opland, Jeff. "*Beowulf* on the Poet." *Mediaeval Studies* 38 (1976): 442–67.

Osborn, Marijane. *Nine Medieval Romances of Magic*. Peterborough, Ontario: Broadview Press, 2010.

Otter, Monika. "'New Werke': *St. Erkenwald*, St. Albans, and the Medieval Sense of the Past." *Journal of Medieval and Renaissance Studies* 24 (1994): 387–414.

Parks, Ward. *Verbal Dueling in Heroic Narrative: The Homeric and Old English Traditions*. Princeton, NJ: Princeton University Press, 1990.

Parsons, John Carmi. "The Pregnant Queen as Counsellor and the Medieval Construction of Motherhood." In *Medieval Mothering*. Edited by John Carmi Parsons and Bonnie Wheeler, 31–61. New York: Garland Publishing, Inc., 1996.

Passmore, S. Elizabeth. "Through the Counsel of a Lady: The Irish and English Loathly Lady Tales and the 'Mirror for Princes' Genre." In *The English 'Loathly Lady' Tales: Boundaries, Traditions, and Motifs*. Edited by S. Elizabeth Passmore and Susan Carter, 3–41. Kalamazoo, Michigan: Medieval Institute Publications, 2007.

Patch, Howard Rollin. *The Otherworld, According to Descriptions on Medieval Literature*. Cambridge, MA: Harvard University Press, 1950.

Peck, Russel A. "Folklore and Powerful Women in Gower's 'Tale of Florent.'" In *The English 'Loathly Lady' Tales: Boundaries, Traditions, and Motifs*. Edited by S. Elizabeth Passmore and Susan Carter, 100–145. Kalamazoo, Michigan: Medieval Institute Publications, 2007.

Pigg, Daniel F. "The Implications of Realist Poetics in the Middle English *Athelston*." *English Language Notes* 32 (1994): 1–8.

Pinner, Rebecca. *The Cult of St. Edmund in Medieval East Anglia*. Woodbridge, Suffolk: Boydell Press, 2015.

Pounds, N.J.G. *The Medieval Castle in England and Wales: A Social and Political History*. Cambridge: Cambridge University Press, 1993.

Pugh, Tison. "Gender, Vulgarity, and the Phantom Debates of Chaucer's *Merchant's Tale*." *Studies in Philology* 114 (2017): 473–96.

Reiss, Edmund. "Symbolic Detail in Medieval Narrative: *Floris and Blancheflour*." *Papers on Language and Literature* 7 (1971): 339–50.

Renoir, Alain. *A Key to Old Poems: The Oral-Formulaic Approach to the Interpretation of West Germanic Verse*. University Park: Pennsylvania State University Press, 1988.

Rouse, E. Clive, and Audrey Baker. "The Wall-Paintings at Longthorpe Tower near Peterborough, Northants." *Archaeologia* 96 (1955): 1–57.

Rouse, Robert Allen. *The Idea of Anglo-Saxon England in Middle English Romance*. Cambridge: D.S. Brewer, 2005.

Rowe, Elizabeth Ashman. "The Female Body Politic and the Miscarriage of Justice in *Athelston*." *Studies in the Age of Chaucer* 17 (1995): 79–98.

Saunders, Corinne. *Magic and the Supernatural in Medieval English Romance*. Cambridge: D.S. Brewer, 2010.

Sayers, William. "*La Joie de la Cort* (*Érec et Énide*), Mabon, and Early Irish *síd* [peace; Otherworld]." *Arthuriana* 17 (2007): 10–17.

Schofield, William Henry. *English Literature from the Norman Conquest to Chaucer*. New York: Macmillan and Co., 1906.

Severs, J. Burke. "The Antecedents of *Sir Orfeo*." In *Studies in Medieval Literature in Honor of Professor Albert Cross Baugh*. Edited by MacEdward Leach, 187–207. Philadelphia: University of Pennsylvania Press, 1961.

Shannon, Edgar F. "Mediaeval Law in *The Tale of Gamelyn*." *Speculum* 26 (1951): 458–64.

Shelmerdine, C.W. "The Pattern of Guest Welcome in the *Odyssey*." *Classical Journal* 65 (3) (1969): 124.

Shutters, Lynn. "Griselda's Pagan Virtue." *The Chaucer Review* 44 (2009): 61–83.

Singer, S. "Arabische und europäische Poesi im Mittelalter." In *Akademie der Wissenschaften*. Berlin: Reimer, 1918.

Smith. Greg M. *Film Structure and the Emotion System*. Cambridge: Cambridge University Press, 2007.

Spearing, A.C. *Medieval Dream Poetry*. Cambridge: Cambridge University Press, 1976.

Steinberg, Glenn A. "Is Ugliness Only Skin Deep?: Middle English Gawain Romances and the 'Wife of Bath's Tale'." *Arthuriana* 31 (2021): 3–28.

Stenton, Doris M. *English Justice Between the Norman Conquest and the Great Charter 1066–1215*. Philadelphia: The American Philosophical Society, 1964.

Stockwell, Peter. *Cognitive Poetics: An Introduction*. 2nd ed. London and New York: Routledge, 2020.

Taplin, Oliver. "The Shield of Achilles within the *Iliad*." *Greece and Rome* 27 (1980): 1–21.

Taylor, Ann M. "Epic Descent in the *Knight's Tale*." *Classical folia* 30 (1976): 40–56.

Thompson, Stith. *Motif-Index of Folk Literature*. Bloomington: University of Indiana Press, 1955–58.
Tompkins, Jane. *West of Everything: The Inner Life of the Western*. New York: Oxford University Press, 1992.
Toohey, Brian. *Reading Epic: An Introduction to Ancient Narratives*. London: Routledge, 1992.
Tracy, Larissa. *Torture and Brutality in Medieval Literature: Negotiations of National Identity*. Cambridge: D.S. Brewer, 2012.
Treharne, Elaine. "Romanticizing the Past in the Middle English *Athelston*." *The Review of English Studies* 50 (1999): 1–21.
Truby, John. *The Anatomy of Genre: How Story Forms Explain the Way the World Works*. New York: Picador, 2022.
Tsai, Christine Li-ju. "Emaré's Fabulous Robe: The Ambiguity of Power in a Late Medieval Romance." *Medieval Forum* 14 (2003).
Tubach, Frederic C. "The *Locus Amoenus* in the *Tristan* of Gottfried von Straszburg." *Neophilologus* 43 (1959): 37–42.
Varty, Kenneth. "Medieval Romance." In *The New Princeton Encyclopedia of Poetry and Poetics*. Edited by Alex Preminger and T.V.F. Brogan, 751–54. Princeton, NJ: Princeton University Press, 1993.
Veldhoen, N.H.G.E. "Floris and Blancheflour: To Indulge the Fancy and to Hear the Love." In *Companion to Early Middle English Literature*. Edited by N.H.G.E. Veldhoen and H. Aertsen, 51–65. Amsterdam: VU University Press, 1995.
Weissman, Hope. "Aphrodite/Artemis//Emila/Alison." *Exemplaria* 2 (1990): 89–125.
Wentersdorf, Karl P. "Iconographic Elements in *Floris and Blancheflour*." *Annuale Mediaevale* 20 (1981): 76–96.
West, G.D. *An Index to Proper Names in French Arthurian Verse Romances 1150–1300*. University of Toronto Romance Series. Vol. 15. Toronto: University of Toronto Press, 1969.
Wetherbee, Winthrop. "History and Romance in Boccaccio's *Teseida*." *Studia sul Boccaccio* 20 (1991–1992): 173–84.
Wimsatt, James. *Chaucer and the French Love Poets: The Literary Background of the Book of the Duchess*. Chapel Hill: University of North Carolina Press, 1968.
Wittig, Joseph S. "The Aeneas-Dido Allusion in Chrétien's *Erec et Enide*." *Comparative Literature* 22 (1970): 237–53.
Young, Helen. "*Athelston* and English Law: Plantagenet Practice and Anglo-Saxon Precedent." *Parergon* 22 (2005): 95–118.
Ziolkowski, Jan. "Avatars of Ugliness in Medieval Literature." *Modern Language Review* 79 (1984): 1–20.

Index

Adam Bell, Clim of the Clough, and William of Cloudesley: Outlaw Gathering type-scene in 91
Aethelred, the "Unready" (978–1016) 180
Agravain 163, 191
Aguirre, Manuel xiv
Albrecht, W.P. 79
Alliterative Morte Arthure: Hero on the Beach type-scene in 66–7
Anderson, David 21, 30
Andreas: Contending Throng type-scene in 25; Hero on the Beach type-scene in 66; Open Heavens type-scene in 89; *Scop*'s Repertoire type-scene and 100; Sleeping After the Feast type-scene and 102; Traveler Recognizes His Goal type-scene in 151, 152
Arend, Walter xv
Arming of the Hero type-scene xiv, xix, xx, xxi, 3–6, 49, 117–20, 149; in *Beowulf* 3–4; in Boccaccio's *Teseida* 117–20; in Chaucer's *Sir Thopas* 6; in Chrétien's *Erec and Enide* 4–5; in Gottfried von Strassburg's *Tristan* 5; in *Sir Gawain and the Green Knight* 5–6
Artes Poeticae xvii, 9, 80
Athelston: and Anglo-Saxon identity 175–78; Crowd of Onlookers type-scene in 31, 127, 131–33; judicial ordeal in 92, 127–29, 131, 180; Outlaw Gathering type-scene in 91–2, 126–28, 179; and the Peasant's Revolt of 1381 184; Wise Woman type-scene in 110, 175–85

Atkinson, Stephen C.B. 21
Aubade *see* Dawn Song

Barnes, Geraldine 154
Barnett, Rod 84
Bartholomeus Anglicus 227
Battle of Brunanburg: Beasts of Battles type-scene in 7
Battle of Maldon: Beasts of Battle type-scene and 7; Contending Throng type-scene in 25
Battles, Dominique 21, 24, 34, 48, 56, 59, 69, 73, 84, 92, 111
Battles, Paul 26, 38, 52, 101, 103, 108
Beasts of Battle type-scene xx, 7–8; and *Battle of Brunanburg* 7; and *Battle of Maldon* 7; in *Beowulf* 7–8; in Chaucer's "*Legend of Philomela*" 7–8; and *Elene* 7; and *Exodus* 7; and *Fight at Finnsburg* 7; and *Genesis A* 7; and *Judith* 7; and *The Wanderer* 7
Bede: *Ecclesiastical History of the English People*: *inventio* type-scene in 68; *Scop*'s Repertoire type-scene in 101
Benoït de St. Mauré: *Roman de Troie* 104; *teichoscopia* type-scene and 104
Beowulf: Arming of the Hero type-scene in 3–4; Beasts of Battle type-scene and 7–8; Contending Throng type-scene in 25; Exile type-scene in 57; Flyting type-scene in 61–2, 64; Hero on the Beach type-scene in 66; Joy in the Hall type-scene in 71; Lady with the Mead Cup type-scene

Index   213

in 72; *Scop's* Repertoire type-scene in 71, 100–1, 138; Sleeping After the Feast type-scene in 3, 102, 136–46; Traveler Recognizes His Goal type-scene in 151–2
Besserman, Laurence 138
Blason type-scene xiii, xviii, xix, xx, xxi, 9–18, 19, 74, 78, 117, 120–23, 136; in Boccaccio's *Teseida* 117, 120–23; in Chaucer's *Book of the Duchess* 16–17; in Chrétien de Troyes, *Yvain* 10–11, 13; in *Erl of Tolous* 15; and Geoffrey of Vinsauf, *Poetria Nova* 9–10; in Gottfried von Strassburg's *Tristan* 12–13; in *Havelok the Dane* 15–16; *Knight's Tale* 16; *Legend of Good Women* 16; in Marie de France's *Lai de Lanval* 11–12, 14; and Matthew of Vendôme, *Ars versificatoria* xviii, 9–10, 17; *Miller's Tale* 16–18; in *Sir Gawain and the Green Knight* 13–15; in *Sir Orfeo* 13; *Troilus* 16
Bloomfield, Morton W. 138
Boccaccio, Giovanni: *Decameron* 98; *Il Filostrato* (Dawn Song type-scene in 35–6; *paraclausithyron* type-scene in 93–4; *teichoscopia* type-scene in 105–6); *Il Teseida* (Arming of the Hero type-scene 117–20, 123; battle in 118; Blason type-scene in 117, 120–23; Catalog of Warriors type-scene in 19–20; Council of the Gods type-scene in 29; Disguise and Infiltration type-scene in 47; funeral games in 166–7; reversal of epic type-scenes in 169–70; Statius' *Thebaid* and 161–2; *teichoscopia* type-scene in 105, 118; Trojan War and 160–74)
Bodel, Jean xv
Bradbury, Nancy Mason 92
Brewer, Derek 6
Byrne, Aisling 80

Canter, H.W. 138; in Boccacio's *Teseida* 19–20; in Chaucer's *Knight's Tale* 20; and Homer's *Iliad* 19; and *Le Roman d'Enéas* 19; in Malory's *Le Morte Darthur* 21; and Statius' *Thebaid* 19; and Virgil's *Aeneid* 19
Catalog of Warriors type-scene xxi, 19–21
Chanson de geste xv, 153, 188
Chaucer, Geoffrey: *Book of the Duchess* (Blason type-scene in 16–17; *locus amoenus* type-scene in 83); Catalog of Warriors type-scene in 20 (Council of the Gods type-scene in 29, 115; Disguise and Infiltration type-scene in 85; Epic Descent type-scene in 54; *locus amoenus* type-scene in 84; *teichoscopia* type-scene and 106); *Complaint of Mars* (Dawn Song type-scene in 36); *Franklin's Tale* (*locus amoenus* type-scene in 84; Rash Promise type-scene in 98, 99); *Knight's Tale* (Blason type-scene in 16); *Legend of Good Women* (Beasts of Battle type-scene in "Legend of Philomela" 7–8; Blason type-scene in 16; *locus amoenus* type-scene in Prologue 84); *Man of Law's Tale* (Crowd of Onlookers type-scene in 31, 132); *Merchant's Tale* (Conciliar Debate type-scene in 22–3; Council of the Gods type-scene in 29; Dawn Song type-scene in 36, 37; *locus amoenus* type-scene in 84); *Miller's Tale* (Blason type-scene in 16–18; Crowd of Onlookers type-scene in 33–4); *Parliament of Fowls* (*locus amoenus* type-scene in 84); *Reeve's Tale* (Dawn Song type-scene in 36, 37–8); *Sir Thopas* (Arming of the Hero type-scene in 6); *Troilus and Criseyde* (Blason type-scene in 16; Conciliar Debate type-scene in 23; Council of the Gods type-scene and 29–30; Dawn Song type-scene in 36–7; *locus amoenus* type-scene in 84; *paraclausithyron* type-scene in 93–4; *teichoscopia* type-scene in 36, 106); *Wife of Bath's Tale* (Loathly Lady Encounter type-scene in 75, 76–7, 98; Rash Promise type-scene in 76, 98–9)

Chrétien de Troyes: *Erec and Enide* (Arming of the Hero type-scene in 4–5; *Ekphrasis* type-scene in 50–1; *locus amoenus* type-scene in 81; Rash Promise in 81); *Yvain, the Knight with the Lion* (Blason type-scene in xiii, 10–11, 13; Flyting type-scene in 62–3, 64; *locus amoenus* type-scene in 80–1; Magic Ring type-scene in xiii, 86)
Christ and Satan: Open Heavens type-scene in 89
Christ I: Contending Throng type-scene and 25
Christ II: Scop's Repertoire type-scene in 100, 101
Chronicle of Evesham Abbey: *inventio* type-scene in 68–9
Clark, George 108
Clover, Carol J. 65
Cnut, King (1016–1035) 180
Cognitive Poetics xvi–xvii
Colby, Alice M. 18
Conciliar Debate type-scene 22–4; in Chaucer's *Merchant's Tale* 22–3; in *Roman de Thèbes* 22, 23; in *Thebaid* 22; *Troilus* 23
Contending Throng type-scene 25; in *Andreas* 25; in *Battle of Maldon* 25; in *Beowulf* 25; in *Christ I* 25; in *Cursor Mundi* 25–6; in *Descent into Hell* 25; in *Seinte Katherine* 25
Coomaraswamy, Ananda K. 79
Council of the Gods type-scene 27–30; in Boccaccio's *Teseida* 29; in Chaucer's *Knight's Tale* 29, 115; *Merchant's Tale* 29; in Statius' *Thebaid* 27–8; in the *Roman de Thèbes* 28–9; in *Troilus and Criseyde* 29–30; in Virgil's *Aeneid* 27
Crowd of Onlookers type-scene 26, 31–4, 127, 131–33; in *Athelston* 31, 127, 131–33; in Chaucer's *Man of Law's Tale* 31, 132; *Erl of Tolouse* and 31; in *Floris and Blancheflour* 31, 32; in *Life of St. Cecelia* 31–2, 131–32; *Miller's Tale* 33–4; *Pistel of Susanna* and 31; in *St. Erkenwald* 31, 33
Crowne, David K. 67

Curry, Walter Clyde 18
Cursor Mundi: Contending Throng type-scene in 25–6
Curtius, Ernst Robert xxiv, xxv, 84

Daniel: Sleeping after the Feast type-scene in 102
Dante Alighieri: *Inferno* (Descent into the Underworld type-scene in 39, 40–1)
Dares and Dictys: *teichoscopia* type-scene and 104
Dawn Song type-scene: in Boccaccio's *Filostrato* 35–6; in Chaucer's *Complaint of Mars* 36; *Merchant's Tale* 36, 37; in Ovidian tradition 35–6; *Reeve's Tale* 36, 37–8; and *Tagelied* 35; *Troilus* 36–7; type-scene 35–8
Descent into Hell: Contending Throng type-scene in 25
Descent into the Underworld type-scene 39–43; in Dante's *Inferno* 39, 40–1; in Homer's *Odyssey* 39; in Ovid's *Metamorphoses* 39; in Shakespeare's *Romeo and Juliet* 42–3; in *Sir Orfeo* 39, 41, 42; in *Thomas of Erceldoune* 39, 41–2; in Virgil's *Aeneid* 39–40
Dickson, Morgan 48
Disguise and Infiltration type-scene xiii, 44–8, 72–3, 87; in Boccaccio's *Teseida* 47; in Chaucer's *Knight's Tale* 47; in the *Erl of Tolouse* 46, 47; in *Floris and Blancheflour* 46, 47; in *Gesta Herewardi* 45–6; in Gottfried's *Tristan* 44–5; in *Havelok the Dane* 46, 47; in Homer's *Odyssey* 44; in *King Horn* 46, 72–3, 87; in *Sir Orfeo* 46–7
Doctor Faustus: *teichoscopia* type-scene and 104
Dream of the Rood 137

Edmund, St. (d. 869) 184
Edward, the Confessor, King (1042–1066) 180
Ekphrasis type-scene 5, 49–52; in Chrétien's *Erec and Enide* 50–1; in *Emaré* 51–2; in Homer's *Iliad* 49;

in *Sir Gawain and the Green Knight* 5, 49–50
Elene: Beasts of Battle type-scene in 7; Hero on the Beach type-scene and 66
Ellzey, Mary Housum 111
Emaré: Ekphrasis type-scene in 51–2; and Exile type-scene 51
Emma, Queen (c. 984–1052) 180
Enright, Michael J. 73
Epic Descent type-scene 39, 53–6, 136; and Boccaccio's *Teseida* 54; in Chaucer's *Knight's Tale* 54; in *Havelok the Dane* 55–6; in Malory's *Morte Darthur* 56; in Statius's *Thebaid* 53–4, 55; in Virgil's *Aeneid* 54
Erl of Tolouse: Blason type-scene in 15; Crowd of Onlookers type-scene and 31; Disguise and Infiltration type-scene in 46, 47; Wise Woman type-scene in 130–31, 182
Exile type-scene 41, 46, 57–9, 97; in *Beowulf* 57; and *Emaré* 51; in *The Seafarer* 57; in *Sir Gawain and the Green Knight* 58; in *Sir Orfeo* 41, 46, 57–8, 97; in *St. Erkenwald* 58–9; in *The Wanderer* 57
Exodus: Beasts of Battle type-scene and 7; Hero on the Beach type-scene in 66

Fell, Christine 59
Fight at Finnsburg: Beasts of Battle type-scene and 7
Floris and Blancheflour: Babylon in 160–61; Crowd of Onlookers type-scene in 31, 32; Dido and Aeneas and 50, 51; Disguise and Infiltration type-scene in 46, 47; Magic Ring type-scene in 87–8, 159–60; Wise Woman type-scene in 110, 147–63
Flyting type-scene xiv, xix, xx, xxi, 50, 60–5, 81, 137; in *Beowulf* 61–2, 64; in Chrétien's *Yvain* 62–3, 64; and Gottfried's *Tristan* 81; in Homer's *Odyssey* 60–1; in *Sir Gawain and the Green Knight* 50, 64–5
Foley, John Miles 71
Friedman, John Block 80

Gaimar, Geffrei, *L'Estoire des Engleis* 55
Gamelyn see *Tale of Gamelyn*
Genesis A: Sleeping After the Feast type-scene and 102; Traveler Recognizes His Goal type-scene and 151, 152
Geoffrey of Vinsauf, *Poetria Nova* 40–1
Gesta Herewardi: Disguise and Infiltration type-scene in 45–6; Lady with the Mead Cup type-scene and 45, 73; Rash Promise type-scene in 45
Geste of Robyn Hode: Outlaw Gathering type-scene in 91
Gifts of Men: Scop's Repertoire type-scene and 100, 101
Gollancz, Sir Israel 52
Gottfried von Strassburg: *Tristan and Isolde* (Arming of the Hero type-scene in 5; Blason type-scene in 12–13; Disguise and Infiltration type-scene in 44–5; and Flyting type-scene in 81; *locus amoenus* type-scene in 81; Rash Promise type-scene in 44, 97–8)
Gower, John: "Tale of Florent," *Confessio Amantis* (Loathly Lady Encounter type-scene in 75–6, 99; Rash Promise type-scene in 75)
Gray, Sir Thomas, *Scalacronica* 173
Green, Richard Firth 99
Greene, Thomas M. 55
Grimbert, Joan Tasker 52
Guido delle Colonne: *Historia Destructionis Troiae* (*teichoscopia* type-scene in 104–5)
Guidry, Marc S. 30
Guillaume de Lorris: *Romance of the Rose* (*locus amoenus* type-scene in 82–4)
Guthlac A: Open Heavens type-scene in 89
Guthlac B: Hero on the Beach type-scene and 66

Haidu, Peter xii, xxv, xxvi
Harrowing of Hell 58, 59
Hatto, A.T. 38
Havelok the Dane 238; Blason type-scene in 15–16; Disguise and Infiltration type-scene in 46, 47; Epic Descent type-scene in 55–6

216   Index

Hayward, Paul Antony 70
Helen of Troy 10, 120
Heliand: *Scop*'s Repertoire type-scene and 100; Traveler Recognizes His Goal type-scene in 151, 152–3
Hero on the Beach type-scene 66–7; in *Alliterative Morte Arthure* 66–7; in *Andreas* 66; in *Beowulf* 66; and *Elene* 66; in *Exodus* 66; and *Guthlac B* 66; and *Judith* 66
Herrick, Samantha Kahn 70
Hibbard, Laura A. 135
Histoire ancienne 104
Hollis, Stephanie 6
Holmes, Sherlock xxi
Homer: *Iliad* (Catalog of Warriors type-scene and 19; *Ekphrasis* type-scene in 49; *teichoscopia* type-scene in 104); *Odyssey* xvii, xix (Descent into the Underworld type-scene in 39; Disguise and Infiltration type-scene in 44; Flyting type-scene in 60–1)
Honneger, Thomas 40
Hopkins, Stephen C.E. 40
Hornstein, Lilian Herlands 111
Howes, Laura 85

Inventio type-scene xxi, 33, 68–70; in Bede's *Ecclesiastical History of the English People* 68; in *Chronicle of Evesham Abbey* 68–9; in *St. Erkenwald* xxi, 33, 69
Islam: medieval Western stereotypes of 149, 153–58, 159–63

Jones, Timothy S. 92
Joy in the Hall type-scene 71; in *Beowulf* 71; and *Scop*'s Repertoire 71
Judith: Beasts of Battle type-scene and 7; Hero on the Beach type-scene and 66; Sleeping After the Feast type-scene and 102, 137; Traveler Recognizes His Goal type-scene and 151
Juliana 137

Kaske, R.E. 38
katabasis see Descent into the Underworld

Kavros, Harry E. 103
Keen, Maurice 128, 134, 196
King Horn: Disguise and Infiltration type-scene in 82–3, 112, 129; Lady with the Mead Cup type-scene in 72–3; Magic Ring type-scene in 87; Outlaw Gathering type-scene in 90
King of Tars: Wise Woman type-scene in 110–11, 149

Lacy, Norris J. 52
Lady with the Mead Cup type-scene 45, 72–3; in *Beowulf* 72; and *Gesta Herewardi* 45, 73; in *King Horn* 72–3; in *Maxims I* 72
Lai d'Haveloc 55
Lewis, C.S. 30
Life of St. Cecelia: Crowd of Onlookers type-scene in 31–2, 131–32
Loathly Lady Encounter type-scene 9, 42, 74–9, 98, 99; in Chaucer's *Wife of Bath's Tale* 75, 76–7, 98; in John Gower's "Tale of Florent," 75–76, 99; in *The Wedding of Sir Gawain and Dame Ragnelle* 75, 77–9, 99; in *Thomas of Erceldoune* 42, 75, 77
Locus Amoenus type-scene xix, 42, 80–5; in *Artes Poeticae* 80; in Chaucer, *Book of the Duchess* 83; in Chrétien's *Erec and Enide* 81; in Chrétien's *Yvain* 80–1; *Franklin's Tale* 84; in Gottfried's *Tristan* 81; in Guillaume de Lorris, *Romance of the Rose* 82–4; *Knight's Tale* 84; in Matthew of Vendôme's *Ars Versificatoria* 80; *Merchant's Tale* 84; *Parliament of Fowls* 84; in *Pearl* 82–3; Prologue to *Legend of Good Women* 84; and *Thomas of Erceldoune* 42; *Troilus* 84
Lomuto, Sierra 111
Lord, Albert B. xv

Magic Ring type-scene xiii, 86–8, 159–60; in Chrétien's *Yvain* xiii, 86; in *Floris and Blancheflour* 87–8, 159–60; in *King Horn* 87; in *Sir Gawain and the Green Knight* 88
Magoun, Jr., Francis P. 40

Malory, Sir Thomas: *Le Morte d'Arthur* (Catalog of Warriors type-scene in 21; Epic Descent type-scene in 56)
Marie de France: *Lai de Lanval* (Blason type-scene in 11–12, 14; Rash Promise type-scene in 96–7, 98)
Matthew of Vendôme, *Ars Versificatoria*: Blason type-scene in xviii, 9–10, 17; *locus amoenus* type-scene in 80
Maxims I: Lady with the Mead Cup type-scene in 72
Minnis, Alistair 30
Moretti, Franco xx
Mursell, Gordon 59

Nibelungenlied: Scop's Repertoire type-scene and 100
Nickel, Helmut 6

O'Briain, Helen Conrad 73
Open Heavens type-scene 89; and *Andreas* 89; in *Christ and Satan* 89; in *Guthlac A* 89; and *Solomon and Saturn I* 89
Opland, Jeff 71
Otter, Monika 70
Outlaw Gathering type-scene 45, 90–2, 126–28, 179; in *Adam Bell, Clim of the Clough, and William of Cloudesley* 91; in *A Geste of Robyn Hode* 91; in *Athelston* 91–2, 126–28, 179; in *King Horn* 90; in *Tale of Gamelyn* 90–1
Ovid (Publius Ovidius Naso): *Amores* (Dawn Song type-scene in 36; *paraclausithyron* type-scene in 93); *Heroides*. 36; *Metamorphoses* 36 (Descent into the Underworld type-scene in 39)

Paraclausithyron type-scene 93–5; in Boccaccio's *Filostrato* 93–4; in Chaucer's *Troilus* 93–4; in Ovid's *Amores* 93
Parks, Ward 65
Parry, Milman xv
Passmore, S. Elizabeth 79
Patch, Howard Rollin 80
Pearl: *locus amoenus* type-scene in 82–3
Peasant's Revolt of 1381 184

Peck, Russell A. 79
Pistel of Susanna: Crowd of Onlookers type-scene and 31
Pugh, Tison 24

Rash Promise type-scene 41, 44, 45, 75, 76, 96–9; in Chaucer's *Franklin's Tale* 98, 99; in Chaucer's *Wife of Bath's Tale* 76, 98–9; and *Erec and Enide* 81; and *Gesta Herewardi* 45; in Gottfried's *Tristan* 44, 97–8; in Marie de France, *Lanval* 96–7, 98; in *Sir Orfeo* 41, 97–8; and "Tale of Florent," 75
Renoir, Alain 67
Richard II 150, 197
Robin Hood *see Geste of Robyn Hode*
Roman d'Enéas: Blason type-scene in 19; and Catalog of Warriors type-scene 19
Roman de Thèbes: Council of the Gods type-scene in 28–9; crusade chronicles and 160–61; Pious Traitor episode in 220–1; Wise Woman type-scene in 109–10

Saunders, Corinne 88
Sayers, William 85
Scop's Repertoire type-scene xvii, 71, 100–1, 138; and *Andreas* 100; in Bede's *Ecclesiastical History of the English People* 101; in *Beowulf* 71, 100–1, 138; in *Christ II* 100, 101; and *Gifts of Men* 100, 101; and the *Heliand* 100; and *Nibelungenlied* 100; and *Widsith* 100
Seafarer: Exile type-scene in 57
Seinte Katherine: Contending Throng type-scene in 25
Severs, J. Burke 59
Shakespeare, William: *Romeo and Juliet* (Descent into the Underworld type-scene in 42–3)
Sir Degrevant: English foreign policy in 163–65, 169, 171–72; and *scoti anglicati* 163; and Scottish Border society 163–75; Wise Woman type-scene in 110, 163–75
Sir Gawain and the Green Knight: Arming of the Hero type-scene in 5–6; Blason type-scene in 13–15;

218   Index

Ekphrasis type-scene in 5, 49–50; Exile type-scene in 58; Flyting type-scene in 50, 64–5; Magic Ring type-scene in 88
Sir Orfeo: Blason type-scene in 13; Descent into the Underworld type-scene in 39, 41, 42; Disguise and Infiltration type-scene in 83–4; Exile type-scene in 41, 46, 57–8, 97; Rash Promise type-scene in 41, 97–8
Sleeping After the Feast type-scene 3, 102–3, 136–46; and *Andreas* 102; in *Beowulf* 3, 102, 136–46; in *Daniel* 102; and *Genesis A* 102; and *Judith* 102, 137; and *Juliana* 137
Smith, Greg M. xx
Solomon and Saturn I: Open Heavens type-scene and 89; Traveler Recognizes His Goal type-scene in 151, 152
Spearing, A.C. 85
Star Wars: A New Hope xxi–xxii
Statius, *Thebaid*: Catalog of Warriors type-scene and 19; Council of the Gods type-scene in 27–8; Epic Descent type-scene in 54, 55
Steinberg, Glenn A. 79
St. Erkenwald: Crowd of Onlookers type-scene in 31, 33; Exile type-scene in 58–9; *inventio* type-scene in xxi, 33, 69

Tagelied 35
Tale of Gamelyn: Outlaw Gathering type-scene in 90–1
Taplin, Oliver 52
Taylor, A.B. 158
Taylor, Ann M. 55
Teichoscopia type-scene 36, 104–6, 118; and Benoît de St. Mauré's *Roman de Troie* 104; in Boccaccio's *Filostrato* 105–6; in Boccaccio's *Teseida* 105, 118; and Chaucer's *Knight's Tale* 106; in Chaucer's *Troilus* 36, 106; and Dares and Dictys 104; and *Doctor Faustus* 104; in Guido delle Colonne's *Historia Destructionis Troiae* 104–5; in Homer's *Iliad* 104
Thomas of Erceldoune: Descent into the Underworld type-scene in 39, 41–2; Loathly Lady Encounter type-scene in 42, 75, 77; *Locus Amoenus* type-scene and 42
Toohey, Brian 30, 106
Traveler Recognizes His Goal type-scene xiii, 107–8; in *Andreas* 107; in *Beowulf* 107; and *Genesis A* xiii, 107–8; in *Heliand* 107; and *Judith* 107; in *Solomon and Saturn* 107
Tsai, Christine Li-Ju 52
Tubach, Frederic C. 85
type-scene: analysis, history of xv–xvii; and *ars poeticae* xvii–xviii; and Cognitive Poetics xvi–xvii; definition of xii–xiv; and emotions xx–xxi; Homeric studies and xv, xvii; Oral composition and xvii; origins of xviii–xix; as tools of innovation xxi–xxii

Virgil, *Aeneid*: Catalog of Warriors type-scene and 19; Council of the Gods type-scene in 27; Descent into the Underworld type-scene in 39–40; Epic Descent type-scene in 54

The Wallace of Blind Hary 173
Wanderer: Beasts of Battle type-scene and 7; Exile type-scene in 57
Wedding of Sir Gawain and Dame Ragnelle: Loathly Lady Encounter type-scene in 75, 77–9, 99
Western genre xviii–xix
Widsith: Scop's Repertoire type-scene and 100
Wimsatt, James 18
Wise Woman type-scene 109–11, 130, 147–98; in *Athelston* 110, 175–85; in *Erl of Tolouse* 130–31, 182; in *Floris and Blancheflour* 110, 147–63; in *King of Tars* 110–11, 149; origins in crusading literature 152, 154–58, 160–61; in *Roman de Thèbes* 109–10; in *Sir Degrevant* 110, 163–75
Wittig, Joseph S. 52
Wright, Charles D. 101

Ziolkowski, Jan 18

For Product Safety Concerns and Information please contact our EU representative GPSR@taylorandfrancis.com
Taylor & Francis Verlag GmbH, Kaufingerstraße 24, 80331 München, Germany

www.ingramcontent.com/pod-product-compliance
Lightning Source LLC
Chambersburg PA
CBHW051355290426
44108CB00015B/2021